Law's Detour

CRITICAL AMERICA

General Editors: Richard Delgado and Jean Stefancic

For a complete list of titles in the series,
please visit the New York University Press
website at www.nyupress.org.

Law's Detour

Justice Displaced in the
Bush Administration

Peter Margulies

NEW YORK UNIVERSITY PRESS
New York and London

NEW YORK UNIVERSITY PRESS
New York and London
www.nyupress.org

Library of Congress Cataloging-in-Publication Data

Margulies, Peter.
Law's detour : justice displaced in the Bush administration / Peter Margulies.
p. cm. — (Critical America)
Includes bibliographical references and index.
ISBN-13: 978-0-8147-9559-0 (cl : alk. paper)
ISBN-10: 0-8147-9559-5 (cl : alk. paper)
1. Law—Political aspects—United States. 2. Executive power—United
States. 3. United States—Politics and government—2001-2009. I. Title.
KF385.M368   2010
973.931—dc22   2009046687

New York University Press books are printed on acid-free paper,
and their binding materials are chosen for strength and durability.
We strive to use environmentally responsible suppliers and materials
to the greatest extent possible in publishing our books.

Manufactured in the United States of America
10 9 8 7 6 5 4 3 2 1

To my soul mate, Ellen Saideman

Contents

Acknowledgments

Many people contributed to making this book possible. At the Roger Williams University School of Law, I received great support from Dean David Logan. Research stipends helped not only to aid this project, but also to validate the challenging work involved. I also owe a debt to associate deans Michael Yelnosky and David Zlotnick, and to colleagues Carl Bogus, Ed Eberle, Jared Goldstein, Tim Kuhner, and Colleen Murphy for helpful conversations and advice. Throughout the process, I benefited from our superb law library, whose staff gladly obtained the many books relevant to the project, and from research assistance provided by our team of expert, dedicated, and thoughtful reference librarians, including Emilie Benoit, Stephanie Edwards, Nan Balliot, and Lucinda Harrison-Cox. Student research assistants Laura Corbin and Jennifer Mota were also exceptionally helpful.

Friends have offered advice and expertise on many of the topics discussed in the book. I'm grateful for conversations and feedback from Muneer Ahmad, Baher Azmy, Jim Campbell, Bobby Chesney, Kathleen Clark, the late and much-missed Mary Daly, Steve Ellmann, Sam Goodstein, Bruce Green, Peter Raven-Hansen, Dan Richman, Mike Ritz, Sudha Setty, Glenn Sulmasy, Brian Tamanaha, Steve Vladeck, and Ellen Yaroshefsky.

While many books have been written about the Bush administration, the inspiration for this one came from Richard Delgado and Jean Stefancic, who looked at the sometimes-impenetrable law review articles I had been laboring over for more than twenty years and saw someone who could write a straightforward book. At NYU Press, editor Deborah Gershenowitz also saw something promising in a mess of academic jargon, and reached out continually with suggestions and encouragement. In addition, I am grateful to NYU Press managing editor Despina Gimbel, copyeditor Nicholas Taylor, editorial assistant Gabrielle Begue, and anonymous peer reviewers, whose comments were invariably useful as I refined the manuscript.

Portions of this book appeared as True Believers at Law: Legal Ethics, National Security Agendas, and the Separation of Powers, 68 Md. L. Rev. 1

(2008) and Guantanamo by Other Means: Conspiracy Prosecutions and Law Enforcement Dilemmas After September 11, 43 Gonzaga L. Rev. 513 (2007). I am grateful to these law reviews for permission to use portions of those articles.

I must also thank my family, whose contributions have been incalculable. My parents, Josef and Lola Margulies, who endured great hardship during World War II before making new lives in this country, taught me from an early age to value justice and question authority. My wife, Ellen Saideman, who like me teaches at Roger Williams University School of Law, has revealed her love, insight, and patience in countless ways, not least by reading many of my early drafts over the past twenty years and never hesitating to ask, "Peter, in this piece, what exactly are you trying to say?" Our daughters, Sarah and Emma, have also asked questions about the book and the policies pursued by the Bush administration, and have tolerated my extensive sojourns in our basement study spent laboring over the manuscript. My wife's parents, Reuben and Beulah Saideman, have brought their energy, goodwill, and inquisitive nature to bear on the book's subject in many conversations, and have tolerated my turns at the laptop during family vacations.

All told, I received enormous help in writing this book. Needless to say, all errors are my own.

Introduction

In June 2007, the Justice Department's elite Office of Legal Counsel
(OLC), whose earlier memos on detention, interrogation, and surveillance
of suspected terrorists had ignited controversy, issued a memo on a more
mundane subject: faith-based charities and employment discrimination.[1]
The Bush administration had long sought to give faith-based organizations
a bigger slice of the pie in antipoverty programs.[2] Among those lining up for
federal aid was a group called World Vision, which informed the government
that, "to maintain identity and strength," it hired "only Christian staff."[3] Giving World Vision taxpayer money raised one problem: federal law prohibits
religious discrimination in anticrime programs.[4]

This obstacle did not deter the eager lawyers at OLC, who advised the
administration that it could simply disregard the antidiscrimination law. The
learned lawyers reached this conclusion through two moves. First, they provided a strained reading of another statute. Second, in case that argument
failed, they proposed to gut the legal definition of religious discrimination.

According to OLC's creative interpretation, another federal law, the Religious Freedom Restoration Act (RFRA),[5] *required* that the government give
money to World Vision despite its discriminatory practices. OLC took this
position even though the RFRA does not address federal funding, and merely
limits bureaucratic rules that interfere with the free exercise of religion.[6] OLC
also suggested that religious discrimination may not be discrimination *at all*,
since it merely allows members of one group the freedom to associate with
that group and reject everyone else.[7] On this narrow view, white employers
who merely wanted to associate with whites and therefore refused to hire
persons of other races would not be practicing discrimination either.

OLC's cheerful evisceration of federal discrimination law was not just an
isolated failure of legal judgment; it was an attempt to undermine a pillar of
American constitutionalism: the separation of powers. The framers created a
federal government with three branches—the legislative, executive, and judicial. To prevent one branch of government from dominating the others, they

reasoned that "ambition must be made to counteract ambition."[8] Implementing this insight, they devised a scheme of checks and balances in which each branch possesses both unique and overlapping powers. For example, while the president proposes a budget, the Constitution gives Congress the power to appropriate funds. The executive spends the money, consistent with conditions imposed by Congress and subject to congressional oversight.

The separation of powers regarding the conduct of war is more complex. Congress has the power to declare war. It may also fashion rules that regulate the uniformed services, captures on land and sea, and the application of international law, including the laws of war. The president is commander in chief, fashioning war strategy. The Constitution leaves room for interpretation on where authorization for war ends and war strategy begins.[9]

The framers foresaw that the legislative, executive, and judicial branches would perennially contend for turf, but also recognize their common stake in furthering deliberation about the common good.[10] The fluid dialog between and among the branches would prevent any one branch from gaining excessive leverage over the others. These checks and balances would also disperse the government's aggregate power, thus protecting individual freedom.[11] The OLC's memo on faith-based charities flouted the framers' carefully wrought separation of powers scheme.

The faith-based initiatives memo illustrated the signature strategy of the Bush administration: the construction of detours around legal barriers. When legislation, legal principles, or decades of historical practice stood in the way of a political or policy agenda, Bush officials sought to circumvent the obstacle. When legal impediments to a regime of detention, interrogation, and surveillance of suspected terrorists threatened to force a change in the administration's plans, officials like Vice President Dick Cheney and his counsel, David Addington, simply procured legal opinions that interpreted away those hindrances. When federal prosecutor David Iglesias of New Mexico refused to use his office to target the administration's political foes, top officials at the Justice Department and the White House removed him. When the financial markets showed clear signs of overheating in the period preceding the subprime mortgage meltdown, senior administration officials viewed regulation as unduly burdensome.

Detours of this kind have adverse legal and policy effects. In keeping with the framers' scheme, the president has maximum legitimacy when he or she acts together with Congress.[12] A president who takes a detour to evade Congress loses legitimacy and institutional credibility. Courts are more likely to hold that such unilateral acts violate the Constitution. In some areas, such as requirements for federal civil service jobs, Congress has the final say. A presidential act that defies Congress on this front, as Bush officials did in seeking to use political tests to fill merit-based slots, is simply illegal.

Detours also have significant adverse policy impacts. Deliberation within and among the branches reduces the role of biases and unfounded assumptions. In contrast, a decision reached without deliberation will often ignore long-term consequences. This failure marked the administration's policy on coercive interrogation, which damaged the United States's moral standing in the world. Decisions that seem expedient in the short run can also trigger opportunity costs—missed chances to invest in other productive initiatives. For example, the Bush administration's increasing focus on prosecuting undocumented aliens diverted resources from the investigation of fraud and organized crime. In addition, detours diminish transparency, making the president less accountable to voters.

Moreover, the secret resort to detours impedes the process of change that makes democracy superior to other, more rigid forms of government. In some cases, established laws or processes should adjust to emerging realities. The wisest course, like the one taken by President Roosevelt with the Lend-Lease Program aiding Britain in World War II, is identifying the problem publicly and mobilizing support for a solution.[13] When government short-circuits this process through secret detours, like the Bush administration's program for coercive interrogation of suspected terrorists or warrantless surveillance, it delays adjustment and consensus.

The flawed detours that symbolized the Bush administration flowed from three ideologies. Bush officials like Cheney and Addington believed that the president should exercise unilateral authority, unconstrained by Congress or the courts. Presidential unilateralism shredded the constitutional scheme of separation of powers, and defied international norms such as the prohibitions on torture and cruel, inhuman, and degrading treatment. Bush officials also championed the unitary executive theory, which held that the president could undermine the independence of any executive branch official who dared to challenge administration policy, and erase the line between merit-based civil service hiring and political appointments. At an agency like the Securities and Exchange Commission, charged with regulating corporate finance, an antiregulatory agenda in tune with White House wishes loosened constraints on investment banks and helped pave the way for the credit collapse of 2008. Finally, September 11 helped legitimize the law and order focus of the administration, which used the specter of terrorism to target immigrants and establish the Department of Homeland Security (DHS).

DHS served as a repository for Bush hangers-on like Michael Brown of the Federal Emergency Management Administration (FEMA). FEMA became a stepchild to DHS's overriding counterterrorism mission, setting up the woefully inadequate federal response to Hurricane Katrina.

While the Bush administration was negligent in addressing risks posed by Katrina, its response to terrorism targeted disfavored groups without discernment or proportion. In the two years after September 11, the Bush Justice Department rounded up and deported thousands of undocumented immigrants from the Middle East and South Asia. Most had no record of violence or connection to terrorism. Nevertheless, the Justice Department detained them for months after investigations cleared them of all but violations of the immigration laws. In domestic immigration enforcement, the government conducted raids that broke apart families. The government also detained hundreds of people found in Pakistan and Afghanistan, eventually shipping many to the U.S. naval base at Guantánamo Bay, Cuba. Often, the only evidence linking these detainees to terrorism came from bounty hunters who craved the cash the government offered. Administration officials also engaged in extraordinary rendition, targeting individuals like Maher Arar, a Canadian national who turned out to be innocent of terrorism, but whom the United States arranged to ship to Syria to endure a protracted and abusive interrogation. Moreover, the administration targeted lawyers who sought to assist these groups, interfering in attorney-client relationships and seeking disproportionate punishments for attorneys whose zeal led them astray.

As the administration targeted others, it vigorously sought to insulate itself from accountability. It set up a law-free zone for interrogation and detention of detainees at Guantánamo Bay because it hoped that courts would not hear cases from those detained there. Lawyers at the Office of Legal Counsel advised Bush and Cheney that efforts by detainees to invoke domestic or international legal norms were a form of "lawfare" exploited by our enemies, and that any treatment of detainees, including maiming, would be appropriate if the president ordered it. The administration also relied on a similar legal opinion to justify a vast program of warrantless surveillance of Americans and those abroad.[14] Finally, administration officials like political guru Karl Rove invoked the doctrine of executive privilege—a mainstay of the Nixon administration during the Watergate scandal—to avoid even appearing before Congress to answer questions about political motives for the firing of United States Attorneys.

Adding to their overreaching, administration officials aimed to centralize Justice Department policy and personnel in a fashion that ignored the local wisdom of federal prosecutors and clashed with legal mandates for merit-based hiring. Working with Republicans in Congress, administration officials tried to blacklist judges who imposed sentences the administration and its allies viewed as soft on crime. Attorney General John Ashcroft and his successor, Alberto Gonzales, sought to promote use of the federal death penalty, even in communities where jurors were unlikely to agree; this pursuit of the death penalty made the exercise of justice slower and more costly. When United States Attorneys cited these community concerns, Gonzales fired them, triggering a scandal that eventually led to Gonzales's resignation. Gonzales's staffers improperly extended patronage hiring to jobs that federal law had long reserved for applicants based on merit, inquiring about candidates' views on abortion or prodding them to name their favorite Bush administration official.

In criminal prosecutions, the administration pushed the envelope to allow conspiracy prosecutions even where evidence was stale or slender. Sometimes the alleged agreement that formed the basis for the prosecution came perilously close to a mere thought crime. Moreover, the administration used informants with agendas of their own, who sometimes seemed to be principal players in the plots they divulged.

Detours were also pronounced in the administration's handling of voting rights and political prosecutions. Under Ashcroft and Gonzales, ideological zealots in the Justice Department shifted voting rights investigations from cases involving suppression of minority votes to the largely anecdotal issue of vote dilution—fear that people ineligible to vote, such as immigrants, would dilute the ballots of eligible voters. Efforts to combat rare incidents of vote fraud overwhelmed efforts to combat vote suppression—in part because vote suppression efforts conveniently targeted traditional Democratic constituencies. The Bush administration also tried to mobilize federal prosecutors, whose decisions should be divorced from politics, into shock troops for partisan interests. Prosecutors like David Iglesias who refused to play ball with the administration's agenda of targeting political opponents were themselves targeted for dismissal.

The Bush administration's approach to economics at home and abroad displayed the same eagerness to aid friends. In Iraq, companies with close ties to the administration, such as Halliburton, received lucrative no-bid contracts but failed to spot obvious, deadly flaws like faulty wiring in showers. Domestically, the administration's commitment to staffing regulators like the Securities and Exchange Commission and the Federal Reserve with champions of market self-policing helped set up the subprime mortgage collapse of 2008.

The Bush administration's use of detours is not entirely unprecedented. Lincoln famously suspended habeas corpus in the early days of the Civil War without congressional authorization. Truman, concerned about possible shortages of steel during the Korean War caused by a labor-management dispute, sought to seize the steel mills. Nixon created an ad hoc White House crew, the "Plumbers," to break into the offices of those linked with political opponents. Reagan sought to raise money to aid the rightist Contras in Nicaragua by selling arms to the Iranian government without approval from Congress.

Lincoln's actions could claim at least an attenuated link to congressional approval. They were also largely transparent, followed closely by disclosure to Congress and a direct request for congressional ratification. The Supreme Court struck down Truman's seizure of the steel mills. The detours of Nixon and Reagan precipitated an impeachment inquiry for Nixon that led to his resignation, and criminal charges for aides in each administration.

While all these detours had their dangers, the secret detours fashioned by the Bush administration stand out for their pervasive character and relentless pressure on the integrity of lawyers and judges. Although Nixon's creation of the Plumbers was more brazen than any single act of Bush, Cheney, and their underlings, Nixon interfered less with local prosecutors, who by and large continued to exercise judgment and do their jobs. Nor did Nixon seek to sabotage the civil service, as did the political zealots at the Bush Justice Department. The scope and breadth of the Bush administration's detours are unparalleled in modern American history. This is an achievement of sorts, but not an achievement that any future president should care to repeat.

Dismay at the Bush administration's detours will not eliminate the temptations that make detours seem desirable. Presidents of both parties will inevitably seek rationalizations for taking wrong turns. Moreover, as the afterword explains, criminal prosecution of Bush officials may only inspire a more partisan politics, and instill risk aversion in public officials who must sometimes take decisive action. As President Obama has observed, the public needs greater transparency, not payback jurisprudence. The account of the Bush administration's detours offered here can help us see the red flags in the future, and stay on the right track.

The Perfect Storm of Politics, Ideology, and Crisis

On September 2, 2005—almost four years after the horrendous attacks of September 11, 2001—President George W. Bush watched a DVD containing news reports of extraordinary human tragedy and loss. The DVD did not portray a terrorist incident. Instead, it compiled news coverage of the devastation caused by Hurricane Katrina.[1] Deadly flooding had begun in New Orleans on Monday of that week, submerging whole communities and inundating tens of thousands of homes. Since that first day, journalists had been reporting on Katrina's deadly consequences. Thousands of the city's residents perched on rooftops awaiting rescue or converged on the Superdome and Convention Center without food, water, electricity, or proper sanitation. Vulnerable residents who could not move because of age or disease perished. While reporters were on the scene, federal officials were absent.

The federal delays had personal and structural origins. President Bush, preoccupied with the war in Iraq, had not watched the wall-to-wall news coverage of Katrina until his staff pressed the DVD on him for viewing during his Friday flight to the Gulf Coast. FEMA director Michael Brown, a patronage appointee with a mediocre resume, did not have the clout or the ability to mobilize relief efforts. Since 2003, FEMA had been a small, subservient part of the cumbersome 9/11-inspired Department of Homeland Security (DHS), run in September 2005 by Michael Chertoff, a veteran counterterrorism and law enforcement official with no experience or demonstrated interest in disaster relief. This combination of official uninterest and unwieldy structure heightened the suffering endured by residents of New Orleans. As we shall see, that ruinous combination stemmed from political moves made by the administration and its allies.

The orphaning of FEMA and the executive indifference and incompetence that caused the federal delays in responding to Katrina were one detour among many from sound policy, practice, and law. In a wide range of areas, detours caused harm to individuals and groups, wasted opportunities for more effective and humane policy choices, and damaged the government's standing at home and abroad. Analysis of these detours entails a survey of the perfect storm of politics, ideology, and official temperament that developed after the September 11 attacks.

Ideology and Politics

In the anxious time after September 11, ideology, politics, and temperament shaped the Bush administration's characteristic response to both national security and domestic problems: the legal detour. Sometimes a detour marginalized an important area, as did FEMA's status within DHS. Sometimes a detour short-circuited checks and balances, producing decisions that were both shortsighted and illegitimate. Confident that detours were producing wise decisions, administration officials rarely revisited their initial choices. The resort to detours blunted internal dissent and evaded outside accountability, producing a feedback loop that perpetuated bad decisions.

Detours from established practice in the Bush administration's approach to law stemmed from three main sources. First was belief in unilateral presidential authority over foreign affairs and national security. Second was devotion to the unitary executive model of politicized and centralized policy decisions. Third was law and order politics. Each distinct ideology had its advocates.[2]

Champions of unilateral presidential power included Vice President Cheney, his counsel David Addington, and John Yoo, the brilliant young Berkeley law professor whose opinions authorizing coercive interrogation were later to become notorious. The concept of the "imperial presidency"[3] is not new—chief executives have found occasions to unilaterally assert power since Lincoln's day, if not before. President Nixon had exemplified the modern imperial presidency as cautionary tale, covering up criminal acts by subordinates, claiming the right to impound funds duly appropriated by Congress, and invading the sovereign nation of Cambodia without congressional consent. Questioned after his resignation by British journalist David Frost, Nixon justified his actions in stark terms: "When the President does it," he informed Frost, "that means it's not illegal."[4]

Dick Cheney, a youthful bureaucrat in the Nixon administration, viewed Nixon's excesses as an inspiration. Ten years later, as a Republican member of Congress from Wyoming, he drew the same conclusion from President Reagan's policy during the Iran-Contra affair. In Iran-Contra, the Reagan administration fashioned an elaborate scheme to aid rebels in Nicaragua against the leftist Sandinista regime. The Democratic Congress believed that the rebel group, called the Contras, had engaged in torture and repression. To deter U.S. entanglement with the group, Congress exercised its constitutional "power of the purse," prohibiting the executive branch from spending federal dollars to fund the Contras.

For proponents of presidential power including Cheney, Congress's move was both ill-advised and an unconstitutional invasion of the president's prerogatives.[5] Reagan took a detour around the congressional ban by selling arms to Iran and diverting the proceeds to the Contras. To plan and execute the detour, Reagan gave enormous power to a small group of staffers, include Lt. Col. Oliver North, who operated in secret. After Reagan's gambit became public, congressional investigations and criminal prosecutions followed. A House Committee Report vigorously condemned Reagan's approach. Cheney authored a "minority report" stating that the Democratic Congress had acted illegally by restricting the president's power over foreign affairs.[6] Assisting Cheney in the preparation of the report was a young lawyer, David Addington, who had cultivated a stubborn conservative streak during the Nixon administration, telling classmates that the United States had withdrawn from Vietnam too early.[7]

Cheney, Addington, and other true believers in executive primacy did not see their efforts as a naked power grab. Instead, they cited the U.S. Supreme Court. Justice George Sutherland's sweeping opinion in *United States v. Curtiss-Wright*[8] described the president as the "sole organ of the nation in its external relations."[9] Upholding a company's indictment for violating a presidential proclamation that banned arms sales to warring factions in South America, Justice Sutherland extolled the president's supreme power in foreign affairs. Supporters of untrammeled executive power also looked to the commander in chief clause found in Article II of the Constitution,[10] asserting that this clause gave the president unchecked authority.

In exalting the president, Yoo and others rejected any binding role for most international law. The foremost academic critic of international law was Jack Goldsmith, who taught at the University of Chicago before being recruited to serve in the Bush administration as a lawyer in the Pentagon and the Justice Department. Goldsmith, who now teaches at Harvard, referred to international law as "lawfare," a perilous tangle used by the United States's enemies to tie us down.[11] According to Goldsmith, nations operated on the basis of interest. Much international law was therefore illegitimate if it required nations to consider values like equality and fair play. Goldsmith focused his intellectual firepower on customary international law, which helps constitute the law of nations through an accumulative process based on experience. Goldsmith critiqued customary international law, arguing that it lacked the approval of Congress and the consent of the countries bound.[12] Discrediting customary international law left fewer barriers to administration policies such as coercive interrogation of suspected terrorists.[13] Eventually, as chapter 3 describes, Goldsmith learned that Cheney, Addington, and Bush lacked the prudence required when barriers disappear.

In addition to embracing the imperial presidency, ideological supporters of the Bush-Cheney approach argued that the president must be a "unitary executive" who would speak for the entire executive branch. Academic champions of the unitary executive theory, including Steven Calabresi of Northwestern University, argued that the president had the power to fire any executive branch employee for any reason, regardless of any constitutional provision or contrary intent expressed by Congress.[14] To protect the unitary executive's authority, Calabresi and others favored narrowing the reach of due process and civil service protections.[15]

Dick Cheney and other political adherents of the unitary executive cited the president's "responsibilities"[16] to justify total presidential control over the federal bureaucracy. For Cheney, the Constitution's structure required this control, since the president alone in the executive branch was politically accountable to the people. This accountability freed the president to take heroic risks. On this view, dissenters within the bureaucracy were either displaying a craven "cover your behind" attitude or engaging in stealthy ideological warfare against the president, seeking to paralyze his agenda. For unitary executive theorists, both bureaucratic stances required stern presidential discipline.

The championing of unilateral executive power and the unitary executive fit the post–September 11 climate. Frightened by the unprecedented nature of the attack, the public demanded strong measures. On the political level, moreover, these two concepts combined with a powerful law and order narrative that had been a dominant force for more than thirty years.

The law and order trope had emerged in the 1960s.[17] Politicians used crime as a centerpiece for their campaigns, aided by the proliferation of media in the 1960s that used crime as a wedge for increasing ratings. As TV news gained force and market share, it required attention-grabbing stories—"If it bleeds, it leads," became the recipe for ratings. Law and order rhetoric started with words that a Democratic president, Lyndon Johnson, had used in signing the Safe Streets Act of 1968, a paradigmatic piece of anticrime legislation that included an authorization for wiretapping and an attempted rewriting of Supreme Court decisions carving out rights for suspects.[18] Johnson had invoked the themes of home and security that have played a powerful role in American politics, noting that the bill "responds to one of the most urgent problems in America today—the problem of fighting crime in the local neighborhood and on the city street."[19] Richard Nixon, running for president in 1968, made "law and order" a centerpiece of his southern strategy, which dominated national elections for the next third of a century.

While high crime rates require a law enforcement response, the law and order narrative often elevated security at liberty's expense. Responding to Warren Court reforms of custodial interrogation, law and order politicians promoted harsh legislation with lengthy mandatory minimum sentences for drug possession.[20] For law and order politicians, the set of harsh police practices known as "the third degree" were not the evil that the Warren Court had decried in *Miranda v. Arizona*.[21] In *Miranda*, the Court sought to combat this official lawlessness by requiring the verbal warnings that have become familiar to generations of crime show audiences. Politicians who criticized *Miranda* saw such judicial intervention as a threat to public safety.

Politicians' praise of coercive interrogation, vagrancy laws,[22] and other mainstays of mid-twentieth-century law enforcement has often overtly or implicitly evoked race.[23] Campaign accounts of violent crime have frequently highlighted defendants who were African American, as in George H. W. Bush's use of the Willie Horton episode against Michael Dukakis in the 1988 election.[24] Politicians manipulated fear of a restive minority population, painting the courts as allies of minority lawbreakers.

Complementing law and order rhetoric, anti-immigration sentiments helped coalesce support behind the Bush administration in the aftermath of September 11. These sentiments sport some of the same pedigree as law and order, particularly when the rhetoric centers on undocumented aliens— migrants from other countries who broke the law by entering the United States surreptitiously or overstaying on a lawful visa. Politicians arguing for more immigration enforcement contended that those who broke the law should derive no benefit from lawless conduct.

While immigration enforcement is a legitimate goal that intersects with national security interests, the nature and scope of enforcement makes a difference. Immigration law has long been an area where the usual constitutional guarantees do not apply. Although the power to regulate immigration has no express textual support in the Constitution, the Supreme Court ruled in 1889 in the Chinese Exclusion Case[25] that Congress is free to make immigration distinctions based on national origin or race. While one might not equate the arrival of migrants from, say, Mexico as posing a national security danger equal to an actual invasion,[26] the Court drew this analogy, noting that threats come not merely from violent onslaughts, but also from "vast hordes of . . . people crowding in upon us."[27] After September 11, politicians repeatedly invoked this trope, citing the attacks to urge harsher treatment of undocumented aliens and narrowing of legal protections for refugees. For example, congressman Jim Sensenbrenner of Wisconsin, Congress's most persistent advocate for restrictive measures, asserted after September 11 that refugee protections, passed to comply with international law, had made the United States a "safe haven for some of the worst people on earth."[28]

Named attorney general as a gesture to conservatives,[29] John Ashcroft had no doubt that the events of September 11 required an aggressive response in which legal niceties took a backseat. This view was an extension of the law and order rhetoric that Ashcroft had used throughout his political career.[30] When Ashcroft ran successfully for the Senate in Missouri, he attacked his opponent, African American representative Alan Wheat, for favoring modest financial support for prisoner education. Ashcroft's campaign charged that Wheat was "kind to murderers,"[31] and wanted to send "killers to Penn State, not the state pen."[32] Ashcroft hewed to the law and order view of judges as saboteurs of effective law enforcement.

As attorney general, Ashcroft spent little time with subordinates in the Justice Department or with United States Attorneys, leaving such matters to his nonlawyer chief of staff, David Ayres.[33] Ashcroft, like his successor Gonzales, had never served as a lawyer with the federal government prior to his selection as attorney general. He had minimal regard for the view that federal prosecutors were ministers of justice, who could use discretion to leaven the harsh effects of the law and order paradigm. As we shall see in chapter 4, Ashcroft also took a dim view of the local knowledge and roots in the community that distinguish United States Attorneys, the face of the Justice Department in each judicial district. For Ashcroft, the Supreme Court's injunction that federal prosecutors should strike "hard blows . . . not . . . foul ones"[34] did not resonate. Instead, Ashcroft surrounded himself, true to his senatorial roots, with a bevy of political advisers who dedicated themselves to polishing his image. Eager young aides like Kyle Sampson—who later became chief of staff for Ashcroft's successor, Alberto Gonzales, and played a key role in the 2006 firings of United States Attorneys—made many of the key decisions in the department. Senior officials such as the deputy attorney general were cut out of the loop.

As Ashcroft's reliance on his political advisers shows, the strident claims to rectitude of law and order politics mask a fastidious devotion to patronage. Politicians have always consolidated power by providing jobs and resources to political friends. Decisions about law enforcement are no different. For example, law and order politicians have benefited from creation of the "prison-industrial complex," including unions of correction officers and rural towns dependent on dollars from local penitentiaries.[35] These constituencies support politicians who assist them, and advocate for further punitive measures to increase their share of the pie. When Congress and the executive take steps to detain more nonviolent immigrants, companies that run detention facilities stand to gain.[36]

The Judicial Response in American History

Although courts have largely deferred to congressional judgments on criminal penalties and immigration policy, leaving these outcomes to the political process, the imperial and unitary executive theories have encountered a far more mixed judicial reception. Consider the track record of the unitary executive. In *Humphrey's Executor v. United States*,[37] the Supreme Court ruled that president Franklin Roosevelt lacked constitutional authority to fire a member of the Federal Trade Commission except upon good cause, as Congress had required. While courts have recognized that the framers did not seek a toothless executive, they have also understood that dialog within the executive branch can flag policies that seem expedient but engender long-term harm. Moreover, many officials in the executive branch enforce legislation through a "quasi-judicial" function,[38] deciding what products are unsafe or when corporate executives have committed securities fraud. These officials are not merely "an arm or eye of the executive,"[39] but require some distance from the overwhelming power of the president to perform their function.[40]

Courts have also tailored the imperial presidency to fit the separation of powers envisioned by the framers. Consider that calling card for acolytes of presidential power, *United States v. Curtiss-Wright*.[41] In *Curtiss-Wright*, President Franklin Roosevelt issued a proclamation prohibiting the sale of arms to certain regions abroad. Roosevelt, however, did not act unilaterally, but instead exercised authority that Congress had expressly delegated to him to avoid U.S. entanglement in foreign squabbles. Moreover, a closer look at the *Curtiss-Wright* Court's clarion rhetoric of presidential prerogative suggests a lack of historical resonance. For example, while the Court quoted approvingly John Marshall's description of the president as the "sole organ of the nation in its external relations,"[42] it neglected to include the rest of Marshall's speech, which recognized that Congress could "prescribe the mode" of policy that governed foreign affairs.[43]

This deference to Congress is clearest in the case of *Youngstown Sheet & Tube Co. v. Sawyer*[44] in which the Court ruled that President Truman lacked the power to seize the steel mills in a labor dispute during the Korean War. The Court noted that Congress had recently passed the Taft-Hartley Act, governing labor disputes, and had declined to give the president authority to seize factories.[45] By acting in the face of Congress's refusal in area where the Constitution gave the legislature authority, Truman had violated the separation of powers. Justice Robert Jackson, in his memorable concurrence, cautioned against allowing the president power to defy Congress unless the most profound exigency required unilateral action. Jackson observed that presidential emergency powers had to be narrowly construed: "Emergency powers," he wryly observed, "tend to kindle emergencies."[46] To avoid usurpation of legislative authority and threats to liberty, Jackson noted that the president has inherent power to act against Congress's wishes only in the direst circumstances.[47]

Jackson set up a tripartite structure that ever since has helped define the relationship between Congress and the president: The first category concerns cases where Congress has expressly or implicitly consented to the president's action. Here, the president has the greatest power, as he allies himself with the legislature. The second category involves cases where Congress is silent, or has acquiesced over time to a pattern of executive action. Generally, courts have insisted on clear proof of acquiescence, often going back through long decades of history. The third category, where presidential power is at its "lowest ebb," entails cases where the president acts in opposition to Congress's intent.[48] Since *Youngstown*, conservatives and progressives alike have accepted Jackson's typology as the best way to ensure a "workable government."[49]

Detours Around the Rule of Law

Cheney and Addington did not view Jackson's structure as helpful. They resolved to either ignore it entirely or distort its guidance. After September 11, this strategy led to dangerous detours around established policy, practice, and process. In the Bush administration, the legal detour became not merely a stopgap device to handle exigent cases, but a crucial mode of governance.

Senior Bush administration officials like Cheney made five key moves in constructing detours. First, backed by legal opinions from John Yoo discussed in chapter 3, they viewed the president's power as expanding to fit every situation. In so doing, they transformed Jackson's third category from a small set of exceptions into an engine of presidential authority on issues such as the establishment of military tribunals and the warrantless terrorist surveillance program.[50] Second, they narrowly construed statutes and provisions of international law that appeared to restrict presidential authority, such as the torture statute[51] and the UN Convention Against Torture. Third, to hedge their bets, they *broadly* construed other laws, such as the Authorization for Use of Military Force (AUMF)[52] against Al Qaeda, as endorsing initiatives like the new surveillance program, even where this broad reading distorted Congress's language and intent. Fourth, Bush administration officials wielded power, including authority newly granted under the Patriot Act, to bypass or eviscerate accountability mechanisms, including grand juries and a board charged with ensuring the accuracy of decisions about political asylum. Fifth, aided by Republican operatives like Karl Rove, they leveraged terrorism as a political issue, particularly in the 2002 congressional elections that hinged on the administration's support for a new Department of Homeland Security.

Based on these moves, detours became the "new normal" in the Bush administration, as they had in the Iran-Contra episode during the Reagan years. Attempts to adapt established practices and processes to the concededly challenging post-9/11 environment were greeted with derision. For example, shortly after September 11, FBI director Robert Mueller, a career prosecutor, warned at a high-level meeting that irregular methods for apprehending, detaining, or interrogating terrorism suspects might taint evidence. Ashcroft dismissed Mueller's doubts, directing that Mueller "stop the discussion right here . . . The chief mission of U.S. law enforcement . . . is to stop another attack and apprehend any accomplices to terrorists before they hit us again. If we can't bring them to trial, so be it."[53]

Ashcroft's response to senators about the president's unilateral establishment of military commissions for suspected terrorists at Guantánamo Bay—discussed in chapters 2 and 3—reflected the racialized dimension of law and order rhetoric, newly adapted to the terrorism landscape. Ashcroft used not-so-veiled references to the O. J. Simpson murder trial to mock those who wanted to preserve some semblance of fairness for the accused. "Are we supposed," asked Ashcroft scornfully, "to read them the Miranda rights, hire a flamboyant defense lawyer, bring them back to the United States to create a new cable network of Osama TV?"[54]

Detention of U.S. Persons

In June 2002, Attorney General Ashcroft made an unusual announcement that illustrated his skepticism about lawyers and other procedural safeguards for terrorism suspects. Speaking from a studio in Moscow, Ashcroft informed the world that the United States had detained a U.S. citizen, Jose Padilla, as an "enemy combatant."[55] Officials believed that Padilla, who had been arrested at O'Hare Airport in Chicago, was planning to obtain a "dirty bomb" that would use conventional explosives to disperse radioactive material. The basis for this belief was information obtained during the coercive interrogation of an Al Qaeda logistics manager, Abu Zubaydah.

Perhaps because Zubaydah had been subjected to waterboarding, a procedure described in chapter 2, the United States did not attempt to prove in court that Padilla had sought to obtain a dirty bomb. Instead, Justice Department lawyers argued that the executive had the power to hold Padilla indefinitely *without* court review. Pursuant to this claim, the administration held Padilla incommunicado for an extended period, not even permitting him access to his lawyers for over a year and a half. This claim to virtually unchecked power was unprecedented in American history.

Generally, prosecution in the criminal justice system is the norm, with detention permissible only in cases of extraordinary dangerousness or when needed to secure a defendant's presence at trial. The Constitution permits other regimes of detention linked in some way to dangerousness, including detention of certain immigrants, persons with mental illness, and sex offenders. But all these modes of detention are subject to regular review by a court to ensure that a continuing basis exists for the individual's confinement.

The political branches have on occasion tried to expand the scope of detention when national security crises emerge. For example, Lincoln suspended habeas corpus in the spring of 1861 to permit federal authorities to address the threat posed by Confederate sympathizers in Maryland, who had burned federal property and sought to prevent Union troops from reaching Washington DC.[56] But Lincoln arguably had legislative authorization to declare martial law, which would have given him the same power he gained by suspending habeas corpus.[57] Moreover, Lincoln went to Congress shortly after suspending habeas, seeking the legislative branch's approval. During World War II, President Roosevelt ordered the detention of two U.S. citizens who had allegedly acted under orders from the German High Command, disembarking off the coast of Long Island with the intent to commit acts of sabotage. Here, however, Roosevelt also arguably had statutory authorization for the detention, which was ordered to ensure the defendants' appearance at a trial by military commission.[58] There was no serious dispute that the defendants had disembarked from a German submarine and changed into civilian clothes, which in itself constituted a war crime. Moreover, the proceedings were subject to judicial review. Roosevelt also ordered the infamous internment of tens of thousands of Japanese Americans in the months after Pearl Harbor. But this action, surely one of the low points of American constitutional history, was expressly authorized by Congress.[59]

In short, no American president had ever taken the far-reaching position taken by the Bush administration. Earlier presidents had obtained advance congressional approval, or sought congressional ratification after the fact. While collaboration with the legislature has by no means quelled controversy about these episodes, it has brought the president within Justice Jackson's first category, where the president has maximum legitimacy. In contrast, the Bush administration's take on this argument, based on the AUMF, was almost an afterthought, mentioned in passing after the administration's reliance on the president's inherent power.

Indefinite detention was not the only mode open to the administration in Padilla's case. Officials could have sought immediately to try Padilla in the criminal justice system, or to hold him as a material witness in a criminal investigation—this would have been a detour, as well, but at least one with a line of precedent behind it. Alternatively, the administration could have tried a sharper detour, but one more modest than the path it chose. Citing the danger of a dirty bomb, the government could have said that it needed to detain Padilla for a reasonable amount of time—say, six months—to sort things out. At that point, the government could have brought charges against Padilla, or released him.[60] Instead, the government stuck with its blanket position, charging Padilla with terrorist conspiracy three and a half years later only to avoid Supreme Court review. As of December 2008, in the closing days of the Bush presidency, administration lawyers continued to take this position in the case of another suspected terrorist, Ali Saleh al-Marri.[61]

Executive Surveillance

After September 11, the administration also acted unilaterally in setting up a vast system of warrantless surveillance. In this domain, the president's defiance of Congress's will is even more clear than it is in the areas of detention and military commissions. The secrecy surrounding the surveillance program also reveals the tendency of the Bush administration to discount or ignore dissent.

Prior to September 11, the government conducted national security surveillance under the Foreign Intelligence Surveillance Act (FISA).[62] FISA, passed in 1978 after revelations about warrantless surveillance in the Nixon administration, imposed checks on wiretapping and other forms of surveillance in national security cases. But Congress also recognized the important role of lawful surveillance in protecting national security. In enacting FISA, Congress acknowledged that acts in this country linked to activity abroad can have high stakes for national security yet be more difficult to monitor and regulate than solely domestic communications.[63] To address this asymmetry between possible threats and existing government tools, FISA provided that the executive could seek a warrant for surveillance from a special court if it suspected that the target of surveillance was an "agent of a foreign power." The FISA court, composed of federal judges, was ready to sit day and night, and indeed virtually never refused a government request. The government could also tap a phone for up to seventy-two hours *without* a court warrant.

After September 11, the administration secretly put in place a warrantless surveillance program that did an end run around FISA.[64] Through the so-called Terrorist Surveillance Program (TSP), the government's top-secret National Security Agency (NSA) colluded with many telecommunications companies to conduct warrantless surveillance on vast numbers of telephone calls and other communications that either originated abroad or involved a foreign recipient of a communication from the United States.[65] Although FISA already modified the Fourth Amendment's usual requirement of individualized suspicion of wrongdoing by requiring that the target merely be an agent of a foreign power, reports of the TSP's scope indicate that individualized suspicion was even less central under the TSP than it was under the already-truncated FISA regime. While concrete information about the TSP remains classified, reports from a range of sources suggest that the program as initially conceived permitted the NSA to eavesdrop without a warrant on electronic communications by thousands of persons in the United States, as long as one party to the conversation appeared to be on foreign soil.[66]

The administration did not even consider asking Congress to amend FISA, although once *New York Times* reporters revealed the existence of the TSP in late 2005, Congress proved willing to enact most of the changes that the administration sought. While administration officials briefed a small group of senators and representatives who served in high positions on each house's Intelligence Committee, the administration did not respond to a 2003 query from Senator Jay Rockefeller of West Virginia, expressing concerns about the program.[67] Vice President Cheney, in an interview in January 2009, made light of Rockefeller's letter, asserting that the senator was merely trying to cover his own behind.[68]

Conscientious executive branch officials who bridled at the program also did not receive a respectful hearing; instead the program's prime movers, particularly Cheney and his aide Addington, simply shut them out of the loop. For example, Ashcroft's deputy, Larry Thompson, viewed the program as dangerously overbroad, and declined to sign off on surveillance requests.[69] White House insiders worked with John Yoo and other true believers at Justice to run a detour around Thompson's reluctance. It took a subsequent revolt of administration lawyers to secure changes in the program. Even with these changes, however, the program seemingly failed to comply with FISA.

The Patriot Act and Monolithic Power

While unilateral presidential action was a staple of the Bush presidency, sometimes Congress was complicit in the creation of detours. This eased constitutional concerns, but nevertheless made for troubling policy. For exhibit A, consider portions of the Patriot Act that made it easier for the FBI to obtain National Security Letters (NSLs).

The Patriot Act, passed with alarming haste after September 11, created a giant detour from the decentralized sites of power that had tempered federal prosecutorial authority in the pre–September 11 environment. Here, as elsewhere, a bipartisan majority of members of Congress enthusiastically endorsed the legislation. It passed after minimal perfunctory debate, itself a detour from typical congressional practice. Congressman Sensenbrenner echoed this bipartisan majority in announcing that "we have to change the way we think about the safety and security of our country and its people. We must develop new weapons for protections against this new kind of war."[70] Discussing some of the useful technological changes in the act, Sensenbrenner argued that the laws then in place had been written for "rotary telephones," not the Internet.

The Patriot Act, which included a variety of provisions designed to enhance law enforcement and better integrate law enforcement and national security, also gave the Federal Bureau of Investigation (FBI) substantially expanded power to seek information. Instead of a grand jury subpoena or a specific showing that the information sought concerned a foreign agent,[71] the government could issue an NSL requesting any and all information "relevant" to a terrorism investigation.[72] The statute also prohibited recipients of NSLs from disclosing their receipt of the letter to *anyone*. The FBI could seek business records, including library records, in the same fashion. The use of NSLs had a major advantage over the localized system of grand juries: it ensured the secrecy of a sensitive ongoing investigation.[73] But this secrecy came at a price: the FBI also was less accountable, creating incentives for lax procedures.

In addition to bypassing grand juries, which provide an important albeit limited check on centralized prosecutorial power,[74] law enforcement could use the Patriot Act to erode the usual decentralized practice for seeking warrants. Instead of going to a federal district judge or magistrate in, say, New York, the Patriot Act gave law enforcement expanded power to invoke FISA. Previously, the government had to show that the information it sought under FISA was "primarily" related to foreign intelligence matters. This condition prevented the government from using FISA to do an end run around the tougher requirements from warrants in the criminal justice system. But as policymakers and politicians became concerned about the "wall" that allegedly had hampered prevention of the September 11 attacks, the Patriot Act changed the standard, allowing the government to seek a warrant under FISA whenever a "significant" purpose of the search was the gathering of foreign intelligence information.[75]

The Patriot Act's changes enhanced the effectiveness of national security investigations,[76] but failed to anticipate the risks posed by weakened accountability. The government requested more than five times as many NSLs after the expansion of this authority in the Patriot Act.[77] For example, the FBI made 56,507 requests for national security information in 2004, and 47,221 in 2005.[78] Federal investigators disregarded their own regulations on the use of NSLs, sometimes requesting information on the wrong people because of typographical errors.[79] In addition, agents were sometimes unaware of legal constraints on information requests, such as federal privacy provisions that bar the use of NSLs to obtain educational records.[80]

The FBI also engaged in a web of deceptive practices in collusion with telecommunications carriers to obtain sensitive information without use of an NSL. Sometimes, agents used broadly worded "exigent letters" sent by unauthorized officials.[81] Many of these situations were not exigent, and did not involve an outstanding investigation, as federal law requires.[82] The letters also contained inaccurate information that provided the telecommunications companies with deniability in case anyone questioned their provision of information to the FBI. Each exigent letter advised the recipient that subpoenas for the information would be duly sent to federal prosecutors.[83] But the inspector general found that the FBI could not show that it *ever* issued NSLs or grand jury subpoenas pertaining to the information requested.[84] In some cases, the FBI subsequently issued "blanket" NSLs that covered a broad swath of information requests without mentioning a specific investigation.[85]

In essence, the FBI abused its NSL authority to collude with the telecommunications companies on a giant fishing expedition through the personal communications data of thousands of Americans. This matter has drawn concern from congressional watchdogs such as Senator Charles Grassley of Iowa, as well as continuing investigation within the Justice Department.[86] Candid disclosures by the Justice Department to a vigilant Congress might have nipped these problems in the bud. Extracting information from Justice, however, was more excruciating than pulling teeth.[87] In addition, a Congress dominated by Republicans for much of the first six years of the Bush administration was not disposed to press the matter. So the Patriot Act created a detour from the normal healthy practices of criminal law enforcement that paralleled the excesses of the Terrorist Surveillance Program.

The Homeland Security Follies

September 11 prompted another structural change that had ramifications beyond the terrorism realm: the creation of the Department of Homeland Security. The instinct behind the creation of the Homeland Security Department was uniting a vast, indeed bewildering, array of agencies that had something to do with homeland security. Here, the term, homeland security, was crucial—who could be against it? As a result, immigration, emergency management, the coast guard, customs, and dozens of other agencies folded into one giant department. The trouble was that the missions of these disparate agencies did not mesh. Inevitably, concerns stemming from the war on terror would drive the department, while other vital tasks would receive short shrift. Those neglected tasks included disaster relief, as the nation discovered in 2005 when a preoccupied President Bush and incompetent or indifferent bureaucrats at DHS botched the federal response to Hurricane Katrina.

To understand how the creation of DHS resonated with counterterrorism rhetoric, one must revisit the 2002 debate about the proposed agency. Republicans repeatedly invoked September 11 in pressing for creation of DHS. Congressman Sensenbrenner of Wisconsin applauded the act because it would result in more immigration enforcement.[88] Representative William Thornberry of Texas warned that any delay in passing the legislation would be time "during which our enemies are plotting and planning against us."

Thornberry suggested that Osama bin Laden opposed creation of the new department, warning that failure to pass the bill will aid "someone who intends to kill more Americans."[89]

Some politicians criticized the idea. For example, Representative Henry Waxman of California warned, "We are getting more bureaucracy . . . at a tremendous cost to the taxpayer . . . the new Department [will have] a vast array of responsibilities that have nothing to do with homeland security"—functions including disaster relief.[90] The congressman charged that the crazy quilt of missions and agendas within the new department "bloats the size of the bureaucracy and dilutes the Department's counterterrorism responsibilities."[91]

The bill creating DHS also rewarded interests friendly to the Bush administration. The statute stripped from children injured after taking small pox vaccines their right to compensation.[92] Immunity also extended to companies that make faulty bomb detectors, gas masks, or other security devices. In addition, the act expressly deprived DHS employees of collective bargaining rights and civil service protections.[93]

The Bush administration used DHS as a battering ram in the 2002 elections. While Democrats cited the structural problems in the proposed department and the risks of giving up employment rights and civil service protections for employees, the administration and its allies hammered away at national security. Voters bought the argument that Democrats warning about structural problems and procedural shortcuts were throwing a monkey wrench into the war on terror. This led to the defeat of Democrats at the polls, including Max Cleland, Democratic senator from Georgia, who had used a wheelchair after being wounded during service in Vietnam. Cleland's opponent pilloried him as being soft on national security, airing a campaign ad in which Cleland's picture morphed into an image of Osama bin Laden.[94]

The creation of DHS after the 2002 elections fulfilled opponents' worst fears. At DHS, units with a counterterrorism mission dominated agencies such as FEMA. The Bush administration's rigid approach to budgeting exacerbated this problem. Counterterrorism was a growth industry, taking an increased share of the budgetary pie. But the Bush administration insisted that other agencies, such as the Coast Guard, keep their budgets flat, eroding their ability to fulfill their missions—missions that conservatives often disliked. The Coast Guard, for example, in addition to combating drug smuggling, regulates marine ecosystems and sets standards for port facilities.[95] Some conservatives also viewed FEMA's mandate to provide food and shelter assistance in the wake of natural disasters as a liberal boondoggle.[96] As a result, agencies like FEMA became bureaucratic orphans, lacking resources or access to top policymakers.[97] Stripped of status, FEMA became a destination for patronage hires, offering job opportunities to mediocre officials such as Michael Brown, who took over FEMA even though his most relevant experience with natural disasters had been his heading up of the Arabian Horses Association.[98]

The lowly status of FEMA in DHS, coupled with the inexperience of FEMA's managers and the lassitude of President Bush, had tragic consequences for a traditional homeland security concern: disaster relief. Natural disasters such as hurricanes cause significant numbers of deaths and massive property damage. They also displace thousands of families, frequently leaving those families without electricity or ready access to food and vital services. Disasters with lingering effects, such as floods, often pose greatest dangers in the aftermath of a storm, as sustenance and support vanish for vulnerable residents, including the elderly. A homeland security policy that fails to prepare for such crises is not worthy of the name. Unfortunately, FEMA's orphaned status in DHS rendered it unable to perform these vital functions.

Hurricane Katrina, which slammed New Orleans two and a half years after the creation of DHS, exposed the structural and personnel problems in the new agency. DHS secretary Michael Chertoff had no experience in emergency management, and had long focused on his chief interest: deterring terrorist attacks. Chertoff was ill-suited to advocate with the White House for a more proactive approach to the storm's deadly aftermath. Brown's ineptitude frustrated relief efforts, as millions of television viewers observed when news crews reached sites like the Convention Center days before federal help arrived. Meanwhile, the unwieldy bureaucracy of DHS insulated the president from contact with officials confronting the disaster.[99] Finally, the president initially seemed to treat Katrina as a distraction from his own focus on Iraq and terrorism, apparently unaware of the dire situation in New Orleans. As a result, the federal government failed to respond effectively to the plight of New Orleans residents.

Conclusion

As much as the administration's stances on detention, interrogation, and surveillance, the administration's policies on immigration and the creation of DHS revealed a chronic tendency to favor detours over established structures, processes, and policies. True believers embraced ideologies like the imperial and unitary executive theories that brooked no constraints on presidential will. In detention, the administration claimed power without limit, ignoring the perils revealed by precedents such as Lincoln's suspension of habeas corpus and the World War II internment of Japanese Americans. In interrogation practices, administration officials like Cheney, Addington, and Gonzales sought to evade the strictures of international agreements such as the Convention Against Torture. In surveillance, the administration defied the specific language of FISA. Law and order politics also played a role, providing the impetus for the Republicans' leveraging of the Homeland Security Act to defeat their 2002 election opponents, whom the Bush administration and its allies portrayed as soft on terror. DHS's ineffective response to the challenge of Hurricane Katrina revealed the downside of the administration's detours: by making everything about counterterrorism and defying constraints, the administration also lost the benefit of the deliberation that constraints encourage.

Targeting Individuals and Groups

In May 2002, the Justice Department accused the environmental activist group Greenpeace of tempting sailors into vice. This charge was odd on any number of levels. First, most sailors probably need no temptation. Second, Greenpeace does not trade in vice. The Justice Department filed charges after Greenpeace boarded a vessel that may have been importing illegally logged mahogany from Brazil into the United States.[1] To transform this into criminal activity, federal prosecutors cited an obscure, 140-year-old statute aimed at aggressive marketing by seaside taverns, which bars boarding a vessel in an unauthorized fashion before it has been "completely moored" at its port of entry.[2]

In a decision of 1890, a federal court had summed up the evil Congress had sought to combat: "Lawless persons [employed by] . . . 'sailor-mongers,' get on board vessels . . . and by the help of intoxicants . . . get the crews ashore, and leave the vessel without help to manage or care for her."[3] While this was clearly a pressing problem in 1890, it seems of limited relevance to the activities of Greenpeace today. Accordingly, the modern court dismissed the charges against Greenpeace,[4] noting that the statute in question "has been gathering dust for over a century."[5] The court further noted that the indictment is a "rare—and maybe unprecedented—prosecution of an advocacy organization for conduct having to do with the exposition of the group's message."[6] For the court, the conjunction of an outspoken group and charges based on an obscure statute suggested that the indictment was "politically motivated due to the organization's criticism of President Bush's environmental policies."[7]

The Greenpeace episode demonstrates how the Bush administration used detours to target individuals and groups. Sometimes Bush officials in the Justice Department, the Pentagon, and the CIA targeted individuals and groups because targeting was expedient, whereas at other times targeting stemmed from bureaucratic mission creep.[8] The Bush administration often targeted individuals, such as lawyers working on national security cases, to send a message: cross us and suffer the consequences. Consistent with this vindictive outlook, administration officials sought to impose disproportionately harsh penalties on lawyers and others for relatively contained wrongdoing.

One cardinal flaw of targeting is the proliferation of false positives: hapless individuals and groups who are in fact innocent. For example, in assembling its detention facility for suspected terrorists at Guantánamo, the government lacked an accurate method for filtering out false positives, resulting in the detention of a significant number of people who harbored no hostile intent against the United States. Some detainees did pose legitimate threats. But dangerousness cannot justify the elaborate regime of coercive interrogation techniques, such as waterboarding, that the Bush administration deployed against three detainees. As the Guantánamo and coercive interrogation stories illustrate, targeting in the Bush administration often injured the public interest, by impairing the deliberation that we expect of federal officials, ignoring long-term costs, and reducing the transparency of government decisions.

Targeting is a natural temptation for federal officials, who have extraordinary remedies at their fingertips. As the Greenpeace case illustrates, federal law is a vast expanse navigated at officials' discretion. Lowly individuals face difficulties in keeping track of all of the statutes, some decades or more than a century old, included in federal criminal law. Moreover, the criminal law is only the beginning. Federal immigration law allows the U.S. government a free hand in controlling and removing aliens from the country.[9] In addition to substantive breadth, federal law provides a prodigious repertoire of methods for controlling, disrupting, and intruding on lives. The federal government can on a showing of probable cause search premises, turning lives and businesses upside-down, even when no criminal charges follow. The government after 9/11 also sought to detain individuals as material witnesses, even though in most cases it could not find grounds that would merit prosecution. In addition, the government has control over information, which it can selectively disclose to discredit critics, as it did in the case of Valerie Plame and Joseph Wilson, who had challenged the Bush administration's handling of the war in Iraq.

The American Way of Targeting

Targeting groups through fear, malice, or overzealous enforcement is far from unprecedented in American history. Government's first response to national security threats has often been the targeting of unpopular individuals and groups. This response results from politics as much as genuine exigency. Targeting individuals and groups allows public officials to deflect suspicions that they were insufficiently vigilant before the emergency struck. This opportunity was convenient for officials in the Bush administration, who had ignored or discounted the threat of terrorism before September 11.[10]

The worst example of this dynamic was the Japanese American internment during World War II. After the attack on Pearl Harbor, unfounded fears grew about the loyalty of the Japanese American population, located principally on the West Coast of the United States. In response, Congress authorized the forced evacuation of Japanese Americans from their homes. The executive followed the evacuation order with an order requiring Japanese Americans to report to facilities where they were interned for much of the war.[11]

The government was less than transparent about the rationale for this harsh measure. Moreover, elite government lawyers were complicit in the deception. The government initially justified the internment by invoking security concerns, including the loaded charge that Japanese American radio transmissions were feeding information to the Japanese military after Pearl Harbor. The government lawyers defending lawsuits brought by Japanese Americans knew that these allegations were false.[12] But these same blue-chip lawyers failed to adequately apprise courts of their knowledge, contributing to the Supreme Court's decision in *Korematsu v. United States* upholding the government order.

No single decision of the Bush administration had the impact of the internment program jointly authorized by the Roosevelt administration and Congress. But the range of policies initiated by the Bush administration also singled out thousands of people for arbitrary reasons. This chapter analyzes those problematic policies.

Immigration and the Bush Administration

Many of the Bush administration's policies fell with particular harshness on those without the political ability to fight back: immigrants and foreign nationals. Using the immigration system to react to crises is relatively easy, given the deference that courts have accorded government decisions in this realm. The Bush administration's responses, however, exhibited the risks behind such deference: if government can appear to be doing something, it will take advantage of the opportunity, even if its actions are not particularly effective. Throughout the Bush administration, officials including Attorney Generals Ashcroft and Gonzales and Department of Homeland Security Secretary Michael Chertoff used immigration as an enforcement safety valve, ratcheting up enforcement when facing scrutiny from the media, the public, or their own allies on the Right. This anti-immigrant bias was natural for Ashcroft, who ran successfully for the Senate in 1994 by accusing his opponent of wanting to give welfare to illegal immigrants.[13] The arrests of hundreds of undocumented immigrants in the immediate aftermath of September 11 reflected Ashcroft's philosophy. Later problems emerged in asylum adjudication, flawed databases that penalized naturalized citizens and lawful residents, draconian workplace raids that split up families, and unsafe detention conditions.

The Post–September 11 Roundup

The Bush administration's response to the September 11 attacks illustrated the pivot toward heightened immigration enforcement. In the two years after September 11, the Justice Department rounded up, detained, and then deported thousands of undocumented immigrants from the Middle East and South Asia.[14] Ashcroft boasted in Senate testimony about the comprehensiveness of his investigation, and the hundreds of immigrants whom he had ordered detained in the months after the attacks.[15] If one looks behind Ashcroft's boasts, however, the evidence does not corroborate the productive investigation that Ashcroft advertised.

The federal Immigration and Naturalization Service, at that point part of the Department of Justice, had little or no evidence that the immigrants arrested after September 11 were involved in terrorist activity. Rather, investigators targeted people based on tips, such as, "There are too many foreign-looking people in this area." The FBI, shortly after the shock of the September 11 attacks, created an investigative operation, the Pentagon/Twin Towers Bombings Investigation, or PENTTBOM.[16] One week after the attacks, the program had yielded ninety-six thousand leads.[17] As the saying goes, however, "Garbage in, garbage out." Leads emerged from an unsavory stew of sources, including neighbors, landlords, and employers settling scores.[18] Among all the reasons that the FBI would receive a tip, actual involvement with terrorism was at the bottom of the list. Moreover, the FBI's lack of focus and anxiety about a subsequent attack quickly transformed the investigation into a dragnet targeting undocumented aliens. When the FBI encountered someone of Muslim or Arab background not in this country legally, they took that person into custody, even if that person was not the subject of the tip.[19] For example, agents arrested one individual after receiving a tip that the man worked in a grocery store "operated by numerous Middle Eastern men."[20] The FBI labeled those they arrested, eventually numbering well over a thousand people, as "persons of interest," regardless of their involvement with terrorism.

Once arrested, the hapless "persons of interest" had to run a procedural gauntlet set up by bureaucratic edict and inertia. Although Ashcroft claimed that all immigrants received access to counsel, in a significant number of cases people had difficulty connecting with lawyers. In many cases the INS delayed for weeks and sometimes more than a month serving detainees with notice of the charges against them.[21] In addition, the department formulated and implemented a policy that classified any alien picked up in the course of a PENTTBOM investigation—including an undocumented alien working in a bakery discovered by happenstance—as a "September 11 detainee" who would be held until cleared.[22] In court, the Justice Department maintained that persons classified as September 11 detainees had ties to or information regarding terrorist activity in the United States.[23] Arrests in the vast majority of cases, however, occurred because of "chance encounters or tenuous connections" rather than because of "genuine indications" of terrorist ties or the possession of useful information.[24]

After the aliens were rounded up, authorities exposed them to danger. According to allegations in a federal lawsuit, guards subjected many of the aliens to physical and mental abuse.[25] Consider the case of Shakir Baloch, a Muslim from Pakistan educated as a physician and a Canadian citizen. On September 19, 2001, agents conducting a PENTTBOM investigation of an apartment-mate of Baloch's arrested Baloch, who lacked a lawful immigration status in this country and also had false immigration documents. Baloch was ultimately cleared of any terrorist ties. While in detention, according to Baloch, he was beaten by five correctional officers, who picked him up bodily and threw him from corner to corner in his cell, punching and kicking him in the back as he fell.[26] The officers also called Baloch a "fucking Muslim terrorist," and threatened him, saying, "You did this to us. We're going to kill you."[27] For the next three months, Baloch alleges he was subjected to comparable harsh treatment, including having officers shove him in the back while his face was pressed against the wall, twist his hands, thumbs, and fingers, and step on the chain that linked his ankle shackles.[28] Baloch was sent back to Canada on April 16, 2002, without personal identification or cash—as of 2006, his belongings had not been returned to him.[29] Baloch says that he continues to suffer from severe depression as a result of his experience.[30] In a similar case, the government settled with a former detainee by paying out three hundred thousand dollars.[31]

The FBI also used intrusive means to target Muslim and Arab immigrants, even after the initial post–September 11 detentions. According to documents recently released to Yale Law School's National Litigation Project, the FBI interviewed over two thousand Muslim and Arab immigrants in the fall of 2004, just before the presidential election. FBI agents used information obtained by the CIA to ask questions about which mosque an interview subject attended, or how the subject felt about the United States.[32] Few if any of the cases involved a particularized factual suspicion that the individual was engaged in terrorism. Indeed, although five hundred of the subjects were arrested for immigration violations, none of the subjects was prosecuted for a terrorism offense. One interview subject, asked his opinion of the United States, stated that he was "living the American Dream and cared greatly for the equal opportunities, rights, and values that are afforded in America."[33] It is unclear whether the interviewee's opinion changed after the government profiled him based on ethnicity and religion.

Asylum and Refugee Policy

The United States has been a leader in refugee policy since it ratified the Refugee Act of 1980, helping to live out the meaning of those eloquent words on the Statue of Liberty. But national security and foreign relations agendas have always intruded to some degree on asylum policy. These factors became even more salient after September 11.

Provisions of the Patriot Act allowed government to exclude aliens who aided foreign terrorist groups.[34] These provisions are arguably constitutional as a means of preventing the flow of human and financial capital to groups like Hamas.[35] These measures, however, have led to a bureaucratic rigidity in handling refugees.

Under the Patriot Act rules, an individual who has provided material support to a terrorist organization is excludable—that is, he cannot receive refugee status. For a number of years, the Department of Homeland Security interpreted this provision to mean that any person who provides anything of value to a terrorist group is barred from asylum, regardless of the harm that person might undergo and the circumstances of the case. For example, if a person provides aid under duress, because the group has threatened that person's life or the lives of loved ones, the person was still barred from receiving asylum. As a result of cramped interpretations of the rule, thousands of refugees from Burma, one of the world's most oppressive regimes, could not obtain refugee status.[36] Congress laid the groundwork for this change in policy, which has the effect of closing the door on those who are arguably at the greatest risk of harm. But the Department of Homeland Security could have interpreted the statute more narrowly, avoiding this calamitous effect. As a result of DHS's broad reading, refugees experienced substantial delays in gaining sanctuary in the United States from persecution abroad.[37] Many are still waiting.

Attorney General Ashcroft also cited national security in detaining refugees who posed no threat. In *In re D-J-*,[38] the Attorney General ordered the detention of more than two hundred Haitian and Dominican migrants who arrived at Miami by sea. Ashcroft made two transparently weak national security arguments to justify detention of people who may have been bona fide refugees, and had no record of violence or other threatening activity. Ashcroft said that the landing of vessels distracted the Coast Guard, and that terrorists could be concealed on such vessels.[39] Of course, the Coast Guard's *job* is to ensure the safety of the waters surrounding the United States, and this includes turning back refugee vessels intercepted before they land. The Coast Guard should probably have more resources to do that job, but it is unclear that detaining people will have any deterrent effect, given the formidable array of factors that push people into a creaky boat to navigate the treacherous seas between Haiti and Florida. Ashcroft also asserted without any concrete evidence that terrorists could use Haiti as a staging ground for infiltrating the United States.[40] Risking one's life in a rickety vessel in the turbulent Caribbean surrounded by scores of bona fide Haitian refugees, however, seems like a markedly inauspicious start to a terrorist infiltration. The argument that terrorists could be concealed on board unduly discounts the history and track record of immigration from Haiti—Haitian refugees flee violence and poverty, so they generally do not seek to perpetrate violence in the United States.

Ashcroft also burdened refugees with unfair procedures that short-changed their claims. He eviscerated a tribunal called the Board of Immigration Appeals (BIA), which had imposed quality control on the notoriously uneven and arbitrary decisions of administrative immigration judges (IJs). Ashcroft dismantled reforms the Clinton administration had put in place to ensure accuracy and fairness in the political asylum process.

The stakes in IJ decisions are high. Decisions by IJs change lives, determining who merits asylum in the United States. An arbitrary decision by an IJ can consign a prospective refugee to an uncertain fate, including arrest, torture, or even death. Unfortunately, IJs sometimes subject asylum claimants to standards that are impossible to meet. In one case,[41] where a gypsy claimed that skinheads and military personnel beat him in his native Bulgaria, the IJ asked the claimant if he knew the technical term for gypsies. The claimant correctly answered, "Roma"—but he took too much time to suit the IJ, who denied asylum.

Before Bush, the BIA acted as a backstop, correcting errors by IJs and making sure that claimants with meritorious cases received a fair hearing. Ashcroft believed that the BIA coddled wrongdoers and undermined counterterrorism efforts.[42] Accordingly, he radically shrank the size of the BIA, rendering it unable to engage in meaningful review of IJ decisions. After Ashcroft was done with his "reforms," most decisions were reviewed by just one BIA member, and more liberal or moderate members were purged. Judge Richard Posner, a founder of the law and economics movement who was sympathetic to Bush on some national security issues, noted that pervasive errors had forced courts to reject immigration tribunals' decisions a "staggering" 40 percent of the time.[43] The result was the wholesale denial of asylum to many worthy claimants seeking refuge from persecution abroad.

As further evidence of the unfair treatment refugees received, consider *Dawoud v. Gonzales*,[44] concerning an asylum seeker who belonged to the minority Coptic Christian sect in Egypt. Dawoud had his wedding aired by a local TV station. Shortly thereafter, he received a visit from members of a group, the al-Gama'a al-Islamiyya (IG), designated by the United States as a terrorist group. The IG contingent confiscated the tape, blindfolded the petitioner, kidnapped him, and beat him until his release ten days later, for associating with "infidels" and failing to ensure that all women on the video were fully veiled.[45] After seeking medical care for his injuries, Dawoud was investigated by Egyptian security forces, who said they had received a report that he had insulted Islam. The police tortured him repeatedly by electrocution until he signed a confession. Dawoud was told that he would be called before a secret tribunal that hears security cases, and fled the country rather than face this uncertain fate.[46]

In assessing Dawoud's asylum claim, the immigration judge chose to largely ignore the facts of the case and refer instead to his own pleasant experiences with tourism in Egypt.[47] The BIA affirmed the denial of asylum, asserting that the Egyptian government and other groups no longer persecuted Coptic Christians quite so severely. To reach this conclusion, the BIA ignored reports from a recognized human rights group, Freedom House, that Egyptian security forces arrested and tortured approximately one thousand Copts in 1998, a couple of years before the events described in the application, and that the Egyptian government acquiesced in the mob killing of twenty-one Christians in 2000.[48] Hundreds of other refugee decisions feature this same pattern of arbitrary decision making, aided by the Ashcroft/Gonzales dismantling of internal quality control.[49]

Overzealous Immigration Enforcement

The Bush administration accelerated the targeting of immigrants over time. In 2006, administration officials stepped up raids and detained over twenty thousand persons for immigration violations without a plan for providing adequate medical care. While many of these people were here illegally and Congress had authorized their deportation, enforcement often was harsh and heavy-handed. Results included family breakups and needless deaths in detention.

Immigration raids have separated young children—many of them U.S. citizens—from their families. In one case, agents working with Immigration and Customs Enforcement (ICE)[50] arrested Saida Umanzor, an Ohio resident, and separated her from her nine-month-old daughter, Brittney, who had not yet been weaned.[51] In all, the raids separated at least five hundred children from their parents. Three-quarters of the children were under ten years old. Two-thirds of the children were U.S. citizens. In some cases, ICE sent parents from the Northeast and Midwest to detention centers in the South and West, thousands of miles away from young children.[52] After raids, many children hid for days in their homes. Family members caring for them often did not seek assistance for the children, fearing that seeking help would result in more arrests.

In one major raid of a factory in Postville, Iowa, prosecutors used tactics that the Supreme Court would subsequently cast into doubt. In the Postville raid, federal officers arrested hundreds of undocumented Guatemalan workers, who had been laboring in squalid conditions. Rather than treating these workers as victims of an unscrupulous employer, prosecutors pressured the workers to plead guilty to immigration fraud charges in exchange for dropping identity theft charges that carried a penalty of at least two years in prison. As a government translator later disclosed, most of the defendants did not understand the charges against them.[53] In addition, the Supreme Court later held, in *Flores-Figueroa v. United States*,[54] that identity theft requires proof that the defendant *knew* that documents belonged to a particular individual. The Postville defendants clearly did not know this. Some of the papers may have been entirely fictitious. The workers, who were unsophisticated in the extreme, only knew that their employer had told them these were the papers they needed. Under the Supreme Court's decision, they could not have been convicted of identity theft. Indeed, their lack of intent to deceive made any kind of fraud charge inappropriate. The government, like the employer, exploited the workers' lack of sophistication. While the employer had used the workers to make money, the government used them to make headlines.

ICE also failed to supply appropriate medical care for detained aliens, who are typically nonviolent individuals. A Chinese national, Hu Lui Ng, detained at an ICE-funded facility in Rhode Island, was viewed as a malingerer by facility staff, who drove him to Connecticut in shackles to see if he would admit to faking symptoms.[55] The man turned out to have both metastasized cancer and a broken spine. He had been complaining of severe pain for months and died soon after the Connecticut ordeal.[56] Months before, a senior Department of Homeland Security official had derided reports of inadequate medical care as "myths."[57]

The ramping up of immigration enforcement often had more to do with augmenting budgets than with achieving results. For example, since 2003, ICE has obtained substantially higher funding for its National Fugitive Operations Program (NFOP), and expanded staffing and operations accordingly.[58] ICE officials obtained increased funding from Congress after promising to target aliens who had been convicted of serious crimes. As ICE increased its arrest quota for its NFOP officers, however, the percentage of apprehended criminals plunged. ICE personnel devoted most of their time to apprehending ordinary undocumented aliens, rather than those who posed a threat. Senior ICE officials never admitted that the focus of the NFOP no longer justified its extravagant funding.[59]

Detainees, Habeas Corpus, and Guantánamo

Fear and overzealous government actions have also spurred the worldwide targeting of suspected terrorists. The United States should work with other countries to combat terrorist groups. But the Bush administration sacrificed cherished values and the United States's reputation while securing uncertain results.

Consider, for example, the detention without due process of hundreds of suspected terrorists at Guantánamo Bay. Particularly in the first four years of Guantánamo, the government detained hundreds of people whose connections to terrorism were attenuated or nonexistent. One compelling example is the case of Murat Kurnaz, a German national who traveled to Pakistan to study Islam, where he was delivered to U.S. forces. Kurnaz was accused of a relationship with one Selcuk Bilgin, whom the United States suspected of participation in a suicide attack.[60] The government held Kurnaz at Guantánamo for over five years. Officials knew early on, however, that they had little or no evidence against him.[61] Once the government alleged in open court that Kurnaz was linked to the alleged suicide bomber, Kurnaz's lawyer within twenty-four hours had affidavits from German authorities acknowledging that Bilgin was neither a terrorist nor a suicide, and was in fact living in Dresden.[62]

The problems at Guantánamo stemmed from reliance on tips provided in exchange for reward money and lack of a process that would separate out the wheat from the chaff. To determine whether these detainees are dangerous, the government resorted to so-called Combatant Status Review Tribunals (CSRTs) and ARBs (Annual Review Boards), which did not permit lawyers or the introduction of evidence and witnesses on the detainees' behalf, and did not allow the detainee to have access to evidence against him.[63] When, despite these obstacles, a CSRT found that a detainee was not dangerous, the government resorted to a second and third CSRT hearing to ensure that it got the "right" result.[64]

Even the former chief prosecutor at Guantánamo warned about the risk of unfairness. Col. Morris Davis alleged that a superior in the Defense Department urged him to move quickly on certain high-profile Guantánamo cases because the cases might have "strategic political value" in the 2006 congressional elections.[65] In May 2008, a military judge disqualified the legal adviser to the convening authority, Brig. Gen. Thomas Hartmann, stating that he had interfered unduly with the prosecution by urging the prosecution to bring "sexy" cases that would be good wedge issues in the campaign.[66]

Ironically, the administration was its own worst enemy on the underlying question of detainees' dangerousness. The unfairness of the procedures at Guantánamo made it easy for administration critics to insist that virtually *all* detainees were victims of misadventure—journalists and humanitarian relief workers in the wrong place at the wrong time.[67] Administration officials countered by labeling Guantánamo detainees as the "worst of the worst."[68] As scholar Ben Wittes of the Brookings Institution wrote in a definitive study, the truth lies somewhere between the extremes. A significant cohort of these detainees boasted of their affiliation with Al Qaeda or the Taliban.[69] In other cases involving years of captivity, however, even the Bush administration eventually had to acknowledge that the detainees were not "enemy combatants."

In one such case, the administration had initially made unsupported claims that appeared three times in raw intelligence documents. According to the government, detail and explanation were superfluous: mere repetition proved the claims' reliability.[70] A federal appeals court disagreed, comparing the government's position to a character from the work of Lewis Carroll, author of *Alice's Adventures in Wonderland*, who had proudly announced, "I have said it thrice: What I tell you three times is true."[71] Procedures likened to Lewis Carroll rarely comport with the rule of law.

Extraordinary Rendition

The Bush administration did not content itself with the Lewis Carroll world of inadequate Guantánamo procedures. Another example of the targeting of suspected terrorists was the practice known as extraordinary rendition. In these cases, the government transferred suspected terrorists, who on some if not all occasions turned out to be innocent, to foreign governments with a track record of torture and human rights violations. In one such case, the subject, Maher Arar, a Canadian national, claimed that he was taken off a flight at JFK Airport, summarily ordered deported from the United States with only token attempts to contact his attorney, and then flown to Syria.[72] U.S. officials claimed that they had obtained assurances that Syria, which has one of the world's worst human rights records, would not torture Arar.[73] Regardless of the assurances, Syria did torture Arar. For almost one year, Syrian officials kept Arar in a cell the size of a grave—six feet by three feet by seven feet. They beat him with an electric cable until he signed a false confession. Eventually, the Syrians sent Arar back to his Canada; Canada, which had fed the United States inaccurate information in the lead-up to the rendition, subsequently paid Arar $10.5 million. Canada conceded that Arar had no terrorist ties—Canadian officials had relied on false information the Syrians had extracted through torture.[74] After Arar spoke on video to a congressional committee, Secretary of State Condoleezza Rice acknowledged that the United States had "mishandled" the matter.[75]

Coercive Interrogation

While coercive methods were used on the innocent, like Arar, they were also used on people who may well have been guilty, including Khalid Shaikh Mohammed, the admitted planner of the September 11 attacks. In a civilized society, however, the suspicion of guilt is not a license for government abuse.

The Bush administration's embrace of coercive interrogation was a departure from established practice within the U.S. criminal justice system.[76] The use of coercion has attracted worldwide condemnation, and prompted charges of hypocrisy that undermined support for legitimate counterterrorism efforts.

The use of coercion has had a mixed history in Anglo-American law and practice. For well over two hundred years—since before the drafting of the Constitution—English judges have held that coercion or inducement used against a prisoner made resulting statements by the defendant unreliable and hence inadmissible.[77] American history has been more equivocal. Courts have long required that confessions be "voluntary."[78] Through the first half of the twentieth century, however, law enforcement authorities often used coercion, colloquially known as "the third degree," to extract confessions.[79] The Supreme Court over time took steps to halt this practice, first barring techniques that "shocked the conscience"[80] and then in *Miranda* imposing affirmative duties on the police to inform suspects of their rights. More recently, Congress enacted the torture statute, which prohibits the infliction of severe pain.[81]

International law also increasingly limited the use of coercion. The Convention Against Torture bars imposition of severe pain for any reason, including obtaining information.[82] Customary international law has made the prohibition on torture a compelling or *jus cogens* norm. In addition, the Geneva Conventions' Common Article 3 bars both torture and "cruel, inhuman, and degrading" treatment.

Torture is not only legally suspect under domestic and international law; it is also of dubious effectiveness. Despite the revival of interest in torture in popular culture, such as television's hit show *24*, in which Jack Bauer regularly beats up on bad guys in custody to save the world, torture and coercion have limitations. Consider the problem of imperfect information. Often the interrogator does not know the bounds of the subject's knowledge. Faced with coercion, the subject may simply say what the subject thinks the interrogator wishes to hear.[83] In contrast, traditional interrogation techniques that are entirely legal in the United States, including rapport building and certain kinds of deceit, often produce better information in the long term, since they permit interrogators to acquire a more finely grained appreciation of their subject.

The Bush administration, however, was impatient with these venerable methods. Supported by the expansive and thoroughly unconvincing opinions of its elite lawyers at the OLC (discussed in chapter 3), it pulled the plug on traditional techniques and embraced the use of coercion. The president and his closest advisers specifically endorsed the shift in strategy.[84] It had disastrous consequences for the United States, undermining legal and moral constraints and also encouraging bad foreign policy choices.

To illustrate the distorting effect of information gained through coercion on policy, consider the case of a senior Al Qaeda detainee, Ibn al-Shaykh al-Libi, apprehended by the United States. Veteran FBI interrogators used traditional, lawful interrogation techniques to get information from al-Libi.[85] They built up rapport with the detainee, at one point praying with him. In return, al-Libi gave them information about procedures at Al Qaeda camps, and even about a plot to blow up the American embassy in Yemen. The CIA, however, was not satisfied. One day, during the FBI agents' interrogation, a CIA officer interrupted the interrogation to threaten al-Libi—"You're going to Egypt," the operative screamed. The agent also advised al-Libi in very harsh language that he intended to find al-Libi's mother and violate her sexually. Interrogators in the CIA moved away from rapport building, to other techniques that involved the infliction of physical and psychological pain. Al-Libi gave the CIA more information. Unfortunately, most of this information was false. For example, al-Libi told interrogators that Al Qaeda and Saddam Hussein had a history of operational ties. The administration, electrified by this revelation, used it as part of its case for intervention in Iraq. But the great weight of evidence has shown that al-Libi invented the Al Qaeda-Iraq tie after U.S. personnel started using coercive methods.

The ignorance of American personnel about Arab language and culture compounded these difficulties. In Iraq, for example, U.S. forces did not effectively screen detainees. One detainee was brutally interrogated for days because his captors heard him talking about a bridge. Later, American forces learned that the man was a dental technician who made bridges to replace bad teeth.[86]

Officials like Cheney, who spoke early on of the need to move to the "dark side," failed to realize that the techniques they embraced broke detainees but often failed to produce reliable information. These consequences were plain to see for anyone who knew the modern roots of the approaches used by Bush officials. Many of the techniques originated in the training provided to United States military personnel to help them withstand the rigors of captivity. SERE (Survival, Evasion, Resistance, and Escape) training came from the playbook of the Chinese Communists during the Korean War, who honed their abusive tactics on captured American personnel.[87]

Shortly after September 11, Bush officials reached out to the Joint Personnel Recovery Agency (JPRA), which ran the SERE training. This outreach included a healthy dollop of patronage. A retired JPRA psychologist who pitched the use of SERE techniques for interrogation joined a firm that received a lucrative contract from the Defense Department.[88] Military psychologists warned Bush officials that techniques used in training were not appropriate for interrogations. One psychologist cited the origins of SERE, reminding officials that the Communist Chinese tactics used on American POWs violated the Geneva Conventions.[89] Another warned that information obtained would likely be unreliable, since "a subject in extreme pain may provide an answer, any answer, or many answers in order to get the pain to stop."[90] Indeed, teaching U.S. personnel to provide such answers to thwart their captors was a prime purpose of the SERE training.[91] But these warnings did not deter policymakers' wholesale incorporation of SERE techniques into interrogations.

One of the techniques borrowed from the SERE program was waterboarding. The Bush administration used waterboarding on three detainees, which may seem relatively measured; however, the technique was used a total of 266 times on two of the subjects.[92] Jay Bybee, John Yoo's boss at the elite Justice Department Office of Legal Counsel (OLC), wrote a detailed memo approving the practice.[93] An interrogator would cover a subject's face with a cloth after strapping the subject to a board with the subject's feet elevated, and pour water over the cloth. The restriction in airflow caused by the cloth's saturation would raise the level of carbon dioxide in the prisoner's blood, intensifying the prisoner's attempts to breathe. Because the saturated cloth hindered breathing, the prisoner would experience "'suffocation and incipient panic,' i.e., the perception of drowning."[94] OLC authorized interrogators to use the technique for up to twenty minutes "in any one application." At the session's end, the detainee would be allowed to recover, and ponder his situation. Then interrogation would resume.[95]

While the methodical description of waterboarding in Bybee's memo is disturbing in its own right, precision often took a backseat in practice. Interrogators conducting waterboarding blurred the line between a subject's "perception" of drowning and drowning pure and simple. As a later legal memo acknowledges, the subject would attempt to "defeat the technique," by twisting his head to one side. When this occurred, the interrogator would clamp down on the detainee's nose and mouth, allowing the water to build up, and making it impossible for the detainee to breathe.[96]

Another technique approved by OLC was "walling." An interrogator repeatedly slammed the detainee against a false wall made of plywood or a similar material.[97] Steven Bradbury, a protégé of Ken Starr who became acting head of OLC in 2005, acknowledged that walling "wears down [the detainee] physically . . . and undoubtedly may startle him." Bradbury main-tained, however, that walling is not "significantly painful."[98] The OLC dis-counted the impact of walling even when informed that a detainee could be "walled . . . twenty to thirty times consecutively when the interrogator requires a . . . response."[99]

A third interrogation technique used in combination with the others[100] was sleep deprivation, accomplished not through nudges or even loud music, but through shackling a standing detainee. As Steven Bradbury of OLC explained in approving this technique, interrogators would shackle a stand-ing detainee's feet to the floor, and cuff his hands in front of his body, attach-ing the handcuffs to the ceiling with a chain. While the detainee's hands were "generally" secured at chest level, Bradbury advised that interrogators could also raise the detainee's hands above his head "for a period of up to two hours."[101] Interrogators would prevent the detainee, who was sometimes nude, from hanging from the handcuffs or using them to support his weight. If the detainee dozed off, he would awaken immediately as a reflexive reac-tion to losing his balance or pain caused by the added tension of his body weight on the handcuffs. While the prolonged standing contemplated by this technique could, Bradbury acknowledged, cause edema or swelling in the feet, CIA doctors asserted that this condition was not painful—even when the swelling developed within tight shackles. Interrogators also insisted that the detainee wear a diaper, because sleep deprivation did not include bath-room breaks. Bradbury claimed that the diaper merely promoted health and sanitation, and was not intended to humiliate the detainee.[102]

While government officials faced pressure to understate the harm caused by "enhanced techniques," they also were tempted to overstate the intelligence benefits. Reports suggest that senior officials overestimated the information available from at least one detainee, Abu Zubaydah, and ordered coercive techniques against the advice of their own interroga-tors. FBI interrogators using traditional rapport-building approaches had already obtained crucial information from Zubaydah. Officials famil-iar with the interrogations acknowledge that Zubaydah provided little or no useful information once the shift toward coercive techniques occurred.[103]

While interrogators used the most intense methods on high-value detain-ees, many of the techniques used in SERE school also made their way to Afghanistan and Iraq. A 2003 "Interrogation Techniques" memo sent by the U.S. Central Command (CENTCOM) authorized techniques such as removal of clothing and the use of dogs.[104] Instructors from the SERE school also went to Iraq after the United States invasion, and applied SERE techniques to captives there. Lt. Col. Steven Kleinman, a trained interrogator in the Air Force Reserves, told the Senate Armed Services Committee that he had witnessed an interrogator train a spotlight on a kneeling detainee and slap the detainee across the face after every question in a half-hour session.[105] Kleinman also saw two interrogators strip a hooded detainee, and leave him standing for twelve hours, shackled by the wrist and ankles.[106] After he reported these incidents, Kleinman's life was threatened. Interrogators informed him that they did not "coddl[e] terrorists."[107] Other officers echoed Kleinman's critiques of the new interrogation paradigm. Noting that the United States had played a pivotal role in establishing the laws of war, Maj. Nathan Hoepner asserted: "We need to take a deep breath and remember who we are. . . . It comes down to standards of right and wrong—something we cannot just put aside when we find it inconvenient."[108] But facing demands that "detainees . . . be broken," this warning carried little weight.[109]

Elsewhere, U.S. officials used other methods of interrogation. Consider the case of Mohammed al-Qahtani, who may have been the missing "twentieth hijacker." American agents took Qahtani to Guantánamo, where he was interrogated for over forty days. A memorandum issued by the Pentagon's general counsel, William "Jim" Haynes, and approved by Secretary of Defense Donald Rumsfeld, authorized techniques such as prolonged standing (not to exceed four hours), cuffing Qahtani's hands and legs, placing him near a menacing dog, and allowing him to sleep only four hours out of every twenty-four. A female interrogator subjected Qahtani to sexual humiliation. He was dehydrated, and rehydrated with an IV while kept in a sitting position for seventeen hours. Qahtani's wrists and ankles grew swollen and sore through prolonged shackling and inactivity. Because of the IV, he urinated on himself.[110] In response to Haynes's signing off on standing not to exceed four hours, Secretary Rumsfeld, who had a specially designed desk in his office that allowed him to stand, wrote in the margin, "I stand for 8–10 hours a day—why are you limiting this to four?"[111] Rumsfeld failed to note that he did not stand in leg irons bolted to the floor.

Debate continues on the value of intelligence data obtained through these interrogation techniques.[112] Some, including former Vice President Cheney, have asserted that the techniques saved thousands of lives.[113] In contrast, President Obama has argued that more traditional rapport-building techniques would have been equally effective.[114] Traditional techniques would not have yielded gross misinformation, such as Ibn al-Libi's fables about ties between Al Qaeda and Saddam Hussein. They would not have compromised the United States's moral authority. Finally, as chapter 3 recounts, rejecting the detour into enhanced interrogation techniques would have preserved the traditional role of the OLC as a source of balanced legal advice to the president.

Material Witnesses

The administration also used detours *within* the criminal justice system, starting with the detention of material witnesses. Detention of material witnesses was used by the administration to hold people who often turned out to be innocent of terrorism, but whom the administration wished to incapacitate. While detention of material witnesses can be a legitimate and effective tool for law enforcement,[115] the administration used it to evade the checks on detention provided elsewhere in the legal system. Here, too, the procedural detour was sometimes accompanied by physical abuse.

Historically, law enforcement has used the detention of material witnesses to secure the testimony of persons with knowledge of crimes who were unable or unwilling to testify in open court. Such testimony provides needed information to grand juries, which decide on charges in the federal system. Moreover, material witness detention is a useful gap filler, particularly in dealing with the special problems of international terrorism investigations. If a suspect in a terrorist conspiracy is about to leave the country, and the government believes it can develop evidence for a criminal prosecution within a reasonably short time, then detaining that individual as a material witness is appropriate.[116] Unfortunately, in a number of cases, the Bush administration used material witness detention not to fill gaps, but as a new mode of confinement.

The detour problem with material witness detentions began after September 11 because the government was interested not only in information, but also often in finding a "hook" for detaining people that it suspected of more serious terrorist acts. Material witness detention became a substitute for an indictment by a grand jury. It was a useful surrogate because some of the protections that surround criminal defendants are not available to the material witness who has been detained. For example, law enforcement must file a charging instrument against a defendant, including an indictment or a criminal complaint, with a detailed description of the defendant's alleged illegal conduct. By contrast, the information provided by law enforcement about material witnesses can be much more sketchy, and judges will often defer to prosecutors on key points, including materiality itself.

The second problem flows from the first. When ordinary protections are not available, law enforcement officials become lazy about facts supporting their actions. In a number of the material witness cases, law enforcement officials provided less information to judges scrutinizing the detention than they should have. Consider the case of Portland lawyer Brandon Mayfield.[117] Prosecutors investigated Mayfield for suspected participation in the Madrid train bombings of 2004, after the FBI matched Mayfield's fingerprints with a print found at the scene. The FBI based its conclusion on a xerox copy of a fax transmission from Spain. Prosecutors submitted an affidavit to the court asserting that Spanish authorities agreed with the fingerprint analysis of the FBI. As a result, a judge apparently approved a covert search of Mayfield's residence and Mayfield's detention for over two weeks as a material witness. In fact, however, FBI agents knew that Spanish authorities *disagreed* with the FBI's fingerprint analysis. Moreover, the FBI's focus on Mayfield may have stemmed from evidence relating to Mayfield's religion and professional associations: Mayfield was a practicing Muslim, and had represented a terrorism defendant in a completely unrelated family law case.[118] In fact, Mayfield had not been out of the country in over fifteen years and had no relationship to the Madrid bombing.[119]

The government can also use the disorienting effect of material witness confinement to trap a suspect into making inaccurate statements under oath. The government clearly has a legitimate interest in discouraging false statements, destruction of evidence, and other misconduct that undermines the integrity of the justice system. But the wide discretion prosecutors have in charging such satellite crimes also creates a risk of abuse.

We can see this problem in *United States v. Awadallah*,[120] in which the government charged a defendant with perjury after the government had held him in terrible conditions as a material witness immediately after September 11. The defendant, a lawful permanent resident and Jordanian national with other family in this country, told federal investigators prior to his detention that he had known two of the September 11 hijackers who had lived in San Diego prior to the attacks. Awadallah's acknowledged acquaintance with two members of the September 11 conspiracy justified the government's interest in Awadallah. What followed, however, was more problematic.

The government secured a material witness warrant without disclosing agents' conversations with Awadallah. The government also failed to tell the issuing judge that the defendant had substantial ties to the San Diego area including a U.S. citizen sibling, that together with his own legal immigration status made him unlikely to flee. Evidence suggested that Awadallah had been badly beaten while in custody. At an appearance before a grand jury, the government asked the defendant if he knew the names of the two San Diego hijackers. After his ordeal, Awadallah said he remembered the name of only one of the men, although he continued to acknowledge that he had known both. The government, which never argued that Awadallah had any role in the 9/11 conspiracy, produced a document showing that at one point Awadallah had known both hijackers' names. Awadallah was charged with perjury. After a mistrial, a second jury acquitted Awadallah in the fall of 2006. Awadallah had spent five years under the shadow of these charges.[121]

Targeting Protesters and Other Ordinary Americans

In addition to targeting those who declined to toe the line within government, the Bush administration and other organizations targeted protesters and critics among the public. The Defense Department, in an echo of abuses from the Nixon administration, compiled dossiers on groups that were critical of the war, including many groups engaging in purely nonviolent and lawful opposition. The New York City Police Department moved from legitimate investigation of terrorist threats to far less appropriate targets, including arts and comedy troupes. In preparation for the Republican National Convention in 2004 to be held in New York, the police investigated a young inventor of a bicycle that could translate Internet text into chalk messages on sidewalks.[122] An agency within the Department of Defense made thousands of requests for information about domestic persons and groups.[123]

Further evidence that the FBI did not "get it" comes from Attorney General Michael Mukasey's guidelines on investigation.[124] These guidelines allow the FBI to question individuals without any reason to believe that the individuals are involved in terrorism.[125] The FBI could continue to question people based on otherwise invidious criteria, such as ethnicity or religion, without having to meet a more rigorous or specific test. The guidelines also grant the FBI untrammeled authority to obtain and compile information on individuals and groups of "possible investigative interest," again with minimal oversight and without any concrete basis for believing that the groups are engaged in terrorism.

In the worst-case scenario, targeting can lead to both false positives and false negatives—individuals breaking laws whom authorities fail to detect, apprehend, and punish. Consider the example of the FBI Terrorist Watchlist. FBI personnel failed to timely list a potential domestic terrorist who subsequently pleaded guilty to stealing ammunition, explosives, and firing devices as a Special Forces soldier in Afghanistan and shipping these items back to the United States. Because of delays at the FBI field office and headquarters, the investigation of the suspect had been open for 147 days before his name made it to the watchlist.[126] Bureaucratic glitches delayed listing of appropriate subjects in 78 percent of the cases studied by the Justice Department's own Inspector General.[127] In over 10 percent of the cases studied, the FBI *never* added an individual's name to the watchlist, even though it had opened a terrorist investigation.[128] The FBI's failure transferred risk to frontline personnel, such as airport security and law enforcement officers in the field, who could have encountered dangerous individuals without adequate warning or preparation. This failure also resulted in "missed opportunities" to detain suspected terrorists and acquire useful intelligence.[129]

While officials running the terrorist watchlist racked up false negatives, they also accumulated large numbers of false positives. Prominent individuals like Senator Edward Kennedy appeared on the list.[130] Fully 72 percent of subjects of closed FBI investigations experienced delays in being removed from the watchlist, even though the investigations had found no evidence of terrorist ties.[131] These delays, which the Inspector General described as far beyond a "reasonable standard," often lasted for months. During the delay, both the individual and anyone with the same name was subject to intensive, inconvenient, and inappropriate scrutiny.[132] In contrast, terrorism subjects improperly left off the list came and went as they pleased.[133]

Targeting Lawyers in the War on Terror

Bush administration officials also targeted lawyers and the attorney-client relationship in the war on terror. At Guantánamo, the government laid down an elaborate grid of formal and informal rules, regulations, and practices that make attorney-client communication very difficult, sow mistrust between attorney and client, and sometimes even punish clients for seeking access to an attorney. Much of this framework stemmed from the Bush administration's view that legal remedies are "lawfare" exploited by our enemies. As Attorney General Ashcroft said, terrorists are "instructed to exploit our judicial process for the success of their operations. . . . [Al Qaeda] abuses individual rights as it abuses jet liners . . . to make weapons of them with which to kill Americans."[134] In other cases, the government pursued lawyers with a fervor out of proportion to their offenses, thus risking a chilling effect on other members of the bar.

When lawyers, including the scores of established lawyers with major firms who now work on terrorism cases, seek to meet with clients at Guantánamo, a protective order limits what the attorneys can say to their clients and how they can say about their interactions regarding their clients with the public and the media.[135] Attorneys must send notes of their conversations to a government office that determines whether the notes involve disclosure of any national security information. Lawyers receive the notes back weeks later, trusting that the team that inspects the notes will not pass on information to officials on the other side of the legal case.

The sometimes draconian workings of the protective order, however, are only part of the grid that affects lawyers working with detainees. The government places more informal impediments in the way throughout the process. The beginning is the path to Guantánamo itself. Attorneys must take a trip that totals well over twelve hours from their home city to Guantánamo. The final three or four hours from the U.S. mainland to the Guantánamo base are spent aboard a small plane with no restrooms, making for an uncomfortable voyage that can become an endurance contest for the participants.[136]

At Guantánamo itself, detainees receive subtle cues that consulting with attorneys is a bad idea. Obstacles start because lawyers cannot talk to detainees who have not already requested an attorney. Attorneys are not permitted to talk to the detainees as a group to inform them of their legal rights. Anecdotal evidence also suggests that U.S. interrogators sometimes masquerade as lawyers, compounding the detainees' mistrust, or seek to exploit ethnic and religious stereotypes, including suggesting that attorneys who are Jewish will not work hard for their Muslim clients.[137] Moreover, there is anecdotal evidence that detainees go to more secure detention facilities, often involving "lockdown" or solitary confinement, for a period of days or even weeks before and after attorney interviews. This more severe confinement deters detainees from seeking legal assistance.

The government also pressured the courageous military lawyers who volunteered to represent detainees to agree to plea bargains without testing the legality of the procedures at Guantánamo or the strength of the government's evidence. Take the treatment of Lt. Cdr. Charles Swift, the lawyer for Salim Hamdan, a Yemeni national who had served as a driver for Osama bin Laden. Hamdan was the first detainee to have his case brought before a military commission, in part because the authorities apparently believed that his case would be easier to prosecute. According to Swift, prosecution lawyers approached him early on, and recommended that he seek a plea bargain that would quickly dispose of the case. Swift informed the prosecutors that he would discuss this with his client, but that he had fundamental concerns with the fairness and accuracy of the procedures for the commissions. The prosecutors were disconcerted by Swift's reluctance to accede to their wishes.[138] Ultimately, Swift and Hamdan's civilian lawyer, Professor Neal Katyal of Georgetown, took their concerns about fairness to the U.S. Supreme Court, and prevailed.[139] Swift, however, was not so fortunate. Instead of receiving kudos for his brave and diligent advocacy, he received a notice that he would not be offered a promotion. Under the military's "up or out" policy, that meant he was forced to retire. While the military insisted that its decision was motivated by other factors, Swift's prominent role in the Hamdan case induces doubts about the military's account.

The war on lawyers has also continued with a triptych of episodes targeting specific attorneys. While justification for action was present in each of the cases, the Bush administration's response betrayed a lack of respect for the institutional role of the bar in representing the unpopular and curbing government overreaching. It also highlighted a lack of proportion that characterized many of the administration's legal decisions.

The first example is the case of Jesselyn Radack, an attorney in the Justice Department's Professional Responsibility Advisory Office who offered unwelcome advice to American interrogators in the case of "American Taliban" John Walker Lindh.[140] Lindh was an American who went to Pakistan and then Afghanistan to learn Islam. He joined the Taliban, although he apparently expressly rejected an offer by an Al Qaeda leader to commit terrorism in the United States.[141] U.S. personnel captured Lindh after the American intervention in Afghanistan. Lindh was also present during a prison uprising in Afghanistan by Al Qaeda and Taliban detainees that resulted in the death of Capt. Johnny "Mike" Spann, although there is no evidence that Lindh was responsible for Spann's death.[142] Lindh was stripped and strapped to a board and questioned both by journalists working for CNN and by U.S. interrogators. Lindh's father engaged a prominent attorney to travel to Afghanistan. Radack was apprised of this by the FBI, which queried whether they could question Lindh. Radack wrote back advising the agents to refrain from further interrogation. The FBI questioned Lindh anyway.[143] Subsequently, Radack became concerned that prosecutors in the case had not apprised the judge of her correspondence, which had apparently disappeared from Lindh's file at Justice.[144]

Soon thereafter, Radack was fired after a hastily arranged negative performance evaluation, even though she had previously received glowing reports.[145] At this point, Radack did something that posed substantial tension with the Lawyers Code of Professional Conduct: she discussed her role in the Lindh case with a *Newsweek* reporter (who proceeded to publish the story),[146] in apparent violation of her duty of confidentiality.

The government then pursued Radack professionally with a ferocity not justified by the violation that may well have occurred. As part of this failure of proportion, the government complained to both the Maryland and Washington DC bar associations. The pendency of the bar complaints made it virtually impossible for Radack to find another job. The Maryland bar complaint was ultimately dismissed; the DC bar complaint was pending for over five years. Other people who by no means shared Radack's ideology took up her cause, including Bruce Fein, a former Reagan administration Justice Department official, who agreed that the Bush administration was more concerned about closing the door on disagreement and perceived disloyalty than on enforcing the rules of legal ethics. Nor did senior officials at the Justice Department limit themselves to seeking Radack's disbarment. They also placed her on the no-fly list, obliging her to prove her loyalty each time she arrived at an airport check-in counter.[147]

The next case in the triptych is the case of Lynne Stewart. A well-known defense attorney, Stewart had defended the "blind sheik," Omar Abdel Rahman, who had been convicted of seditious conspiracy during the Clinton administration because he had urged an associate to kill Egyptian president Hosni Mubarak and attack U.S. Army installations.[148] Justice Department officials were concerned that supporters of the sheik abroad had engaged in violence to seek his release, including attacks at Luxor, Egypt, that killed over sixty tourists.[149] To stop possible coordination between violent sympathizers abroad and the sheik, the government had imposed Special Administrative Measures, or SAMs, on Stewart, which barred her from conveying messages from supporters to the sheik, or conveying messages from the sheik to supporters.[150] Stewart signed an affirmation pledging to honor these restrictions. Nevertheless, she called a press conference in the spring of 2000 to announce to the world that the sheik was considering withdrawing support for the cease-fire that his organization, the Islamic Group, had entered into after the outcry about the Luxor attacks.[151]

Stewart's press conference had little practical impact. The Islamic Group operatives observing the cease-fire heatedly disputed Stewart's message from the sheik, asserting publicly that they *still* believed that nonviolence was the best path, in light of their focus on the political process in Egypt. Perhaps as a result, the Clinton administration had not sought to prosecute Stewart.[152]

The Bush administration, however, was not so forbearing. Despite the absence of concrete harm here, Attorney General Ashcroft approved Stewart's indictment, describing her case as a milestone in the war against terror. Stewart was ultimately convicted of material support of a terrorist group.[153] While Stewart's actions violated the law[154] and Stewart herself acknowledged that she had acted unwisely, the government had other paths. It could have barred Stewart from the federal prison where the sheik was incarcerated or sought disciplinary action against her. Moreover, the government's proposed thirty-year sentence for Stewart, a sixty-five year-old grandmother with cancer, seemed like a stretch, in light of the lack of connection of her conduct to actual harm.[155] The government also failed to consider Stewart's long history of capable criminal defense work and the chilling effect a harsh sentence might have on the defense bar. Fortunately, the judge in the case rejected the government's sentencing recommendation, instead imposing a far more reasonable sentence of twenty-eight months.[156] Particularly in the sentencing phase, the episode was yet another demonstration of the administration's draconian approach to lawyers.

The third story in the triptych involves the case of Lt. Cdr. Matthew Diaz, a JAG lawyer at Guantánamo. Diaz came to the detention center in 2004 to do legal work for the government. He rapidly became convinced that the Defense Department was not complying with the spirit or the letter of the Supreme Court's opinions in *Hamdi v. Rumsfeld* and *Rasul v. Bush* that allowed detainees to obtain some measure of process and seek legal assistance.[157] In particular, he was concerned that the government was imposing blanket secrecy on the detentions, not letting family members or lawyers know whether their loved ones/clients were detained there. Ultimately, Diaz took a step that was both misguided and illegal. He sent the names, on a form he had received that also contained coded information about the detainees' interrogation, to a nonprofit law firm, the Center for Constitutional Rights (CCR) in New York. After CCR informed a federal judge, the government traced the letter back to Diaz, and convened a court-martial. Prosecutors charged Diaz with multiple offenses that could have resulted in decades of imprisonment. The military jury convicted Diaz on a less serious charge, and sentenced him to six months in the brig. Here, too, however, the government could have been more measured, particularly because it disclosed the names of virtually all Guantánamo detainees in 2006. The absence of evidence that this disclosure damaged national security demonstrates the harshness of the government's approach.

Targeting Administration Critics: The Case of Valerie Plame

The administration also targeted opposition inside and outside the federal government. Vice President Cheney and his chief of staff, Lewis "Scooter" Libby, tried to destroy the reputation of Valerie Plame, a CIA covert operative, after Plame's husband, ambassador Joe Wilson, wrote an article that was critical of the administration's case for war. Ironically, while the administration jealously guarded its own secrets, Cheney and Libby were negligent in failing to safeguard Plame's covert identity.

Cheney and Libby used a novel detour to target Plame and Wilson. Wilson wrote publicly that he had traveled to Niger for the government to investigate claims that Saddam Hussein had sought uranium from the African country, and had found no basis for the claims. Cheney and Libby were determined to discredit Wilson. They decided that it would be useful to leak portions of the National Intelligence Estimate (NIE) drafted by the CIA, which also contained the claim that Saddam had contacted Niger. There was one obstacle: the NIE is classified, and disclosing its contents is a crime. Moreover, the CIA's director, George Tenet, believed that it would be inappropriate to leak the NIE's contents.

Not to be stymied by such legal niceties, Cheney and Libby found a way around the CIA's reluctance. At Cheney's behest, Libby went to David Addington, Cheney's counsel, and asked if the president could declassify a document without the CIA's knowledge or approval. Addington, never one to turn down an opportunity to augment presidential power, readily agreed, and was prepared to give Libby a lengthy exegesis on the president's authority. Libby indicated that Addington should keep his voice down, lest this detour scenario get back to the CIA before it could be consummated. Subsequently, Cheney approached Bush at one of their regular private meetings, and sought Bush's permission to declassify the document; Bush approved the request. Libby subsequently was seen on the phone, chatting with journalists with the NIE open on his lap, reading from its contents in an attempt to bolster Cheney and discredit Wilson.[158]

Sound judgment about security matters would have dictated bringing the CIA into the process before declassifying the NIE. Cheney's maneuver around the CIA demonstrated the priorities of the administration. Secrecy was used to shield the group around Cheney from questioning both inside and outside the executive branch; however, when keeping secrets would have impeded crushing of a critic, Cheney's coterie simply arranged a detour.

Conclusion

In sum, the detours of the administration often led to targeting groups of people without achieving significant policy goals. Targeting led to less transparency, as in the 9/11 detentions, where the government made a show of rounding up terrorism suspects, but actually engaged in an immigration dragnet focusing on cab drivers and employees at Middle Eastern establishments. The same problem plagued the government's efforts at Guantánamo, where the six hundred detainees who passed through the facility included some with terrorist ties, but others with no connection to terrorism.[159] The use of detours to target groups also produced significant opportunity costs. Questioning immigrants based on ethnicity is often unproductive, crowding out more focused efforts. A similar calculus applies to coercive interrogation. By using torture on a detainee such as Ibn al-Shaykh al-Libi, interrogators skewed U.S. policy, since al-Libi's fraudulent description of links between Saddam Hussein and Al Qaeda helped make the Bush administration's case for war with Iraq. In addition, detours in interrogation, detention, and surveillance created a perception of unfairness. When the United States seeks cooperation from other nations, those nations can argue that we have relinquished moral leadership.

The Architecture of Impunity

In November 2007, members of the Senate Judiciary Committee were intently questioning Michael Mukasey, a former federal judge whom Bush had nominated to be his third attorney general. Senator Sheldon Whitehouse of Rhode Island, himself a former federal prosecutor, asked Mukasey whether waterboarding was torture. Mukasey had difficulty answering the question with a simple, "Yes." Instead, he said that torture is illegal, and that the United States no longer resorts to waterboarding. While agreeing that waterboarding was "repugnant," Mukasey gave two reasons for failing to answer the senator's question straightforwardly: he had not been fully briefed, and he did not want to pave the way for "personal legal jeopardy" for officials who had used this tactic or ordered its use.[1]

The most disturbing aspect of the Mukasey-Whitehouse exchange was its link to a series of legal memos by elite Justice Department lawyers justifying harsh interrogation practices and providing legal cover to government officials.[2] These legal opinions were typical of Bush officials' efforts to orchestrate impunity—to insulate themselves from the sanctions established under domestic and international law. For true believers like Cheney, David Addington, and John Yoo (the author of most of the "torture memos"), the existing legal rules were illegitimate on principle and indefensible as policy. On this view, the legal rules were merely roadblocks that impeded progress. But the quest for impunity also had ruinous ramifications that Cheney, Addington, and Yoo failed to consider.

The principled basis for rejecting impunity rests on the framers' scheme of separation of powers described in the introduction and chapter 1. Powers overlap so that each branch can in some measure check the ambitions of the others.[3] The framers' scheme does not invariably require imposition of criminal and civil liability on executive officials—there are principled and policy reasons to limit liability in particular circumstances. A categorical license to act without repercussions, however, would be anathema to the framers' intent.

The policy consequences of categorical impunity are also dire. Accountability underwrites the United States's most precious asset—its ability to project the "soft power" that persuades the world of the rightness of our cause.[4] Sending the message that no one is above the law confirms the legitimacy of government, and invites broad assent both domestically and internationally. Holding officials accountable ensures that those who follow at home and abroad do so as a matter of consent, not coercion. While force is sometimes necessary, constituencies built on consent are bound by ties of loyalty and shared stake that are ultimately far more durable.

Just as important, categorical impunity creates moral hazard for policymakers. Economists warn that the availability of insurance can encourage people to take unwise risks. Under Cheney and Addington's direction, Yoo concocted legal opinions that amounted to a roving insurance policy for government overreaching. In relying on this dubious form of insurance, officials took risks with the United States's reputation and values.

This chapter explores the Bush administration's attempts to orchestrate and enforce impunity. It first addresses the machinations of Cheney, Addington, and company to arrange impunity before the fact. That effort started with the selection of sites for detention outside the United States as "law-free zones." It continued with legal opinions that used strained (some would say "tortured") readings[5] of statutes and the Constitution to insulate officials from accountability for coercive interrogation and eavesdropping. Bush officials also argued for impunity after the fact, asserting that evidence needed for a lawsuit was a "state secret." Moreover, officials claimed immunity from lawsuits. To shield themselves, they either argued for absolute immunity or sought cover behind their rank and the lack of specific case law on matters like torture abroad. To shield allies, they persuaded Congress to grant immunity to the telecommunications companies that had assisted in the government's program of warrantless surveillance. To thwart investigation of political pressure on eight fired United States Attorneys, the White House invoked executive privilege, a muddled doctrine that President Nixon had unsuccessfully sought to use to cover up misconduct during the Watergate scandal. Few if any previous administrations have sought to orchestrate impunity with such breadth and persistence.

Accountability and Geography

Soon after September 11, the Bush administration sought to frustrate accountability through arguments based on geography and exigency. The audacity of the administration's attempts triggered a comprehensive rebuff from the Supreme Court. In a series of landmark cases, the Court rejected the administration's claim that geography and exigency permitted the indefinite detention and unfair trial of suspected terrorists. To understand the consequences of these cases, however, we must understand the landscape of precedent on geography, exigency, and government power.

The use of geography started a century earlier, with the Insular Cases. In *Downes v. Bidwell*,[6] the Court held that the Constitution's provisions did not extend to unincorporated territories such as Puerto Rico, which the United States had acquired in the Spanish-American War. Congress could impose tariffs on goods originating in these territories, even though goods shipped from one state to another cannot be subject to tariffs. Also, residents of the territories need not be given the right to vote in U.S. presidential elections. But, the Court said, some basic residue of due process remained—although the Court revealed little about its content.

In a case after World War II, *Johnson v. Eisentrager*,[7] the Court deferred again to geography's dictates, holding that a German military officer accused of war crimes in the Pacific theater was not entitled to habeas corpus relief. The Court stressed the logistical and practical difficulties of calling military personnel to testify. Finally, in *United States v. Verdugo-Urquidez*,[8] the Court held in 1990 that the government could seize an individual in Mexico without a warrant and bring that person to the United States to stand trial. Here, too, however, Justice Anthony Kennedy's concurrence stressed that some basic procedural protections might prevail in spite of geography, and emphasized that the person seized would still be entitled to a jury trial within the United States.

The Bush administration sought to link its policies with these precedents, thereby avoiding judicial review. It also sought to evade constraints built into international law. The administration refused to establish a "competent tribunal" under the Geneva Conventions[9] to determine whether a detainee caught after September 11 was a POW whom the government would have to release at the conclusion of hostilities. Instead, the government merely decided on a blanket basis that no detainee met the criteria for POW status. The administration's legal argument was stark. First, neither the Taliban nor Al Qaeda were parties to the Geneva Conventions. Al Qaeda was an organization, not a state, and the Taliban represented what administration lawyers conveniently called a "failed state," which similarly could not be a party to Geneva.[10] Second, according to the administration, the Taliban and Al Qaeda did not meet the requirements for POW status: they did not wear uniforms, use a fixed command structure, carry arms openly, or refrain from killing civilians.[11] As a result, they were unlawful combatants, not POWs. But the administration missed a step: under Geneva, a "competent tribunal" must find that a detainee is an unlawful combatant. By simply decreeing that *all* detainees were unlawful combatants, the administration took a detour around this crucial requirement.

Similarly, the government also decided early on that no detainee qualified for protection under another provision of the Geneva Conventions known as Common Article 3,[12] which bars torture and cruel, inhuman, and degrading treatment. According to the administration's lawyers, Common Article 3, which only bars conflicts "not of an international character," neatly exempted a conflict between the United States on one side and Al Qaeda and the Taliban on the other. Common Article 3, on this view, applied only to civil wars. Since the United States was not fighting a civil war with Al Qaeda, Article 3 did not apply.[13]

Here, as elsewhere, the administration's legal arguments resembled the fine art of self-fulfilling prophecy. Administration lawyers narrowed the scope of the Geneva Conventions provisions until those provisions appeared irrelevant to the administration's actions. As those narrow legal opinions marginalized the Conventions, lawyers like then White House counsel Alberto Gonzales triumphantly declared that September 11 had made Geneva "obsolete."[14]

The constitutional arguments made by the administration were just as sweeping. Administration lawyers argued that the president had inherent power to lock up suspected terrorists without seeking approval or review from either Congress or the courts. Indeed, said the lawyers, Congress would be acting unconstitutionally if it sought to restrain that presidential power over treatment of detainees by broadly construing international law.[15] The administration's lawyer told the Supreme Court that the president could handle this unfettered authority. Responding to a question about the tactics that American personnel might use in interrogating suspected terrorists, the lawyer assured the Supreme Court in April 2004 that the administration would never torture detainees.[16] That same day, network news broadcasts first showed photos depicting abuse of detainees at the Iraq prison of Abu Ghraib.[17]

A couple of months later, the Supreme Court issued the first of its decisions rejecting the Bush administration's positions on terrorism, by holding in *Hamdi v. Rumsfeld*[18] that the Constitution did not provide the president with a "blank check."[19] Justice Sandra Day O'Connor, writing for the Court, warned that an unaccountable executive could make mistakes, including detaining people who were merely in the wrong place at the wrong time.[20] In O'Connor's words, "History and common sense teach us that an unchecked system of detention carries the potential to become a means for oppression and abuse of others."[21] As a result, the Court held, the administration had to provide due process to an American citizen, Yaser Hamdi, who had been apprehended in Afghanistan during the United States's military intervention to remove the Taliban. The government released Hamdi soon thereafter,[22] although it continued to hold hundreds of detainees at Guantánamo and many more in Iraq and Afghanistan.

The administration also established military commissions to try detainees without consulting Congress or providing basic procedural rights. In *Hamdan v. Rumsfeld*,[23] decided in 2006, the Supreme Court rejected the president's claims to such unilateral authority. Justice John Paul Stevens's opinion in *Hamdan* invoked the precedent of the *Steel Seizure Case*,[24] in which the Court had ruled that President Truman lacked authority to seize the steel mills during the Korean War in the face of a federal statute that seemed to preclude such unilateral action. In *Hamdan*, the Court said that the president had to comply with Congress's mandate that military commissions, whenever "practicable," offered the same procedural protections as courts-martial used to try American service personnel. Similarly, according to *Hamdan*, Congress intended to subject military commissions to the laws of war, including the Geneva Conventions, which require that detainees have access to a tribunal with rules acceptable to "civilized peoples."[25] Because the military commission rules permitted departures from these basic norms, including blanket authority to exclude a detainee from his own hearing, the president's rules did not meet the Geneva standard. In a trenchant if unspoken allusion to the abuses at Abu Ghraib, Justice Stevens noted that the government had charged Hamdan with conspiracy to assist Al Qaeda, not with the commission of specific war crimes such as torture and the use of dogs to terrorize prisoners.[26]

The administration also argued that U.S. courts had no jurisdiction over Guantánamo Bay. According to administration lawyers, Guantánamo was under Cuban sovereignty, and therefore outside the reach of federal courts.[27] The fledgling government of Cuba leased Guantánamo Bay to the United States shortly after the Spanish-American War in a treaty that the Castro government has sought to repudiate. Under the terms of the lease, the United States recognized Cuba's sovereignty over Guantánamo.[28] But the lease also provided that the United States would exercise "complete jurisdiction and control" over the leased area. For the administration, this was a tempting twofer indeed: the administration would get to do what it wanted with detainees, but Cuba's nominal sovereignty would deflect the prying eyes of American courts.

After the Supreme Court struck down Bush's military commissions and questioned whether Guantánamo was beyond the courts' purview, the administration upped the ante with the Military Commissions Act of 2006 (MCA).[29] In pushing the Congress to enact the MCA weeks before the 2006 elections, the administration again turned to law and order rhetoric, making it clear that a vote against the bill would demonstrate legislators' softness on terrorism.[30] The MCA set out rules for military commissions that appeared to permit evidence obtained through coercion.[31] It also stripped federal courts of jurisdiction over petitions for habeas corpus brought by detainees, instead channeling efforts at judicial review into a narrower proceeding where courts could not hear new evidence regarding a detainee's innocence. Habeas corpus is perhaps the most important pillar of democracy, which allows the individual to seek release from arbitrary imprisonment at the government's hands. So important was habeas that the English barons made it a centerpiece for the Magna Carta, signed by King John at Runnymede centuries before the Constitution. The MCA's jurisdiction-stripping provision flouted this long history, and risked making courts into a rubber stamp for the government's Combatant Status Review Tribunals, which did not give the detainee access to adverse evidence or provide an opportunity to present evidence that was favorable.

The afterword of this volume discusses the Supreme Court's reckoning with the MCA in June 2008 in the landmark decision of *Boumediene v. Bush*. Here is the place to offer some tentative conclusions about the administration's resort to Guantánamo. In the short term, using Guantánamo was an attractive expedient. In the longer term, however, it had the effect of many other detours: It diminished the legitimacy of the United States's efforts, and so therefore reduced the "soft power" the United States could bring to bear around the rest of the world. It also encouraged bad habits among officials, who did not have to ask the difficult questions about what to do with detainees once we apprehended them.[32] With "send them to Guantánamo" as the answer, officials could avoid formulating an exit strategy. It took the administration a number of years to appreciate that in some cases they would need evidence that was obtained lawfully to present to a tribunal. Responding to this concern, the administration sent out FBI "clean teams" in late 2006 to retrace the steps of intelligence and military personnel.[33] At that point, however, the trail had gone cold, witnesses, documents, and other evidence had sometimes disappeared, and the task was far more challenging that it would have been otherwise.

Moreover, Cheney, Addington, and the rest failed to appreciate that American governance, because of the framers' insistence on the separation of powers, is dynamic. Even when the executive acquires greater discretion in the short term because of a crisis, eventually the pendulum swings back. Executive officials who have practiced consultation with the other branches all along are in a better position to manage that backlash.[34] Officials who have counted on a detour like Guantánamo to insulate them from accountability will experience an even greater blowback from other branches and constituencies long ignored.

As we shall see, winding down Guantánamo presented serious problems. The administration had to worry increasingly about where to put people as pressure built to close the camp. Sending people back to some countries was difficult because of concerns about the Convention Against Torture that the administration had discounted in its own conduct of interrogations. It is to that sorry story that we now turn.

Coercive Interrogation and Legal Advice

In one of the most shameful episodes in the annals of American law, the Bush administration used the Justice Department to shield itself from accountability for coercive interrogation. After September 11, interrogators at the Pentagon and the Central Intelligence Agency wanted to know how far they could go. One CIA lawyer advised that the definition of torture is "basically subject to perception. If the detainee dies, you're doing it wrong."[35] To those seeking guidance, this advice was less than helpful. The Justice Department's elite OLC provided more definitive answers.

Into the post–September 11 vacuum stepped John Yoo, the OLC attorney and Berkeley law professor who had outlined the philosophical case for unilateral executive power. Yoo was part of a group dubbed the "War Council"[36] that mapped strategy on detention and interrogation starting shortly after September 11. Other members of the War Council included Alberto Gonzales, then White House Counsel and subsequently Bush's second Attorney General; David Addington, then counsel to Vice President Cheney; and William "Jim" Haynes, Pentagon general counsel.

To set parameters for permissible interrogation techniques, Yoo drafted a remarkable piece of legal reasoning, now generally known as the Bybee Memo.[37] In this legal opinion, Yoo sought to narrow interpretation of the torture statute,[38] which prohibited U.S. personnel from engaging in torture overseas. The contortions in Yoo's opinion suggested that he wished to make prosecutions for coercive interrogation impossible. Unfortunately, Yoo's interpretations were so strained that, as one commentator has observed, they amounted to "torturing the law."[39]

Yoo justified his advice with analogies that defied common sense. For example, the torture statute follows the lead of the international Convention Against Torture in defining torture as the infliction of "severe pain." To interpret this term, Yoo cited a statute on medical care for undocumented aliens.[40] Undocumented aliens are a perennial political football, and Congress denied coverage for routine illnesses of the undocumented population.[41] In emergencies, however, where a patient is near death, experiencing severe pain equivalent to organ failure, Congress authorized coverage. This may or may not be good policy in the health care realm, but the trade-offs considered by Congress in that domain have little to do with torture. Ignoring this mismatch of policy concerns, Yoo asserted that "severe pain" under the torture statute should be judged by the same "organ failure" test. But Yoo's analogy was flawed. In essence, Yoo argued that Congress's refusal to reimburse medical treatment of a nonemergency condition authorized government to *create* such a condition. Put another way, suppose that Congress refused to reimburse medical treatment for harm caused by a punch in the nose. Few people would believe that punching someone in the nose is therefore appropriate. Few people, that is, apart from John Yoo.

Finally, Yoo argued that the statutes do not really matter. The president, he claimed, has the power to order torture, by virtue of being commander in chief. Indeed, in an interpretive leap that no administration official asked Yoo to make, Yoo volunteered in a later opinion that actions clearly otherwise illegal under federal law, including maiming someone by cutting off an ear or throwing acid in someone's eyes, would be legal if the presidents says so.[42] Yoo asserted that any statute that says otherwise would be an unconstitutional power grab *by the legislature*. Therefore, Yoo claimed, he was actually on the side of the Constitution, avoiding an interpretation that would have triggered constitutional questions. Unfortunately, Yoo's position here is against the great weight of precedent. Yoo failed to mention the Supreme Court's *Youngstown* opinion, which holds that the power of the president is at its lowest ebb when the president acts against the wishes of Congress on a matter committed to both branches. Congress has the power under the Constitution to declare war and regulate the army and navy, as well as provide for redress of violations of the law of nations. A lawyer for the executive branch providing advice on military operations in light of international law must consider the limits imposed by *Youngstown*. Failing to acknowledge those limits does not make them disappear. Yoo also failed to discuss *United States v. Lee*,[43] in which a federal appeals court had repeatedly described waterboarding as "water torture."

Some lawyers were taken aback by the policies on interrogation pursued by the administration. For example, Alberto Mora, general counsel of the Navy, confronted Haynes after Mora learned belatedly of the techniques, such as prolonged standing and sleep deprivation, authorized for Mohammed al-Qahtani, the alleged "twentieth hijacker."[44] Haynes and Rumsfeld withdrew permission for these techniques in January 2003. That is only the end of one chapter, however, in this dismal narrative.

Haynes and Rumsfeld subsequently authorized creation of a Working Group of Pentagon lawyers to examine interrogation issues. The Working Group was chaired by Mary Walker, counsel for the Air Force, who was a bureaucratic ally of Haynes. Taking no chances, Haynes also arranged to receive a memo from Yoo, which Haynes showed to the astonished Mora in draft form in January 2003.[45] This later opinion from Yoo ratified everything done with Qahtani.[46] It stated that interrogators acting with the president's approval could do virtually *anything*, including maiming or biting. Here, too, Yoo did his constitutional two-step. He argued that one must read provisions like the anti-maiming statute to permit the president to personally order exceptions, or else those statutes were simply unconstitutional curbs on the president's authority as commander in chief. The Working Group Report, although Haynes claimed that it curbed interrogation practices, left a large loophole for practices approved in individual cases by Rumsfeld.[47]

Moreover, the Working Group Report was not a deliberative document arising from give-and-take among its members, who included top military lawyers who were uniformly opposed to "enhanced" techniques. Alberto Mora only learned about the final Working Group Report a year later, after news surfaced about abuses at Abu Ghraib.[48] As Senator Lindsey Graham, Republican of South Carolina, put it, if group members did not see the work product, "I'm not so sure that's much of a working group."[49] Reflecting this absence of deliberation, the Working Group's report was a cut-and-paste job that cribbed from Yoo's work. Substantial portions of the report addressing legal authority for coercive interrogation in fact came directly from the Bybee Memo and from Yoo's even broader memorandum of March 2003.[50]

The pursuit of impunity encountered a roadblock when Jack Goldsmith took over as head of the Office of Legal Counsel in the fall of 2003. Goldsmith got the job because he had helped fashion the unilateralist model of presidential power by questioning the legitimacy and relevance of international law and the wisdom of a pioneering Supreme Court decision striking down arbitrary cold war travel restrictions.[51] During and after his time at OLC, Goldsmith defended the interrogation techniques approved by senior officials for use at Guantánamo[52] and also allowed the CIA to remove non-Iraqis from that country for purposes of interrogation.[53] Nevertheless, Goldsmith was a far more discerning lawyer than Yoo. Moreover, Goldsmith backed his discernment with the courage to face down bureaucratic foes like David Addington.

Goldsmith's prudence and courage did not always limit his willingness to interpret international law narrowly to suit the administration's ends. Goldsmith conceded too much ground to the forces pushing for impunity when he allowed the CIA to remove non-Iraqis from Iraq.[54] In his draft opinion,[55] Goldsmith stated that Article 49 of the Fourth Geneva Convention does not bar the deportation of undocumented aliens from occupied Iraq, or their "brief" detention elsewhere for purposes of interrogation. But these conclusions do not square with the text or context of Article 49. Article 49 prohibits "transfers" or "deportations" of "protected persons" by an occupying power. While this provision is not free from ambiguity, the International Committee of the Red Cross (ICRC), which merits deference as the organization charged with responsibility for monitoring compliance with the Geneva Conventions, views Article 49 as an absolute prohibition designed to bar "disappearances" wrought by an occupied power. This reading serves a preventive purpose: it ensures that in the fluid period of an occupation, an occupying power will not be able to spirit troublesome persons out of the country.[56] Moreover, Article 49 works in tandem with other provisions of international treaty and customary law that bar cruel, inhuman, and degrading treatment and torture. If an occupying power can transfer residents of one state to another, it also can hide them from view, and then engage in abusive interrogation techniques with impunity. In ignoring this concern, Goldsmith failed to give Article 49 the purposive reading that customary international law requires.[57]

Nor was this the only time that Goldsmith ignored the ominous context surrounding requests for authority from his governmental clients. Goldsmith approved a list of twenty-four interrogation techniques issued by the Pentagon in April 2003 after the Working Group cribbed much of its final report from Yoo's memos. According to Goldsmith, none of these techniques entailed "anything rough."[58] But this conclusion masks warning signs within the list of techniques. For example, item E is titled "Fear Up Harsh"; it contemplates "significantly increasing the level of fear in the detainee."[59] The item's description does not specify what measures the interrogator might take to heighten the detainee's fear. Item U permits "environmental manipulation," including adjusting temperature to produce "moderate discomfort."[60] Moreover, a rider to the list notes that the techniques may involve "physical contact, stress or, . . . physical pain and harm."[61] A rider of this kind should have been a red flag: how could techniques consistent with "humane" treatment[62] produce "pain and harm"? Nevertheless, Goldsmith has written that he had a "relatively easy time" concluding that the techniques were legal.[63]

Despite his willingness to ignore these red flags, however, Goldsmith had a saving grace: he lacked Yoo's zealous certitude about presidential power. For Goldsmith, clear statements by Congress generally trumped the president's authority. Reading Yoo's memos through this lens, Goldsmith reacted with dismay, describing Yoo's analysis as "lacking detachment" and "wildly broader than was necessary."[64] One can imagine that Yoo's "blank check"[65] for maiming and biting in the March 2003 opinion left Goldsmith particularly appalled. Goldsmith never wished to expand the scope of an opinion beyond what was absolutely needed.[66] Since none of the disclosures about interrogation even hints that the administration ordered an interrogator to maim or bite a detainee, Goldsmith perceived advice on this subject as gratuitous, if not perverse. Goldsmith took this tack even though he continues to maintain that a more precise analysis would not have barred any technique actually used by the administration, including prolonged standing, sleep deprivation, sexual humiliation, and waterboarding.[67]

When Goldsmith's concerns led him to withdraw Yoo's opinions,[68] Addington pushed back. Referring to Goldsmith's finding that another counterterrorism initiative, presumably the Terrorist Surveillance Program, lacked legal support, Addington told Goldsmith that "the blood of the hundred thousand people who die in the next attack will be on *your* hands."[69] Addington admonished Goldsmith that his withdrawal of Yoo's memos on interrogation was a grave disappointment to the president.[70] After Addington's observation that the president and others had "lost faith" in Goldsmith, Goldsmith quit OLC and assumed a professorship at Harvard.[71]

With Goldsmith's resignation, negotiating the conflict between sound legal advice and the White House's pursuit of impunity fell to a veteran national security lawyer, Daniel Levin. Levin, whom the White House named as acting head of OLC, was a lawyer's lawyer who early in his career had done pro bono work for people with mental disabilities.[72] Levin's memo on interrogation techniques, issued in December 2004,[73] marked a clear improvement over Yoo's tone, but conceded key ground to Addington. Levin opened with welcome clarity, asserting that "torture is abhorrent." As Levin turned to defining torture, however, clarity faded. Levin asserted that torture has a durational component—mere transitory harm cannot be torture. This convenient qualification was less far-fetched on the surface than the arguments made by Yoo, but potentially left loopholes just as large. Waterboarding is often brief, as the subject begins to ingest more and more water in a vain attempt to breathe, and panic takes over. Under the circumstances, the brevity of the experience does not remove it from torture's realm.

Levin also included a footnote to mollify White House Counsel Alberto Gonzales, whose nomination to be Attorney General might have been imperiled by a straightforward condemnation of previous interrogation practices. Lawyers earn their living with footnotes and fine print, and Levin's footnote placated Gonzales. In the footnote, Levin acknowledged differences with earlier OLC opinions, but stated that the conclusions reached in those memos would not have been different under the criteria that he outlined.[74]

Despite this apparent cave-in, Levin could not quell his doubts about the legality of waterboarding. Since Levin was a diligent lawyer who disliked loose ends, he went to extreme lengths to explore these reservations. To gain better insight into the real-world consequences of the Justice Department's legal opinions, Levin experienced waterboarding himself.[75] Sources suggest that afterward, Levin called for more stringent regulation of the practice.[76] Evidence also suggests that harsh tactics diminished after Levin's memo.[77] This positive change justified the footnote that Levin's superiors forced him to include. Overall, Levin showed a willingness to learn, grow, and say, "No." The administration could not tolerate such temerity, and declined to nominate Levin to be permanent head of the Office of Legal Counsel.[78]

To replace Levin, the White House settled on an ambitious young lawyer, Steven Bradbury, who came with a decisive endorsement: Levin had warned Gonzales that Bradbury was too receptive to pressure from senior officials.[79] Demonstrating Levin's gift for predicting the future, Bradbury issued a string of opinions giving Cheney and Addington all they wanted. Bradbury repeatedly invoked the durational standard that Levin had devised, asserting that no approved technique had caused prolonged harm. For facts underlying this assessment, Bradbury turned to the medical personnel who had been present when earlier interrogations took place. Medical personnel asserted that none of the detainees subjected to waterboarding had displayed "any evidence" of lasting harm. Moreover, Bradbury insisted that medical personnel had imposed strict time limits on waterboarding, and "closely monitored" the interrogations. [80] But Bradbury's assertions are like a three-legged stool: if one leg breaks, the entire stool collapses.

First, a conscientious lawyer would have recognized the self-serving nature of the medical personnel reports. Presumably, the reporting personnel knew that if they offered a different opinion on the harm caused by enhanced interrogation techniques, they and their colleagues could be prosecuted for violation of the torture statute. The effect is a bit like that reported in the classic movie *Anatomy of a Murder*, in which a client tells his lawyer, played by Jimmy Stewart, that he has just committed a homicide. Stewart explains to the client how the insanity defense works: if the client was so distraught that he did not know right from wrong, he could not be found guilty. After this explanation, Stewart asks the client to tell him what transpired. The client's story tracks Stewart's explanation, word-for-word.[81] In real life, the lawyer will suspect that this coincidence is probably too good to be true. Bradbury's advice was meant not for the real world, but for the world of detours that Cheney and Addington had constructed.

Common sense should have tipped off Bradbury that medical personnel were viewing the interrogations through rose-colored glasses. Bradbury acknowledged that waterboarding could cause "spasms of the larynx" that would prevent breathing even after cessation of the technique.[82] The prudent lawyer might have become alarmed at this risk, and required more facts before finding no prolonged harm. Bradbury, however, termed the risk "remote."[83] Bradbury also saw no likelihood of lasting psychological harm when an interrogator performing waterboarding on a resistant detainee cupped his hands around the detainee's nose and mouth, forcing the detainee to swallow "significant quantities" of water that prevented breathing.[84] Moreover, Bradbury accepted the CIA's claim that substantial edema or swelling in the ankles caused by extended standing sleep deprivation was not painful, even when the detainee's feet were shackled.[85] Here, too, Bradbury failed to even consider that such tactics could cause long-term, debilitating trauma.

The canyon in Bradbury's common sense accompanied a second problem, this one with the facts. Bradbury's analysis of waterboarding hinged on interrogators' compliance with limits. But Bradbury surely knew that interrogators in earlier episodes of waterboarding had blown through those constraints.[86] While Bradbury's mention of limits, parsed closely, could apply only to *future* interrogations, this sentence immediately followed and reinforced his claim that previous waterboarded subjects had not suffered lasting harm. Bradbury's approach here echoed the word games played by the elite Justice Department lawyers in the Japanese American internment litigation during World War II, who twisted language to avoid calling the Court's attention to flaws in an inflammatory government report.[87]

Third, Bradbury must have known that past medical monitoring had been ineffectual. Interrogators had exceeded the guidelines egregiously, suggesting that medical monitors had been either inattentive or complicit. Even assuming that medical monitoring could *ever* excuse or mitigate techniques that would otherwise be torture,[88] the track record of medical monitoring on interrogations did not pass muster.

When three legs on a stool are broken, adding a fourth will not be much help. But that was what Bradbury did. He authorized the combination of techniques—for example, using waterboarding and sleep deprivation in tandem.[89] Bradbury discounted the risk that waterboarding could exacerbate the hallucinations caused by standing sleep deprivation.[90] For support, Bradbury relied again on the broken three-legged stool, citing previous CIA interrogations and "diligent" medical monitoring. Mental suffering would be purely short-term, Bradbury opined, since hallucinations would cease during pauses in the interrogation sessions and medical personnel would intervene "at the first signs of hallucinatory experiences." Here, too, Bradbury failed to concede the ineffectiveness of medical monitoring or consider whether repeated hallucinations experienced under duress would create lasting trauma.

In addition, Bradbury fashioned a sliding scale for coercive interrogation, in which the ends justify the means. According to Bradbury, most interrogation tactics fall within a sliding scale, where the purpose of the interrogation may justify greater levels of coercion. Attempts to prevent a terrorist attack, for example, might justify a range of more intrusive tactics.[91] The good news for detainees was that the Justice Department acknowledged that certain techniques—including "forcing an individual to perform sexual acts, threatening an individual with sexual mutilation, or using an individual as a human shield"[92]—were per se inappropriate. But the bad news was that apparently virtually anything else was OK. The only constraint Bradbury acknowledged was the Supreme Court's "shocks the conscience" test,[93] which is highly amorphous and imposes only modest practical limits on interrogations.[94]

To reach this result, the administration again tortured the law. The case cited by the administration in a 2008 letter to Congress, *Prosecutor v. Aleksovski*,[95] said *nothing* about the purpose of interrogation. The Convention Against Torture states that torture includes abuse for interrogational purposes, and that such abuse is not excusable for "any reason whatever." *Aleksovski* does not depart from this bedrock principle; it merely says that whether a given kind of treatment is inhumane or degrading depends on the *victim's* circumstances, including the victim's gender, age, and medical condition.[96] As a basic example, forcing a young male to strip to the waist might be appropriate, but forcing a female to do so would not be. The Bush administration's spin would have opened the floodgates to continued abuse of the kind that had already tarnished the United States's reputation.

Coercion and Impunity: The Lawyers' Testimony Before Congress

The search for impunity knows no stopping point. Arranging for impunity before the fact is one dimension, diligently worked by Yoo and Bradbury at Addington's behest, with the brief interlude of more conscientious lawyering offered by Goldsmith and Levin. Another dimension is the scramble for impunity after the fact. In the case of policies and legal opinions on coercive interrogation, this latter effort entailed testimony before Congress that was frequently unhelpful and sometimes appeared to be misleading. It also involved the destruction of videotapes of interrogation sessions, actions that could constitute obstruction of justice.

After the election of 2006, the new Democratic Congress was determined to investigate and document the evolution of the Bush administration's justifications for coercive interrogation. To that end, the Senate Armed Services Committee, chaired by Michigan's Carl Levin, and the Constitution, Civil Rights, and Civil Liberties Subcommittee of the House Judiciary Committee, chaired by Representative Jerrold Nadler of New York, convened hearings in 2008 to seek testimony from the participants in the formation of this legal strategy.

Before discussing the testimony, a brief analysis of the law on lying to Congress is in order. Witnesses testifying before Congress may decline to answer specific questions because of attorney-client or other privileges, although the Bush administration went further, as we shall see later in this chapter, by refusing to permit White House adviser Karl Rove or former counsel Harriet Miers to even show up. Witnesses who lied to Congress or withheld information have been convicted of a federal offense.[97] The Bush lawyers sometimes claimed attorney-client or executive privilege, but also claimed failure of memory. Those who do not wish to be forthcoming often seemed to believe that asserting amnesia would effectively immunize them from perjury charges—by saying, "I don't recall," a witness avoids a categorical "Yes" or "No" response that investigators may find easy to disprove, and sets the matter in the recesses of the witness's mind, where an investigator may not wish to follow. But suspects have been found guilty of perjury in connection with false claims of memory loss, where the surrounding context made that falsity plain beyond a reasonable doubt.[98] In addition, courts have on occasion found that circumstances rendered claims of memory loss utterly incredible, and have imposed sentence enhancements for obstruction of justice.[99]

Both a perjury conviction and a sentencing enhancement require that a defendant's false claim of a particular mental state be both intentional and material. In other words, the false claim must be the product of conscious design, not mere inadvertence. Moreover, the false claim cannot be merely incidental—instead, it must concern a core issue in the proceeding.

In the Senate Armed Services Committee hearings, memory loss was the dominant motif for former Pentagon general counsel William Haynes. Haynes is a complex figure,[100] who at the close of his testimony expressed ambivalence about the interrogation techniques that he recommended in the case of suspected "twentieth hijacker" Mohammed al-Qahtani. But Haynes's testimony before the Committee did not resemble the testimony of someone with little or nothing to hide.

Haynes cited memory problems in his first answer to the committee, advising committee members that his recollection was "not perfect." He alluded to memory problems over thirty times throughout the hearing. For example, the only legal memo that Haynes recalled seeing before he drafted the November 2002 memo on questioning Qahtani was an unsophisticated effort by Lt. Col. Diane Beaver.[101] Senators seemed puzzled that Haynes would approve a significant departure from previous military practice on interrogation based on one memo from a relatively junior officer without seeking other legal input from senior military counsel or from the Justice Department. Haynes maintained, however, that he could not recall seeing any other memos, including the OLC's Bybee Memo or memos from military lawyers bitterly criticizing proposed interrogation techniques.[102]

While Haynes's memory issues may have stemmed from the extraordinary demands of his job, they clashed with his striking grasp of detail on other matters concerning detainee interrogation. For example, in his testimony Haynes minutely dissected a Pentagon report on interrogations, claiming that the report inaccurately described the use of dogs in Qahtani's interrogation.[103] Haynes also vehemently objected to reports that detainees were stripped naked pursuant to Rumsfeld's instructions. According to Haynes, Rumsfeld only authorized forced removal of clothing. In a particularly fine distinction, Haynes maintained that "removal of clothing [was] not nudity."[104] Haynes's laser-like recall on these matters belied his claims of amnesia about the genesis of the interrogation policy.

Haynes's testimony that he could not recall having read the Bybee Memo before drafting his November 2002 recommendations also raises more questions than it answers. Since, as Senator Levin of Michigan and Haynes agreed at the hearing, the Bybee Memo was authoritative for the executive branch, and Haynes had been a key player on these issues since late 2001, Haynes would naturally have come across it. Further, both Yoo and Haynes were members of the aforementioned War Council.[105] In addition, Haynes had asked Yoo for a memo in February 2002 on legal constraints governing interrogations of prisoners captured in Afghanistan.[106] Under these circumstances, it would have been odd for Haynes to be unfamiliar with the Bybee Memo. Other reports suggest that Haynes was a close associate of Yoo's, even asking for legal opinions during sports matches,[107] making Haynes's claim of memory loss even more curious.

While Haynes's claims of memory failure may seem unimportant, they actually were material to the committee's investigation. The questions Haynes faced dealt with the committee's core concern: how did interrogation policy develop? The answer to this question hinged on whether Haynes's November 2002 memo on questioning Qahtani was a one-shot deal, triggered by understandable concerns about Qahtani's possible knowledge of future attacks,[108] or part of a pattern of decision making by senior officials aimed at undermining the executive's compliance with law.

The testimony of Addington and Yoo relied less on memory failure and more on impatience with Congress's presumption in questioning the executive (Addington) or on polite invocations of attorney-client privilege (Yoo). At a House committee hearing in June 2008, Addington denied that he would have any legal or moral responsibility for harm that might have befallen subjects of interrogation who were waterboarded. Addington's response to the committee suggested that "moral" responsibility was absurd, either because virtually anything done to suspected terrorists was inherently moral or because the entire realm of argument struck Addington as soft. Asked whether it would be legal to torture a detainee's child to obtain information, Addington responded curtly, "I'm not here to render legal advice to your committee."[109] Yoo, for his part, repeatedly invoked attorney-client privilege when asked about specific interrogation techniques. He did eventually observe that whether waterboarding is torture "would depend on the circumstances."[110] This view echoed the sliding-scale argument Bradbury made in his letter on interrogation techniques.

Daniel Levin's testimony before Congress reflected both more authentic insight into the long-term costs of coercive interrogation and his own brand of legalistic explanation. Levin forthrightly acknowledged that an interrogator who had relied on the Bybee Memo and "went up to the limits of what it allowed . . . would be violating the law."[111] Levin also implicitly confirmed that he had voluntarily undergone waterboarding, and noted that his clear statement that "torture is abhorrent" and his growing doubts about waterboarding had changed administration policy for the better. Levin had an unsatisfying explanation, however, for the footnote in his memo stating that he would have left intact the conclusions reached in the Bybee and Yoo memos. Levin testified that the footnote meant only that John Yoo could have applied Levin's definition and nevertheless approved harsh interrogation techniques, because of Yoo's belief in unlimited presidential power.[112] On this reading, the footnote merely described Yoo's subjective state of mind, as in the observation that cats like canaries. It seems hard to believe that Levin could have contemplated such a trivial goal for a footnote that he knew carried such high stakes.[113]

Other Efforts at Impunity on Interrogations

The administration also stifled earlier efforts to investigate the interrogation issue. FBI agents early on appreciated the problems with the tactics used at Guantánamo and elsewhere.[114] Agents reported their concerns to their superiors, and even assembled a "war crimes file."[115] Their superiors, however, told them to close the file, apparently fearful of embarrassment or worse. Subsequently, the CIA denied the Justice Department's Inspector General access to senior Al Qaeda detainee Abu Zubaydah, one of the three detainees that the government waterboarded. According to the Inspector General, the CIA's refusal hindered his investigation.[116]

Administration officials also apparently tried to cover up possible wrongdoing through destruction of evidence. The CIA had taped many of its interrogation sessions, apparently including those involving waterboarding. For several years, the CIA asked for permission to destroy the tapes.[117] When consulted, White House lawyers sent mixed signals. A couple of lawyers, including John Bellinger, then counsel to the National Security Council and later legal adviser to Secretary of State Condoleezza Rice, recommended that the CIA preserve the documents. But reports indicate that other White House lawyers vigorously argued for the tapes' destruction.[118]

State Secrets

The government has also used a broad doctrine known as the state secrets privilege to frustrate transparency about the surveillance and interrogation of suspected terrorists. The state secrets doctrine is not new; indeed, it has been used by both Democratic and Republican administrations.[119] The breadth of both the state secrets doctrine and Bush administration claims about executive prerogative, however, have produced a powerful threat to government accountability.

The state secrets privilege actually includes two doctrines. One is a standard evidentiary doctrine, like the attorney-client, physician-patient, or clergy-penitent privilege, which shields information from public view to give the participants in conduct maximum flexibility and to avoid chilling socially useful or necessary conduct. Part of government's obligation is safeguarding security, and some secrets are necessary for this task. Officials who operate under a 24/7 microscope may shy away from the difficult calls that national security interests require. The other aspect of state secrets doctrine is even more sweeping. The dimension makes state secrets an absolute defense to certain kinds of litigation, stopping accountability before it even gets started. In other words, if the government pleads the state secrets defense, the court will dismiss the lawsuit, regardless of the merits asserted by the plaintiff.

The difficulty with both the evidentiary and substantive state secrets doctrine is the handy escape route from accountability that it provides. The government has invoked the privilege to cover up the incompetence of its own personnel. For example, in *United States v. Reynolds*,[120] plaintiffs sued about a plane crash involving government personnel. The Supreme Court upheld a claim of state secrets, but documents subsequently uncovered showed that simple human error caused the crash.[121]

The state secrets doctrine, like other detours, does more than merely impair redress and transparency after an event. Just as important, it causes moral hazard for policymakers. When officials know *ex ante*—before the fact—that their accountability is limited, they shed the discipline and sound habits that accountability promotes. Rather than protecting conscientious decision makers, the state secrets doctrine can promote complacency and allow unwise options to flourish.

The Bush administration has used the state secrets privilege in two major types of cases: the first concerning the government's Terrorist Surveillance Program (TSP), and the second concerning the extraordinary rendition of terrorist suspects to countries such as Syria and Morocco, where these individuals allegedly suffered torture. The extraordinary rendition cases receive attention below; here I will briefly discuss judicial response to invocation of the doctrine in cases regarding the TSP.

The government has asserted the state secrets doctrine to shut down most suits regarding the TSP at an early stage. Courts require that a party seeking redress demonstrate standing to sue. Standing entails a showing that the party bringing the lawsuit has experienced harm as a result of the policy that triggered the lawsuit. Proving standing is tricky in the TSP cases, since the surveillance is covert. People subject to surveillance generally do not *know* if the government is watching them, and the government does not confirm or deny individuals' suspicions. When parties bringing lawsuits have sought more definitive information to show standing, the government has resisted these efforts by citing the state secrets privilege. Indeed, in one well-known case, the organization bringing the case had inadvertently received information from the government that showed it might have been a target of surveillance. But the court held that the privilege applied to this information, too. Without the information, the plaintiff could not show standing.[122]

While it is easy to condemn the government's use of the state secrets privilege in such cases, the question is a difficult one. Courts should not force the government to disclose sensitive information about technological innovations or particular search criteria used for combing through vast pools of information. Such disclosures would allow genuine terrorists to gauge our defenses, and game the system. At the same time, some check is needed to prevent the government from using the state secrets privilege to shield incompetence and overreaching.

Congress is considering legislation, entitled the State Secrets Protection Act,[123] which received support from Senators Edward Kennedy, Arlen Specter, and others, to ameliorate this difficulty. This legislation would allow greater in camera review by courts. When the government asserted the state secrets privilege, a court would review the relevant material in private without disclosing it to the other side. If the material fit the privilege, the government would prevail. If the court was not satisfied that the material fit within the state secrets privilege, however, the court would entertain further proceedings on the matter. In addition, the proposed bill would require that courts consider whether the government could submit a substitute for the privileged information, such as a summary or a stipulation that would not injure national security. An existing law, the Classified Information Procedures Act (CIPA),[124] works well, by giving courts discretion to devise such substitutes with the cooperation of the parties. The proposed bill would mitigate the catch-22 that litigants now face.

Claiming Immunity in Court

In addition to doctrines like state secrets that shield information, Bush officials also advanced a phalanx of reasons for why they could not be sued *at all*. In some cases Bush officials claimed that even if all the misconduct alleged by their adversary had happened, their adversary lacked a legal vessel or "cause of action" to carry his claims to court. In other cases, Bush officials said a court could consider the lawsuit, but was obliged to dismiss it because officials had immunity. These arguments against accountability are not new, and indeed are sometimes necessary to prevent officials from being "chilled" in their job performance. But Bush officials sought to expand these doctrines to provide additional insulation to wayward officials.

Consider first the argument of Bush officials like Attorney General Ashcroft in the case of Maher Arar that the alleged victim of overreaching had no legal vessel available to him to seek redress.[125] In *Bivens v. Six Unknown Federal Agents*,[126] the Supreme Court held that an individual subject to a violent, brutal, and flagrantly illegal search by federal officials could sue federal officials directly under the Constitution, instead of depending on Congress to pass a statute that provided a cause of action. *Bivens* suits, as they are called, have gone forward in many courts since then to remedy wrongs that would otherwise go unaddressed. The Supreme Court, however, has been reluctant to expand the categories of cases in which *Bivens* suits are appropriate. In checking the development of this area of law, the Supreme Court has said that courts should consider that "special factors" might make a *Bivens* lawsuit particularly disruptive in a category of cases, thereby rendering it inadvisable to provide a remedy.

The government relied on this "special factors" test to contest accountability in the extraordinary rendition case of Arar, a Canadian citizen whom American officials removed to Syria, where he was tortured. First, the government argued that one "special factor" was Arar's failure to invoke his rights under the Immigration and Nationality Act, which permits those facing deportation to seek judicial review. According to the government, granting Arar a *Bivens* remedy would undermine the Immigration Act's comprehensive scheme. The government undercut its argument, however, by impeding Arar's ability to seek recourse under the statute, misleading his attorney about his whereabouts and officials' intent to summarily deport him to Syria.

The government's second argument was that a *Bivens* remedy would result in the inappropriate disclosure of communications between sovereign states about national security matters. According to the government, possible damage to U.S. foreign relations caused by such disclosure was a "special factor counseling hesitation" in creating a right of action under *Bivens*. This argument, however, ignored the elaborate gestures of redress that Canada had already engaged in, including a scathing commission report and the payment of ten million dollars. Surely, whatever the merits of this defense initially, changed circumstances had made it less compelling. In contrast, the importance of clearly articulating values to avoid such nightmarish incidents seems more compelling than ever. At an oral argument in the case, Second Circuit judge Guido Calabresi, a former dean of the Yale Law School, observed that holding American officials liable for deporting an individual to effectuate torture would further reciprocity in foreign affairs, enhancing the United States's ability to deter abuses by foreign governments.[127]

The *Arar* defendants also argued that they were protected by the doctrine of qualified immunity. By claiming to be immune from a legal process, including a lawsuit or a subpoena to appear before Congress, an official acknowledges that other persons might be accountable, but asserts that the official's status renders him impervious to the process's reach. While some form of immunity is necessary to avoid second-guessing of government officials, the Bush administration asserted immunity to escape accountability for particularly egregious activity.

Courts have recognized two kinds of immunity for government officials. The first, absolute immunity, is conferred on officials where the prospect of legal action would fundamentally impair officials in doing their jobs. One example is the constitutional immunity that legislators possess under the speech and debate clause of Article I.[128] Another is the immunity granted prosecutors regarding decisions about bringing charges or calling witnesses.[129] Courts confer a second kind of shield—qualified immunity—on officials who did not violate "clearly settled" law. According to the Supreme Court, requiring officials who had complied with law to the best of their ability and with the best knowledge at the time to be answerable in damages would unfairly subject officials to the 20/20 hindsight of juries and trial lawyers, and also encourage undue risk aversion by officials making difficult choices. Under qualified immunity, an official is liable only if he violates a "clearly established principle" of law.[130]

In Arar's case, the officials did not fit within the narrow class of cases conferring absolute immunity, so they instead asserted that they were entitled to qualified immunity. According to the officials' strained reading, no settled precedent had held officials liable for deporting aliens to facilitate their torture. This argument, if accepted, would provide a windfall to officials who walk on the wild side. In its 1997 decision *United States v. Lanier*,[131] the Supreme Court noted that the touchstone of qualified immunity is "reasonable warning." In *Lanier*, Justice David Souter commented that while no case has accused a state official of "selling foster children into slavery," every reasonable official would regard such a scheme as unlawful.[132] The same analysis should apply to officials who willfully send an individual abroad to be tortured. Any other result would transform qualified immunity from a doctrine that reduces chilling effects on legitimate policy choices to a license for official overreaching.

Ashcroft and other officials also claimed qualified immunity in a case, *Ashcroft v. Iqbal*,[133] involving the detention of aliens after September 11. In *Iqbal*, undocumented aliens detained in the post–September 11 roundup alleged that Attorney General Ashcroft and other senior officials had established a policy that called for the plaintiffs' abusive treatment. Strong evidence, including a report from the Justice Department's Inspector General, demonstrated that the plaintiffs had been beaten by inmates and guards after their detention, and that the facilities where the abuse occurred were under the supervision of the Attorney General. Moreover, senior officials were aware of reports of detainee abuse within two weeks.[134] The failure to investigate reports of abuse could have helped to prove a claim of "deliberate indifference," which courts had held to be actionable under *Bivens* and outside the scope of officials' qualified immunity.

The Supreme Court shut the door on plaintiffs in a 5–4 decision ruling out "deliberate indifference" claims against senior officials. The Court, in an opinion by Justice Kennedy, held that a plaintiff suing a senior official had to make specific claims in his initial complaint that the official actively ordered the conduct underlying the lawsuit. Only this specificity requirement, Justice Kennedy reasoned, would protect senior officials' from burdensome litigation.[135] The Court discounted the protection that rules currently afford against litigation abuses.[136] Moreover, the Court placed plaintiffs in a catch-22. Plaintiffs need to use the discovery phase in litigation to help develop information about the role of defendants. If plaintiffs must plead specific facts in their initial complaint, however, they will never get to the discovery phase. The statute of limitations will expire, and senior officials will not be called to account. The Court's decision therefore placed a thumb on the scales of justice, leaving victims without redress and permitting officials to abuse their power with impunity.

Impunity and the United States Attorney Firings

Impunity and its pursuit has not stopped at national security matters. In largely domestic matters, the Bush administration also sought to use any means at its disposal to defeat investigations by Congress. The best example of this was the invocation of executive privilege and the campaign of selective amnesia to cover up evidence of political influence in the United States Attorney firings of 2006.

In December 2006, the DOJ fired nine United States Attorneys. Those fired included David Iglesias of New Mexico, who had refused to make his office a political arm of the New Mexico Republican Party by targeting foes of prominent New Mexico Republicans.[137] Another fired prosecutor was Todd Graves of Missouri, who had refused to target ACORN, a community organizing group regarded as a mortal foe by Republicans, and had also insisted on tough penalties in a cross-burning case. Still another was John McKay of Washington State, who had refused to use his power to alter the outcome of the closely contested gubernatorial race. In yet another case, the White House pressured the Justice Department to remove the federal prosecutor for Arkansas, Bud Cummins, to secure a plum position for a protégé of Karl Rove. When pressed to explain the dismissals, senior Justice officials claimed that those dismissed had been subpar performers, even though most had received favorable performance reviews. In the wake of the controversy, an even more troubling plan sponsored by the White House and senior Justice Department officials came to light, spearheaded by the politically connected and overzealous Bush partisan Monica Goodling, to undermine laws that required merit-based hiring for civil service positions.

To fully investigate the controversy and exercise oversight, Congress wished to call a number of White House officials, including Harriet Miers, former White House counsel; Karl Rove, adviser to the president and former deputy chief of staff; and Sara Taylor, who was an official in the White House political office.[138] The White House directed that Taylor invoke executive privilege when she testified. In an even more sweeping contention, the White House argued that senior officials such as Miers and Rove were *absolutely immune* from even being called as witnesses by Congress. The Senate Judiciary Committee went to court to enforce the subpoenas of Miers and Rove.

To understand the White House's detour from accountability and oversight, some background on executive privilege is helpful. Many presidents have claimed some sort of privilege rooted in the same policy concerns as attorney-client, physician-patient, and priest-penitent privilege—the notion that keeping communication confidential encouraged the free flow of information and advice. At least one prominent academic, Raoul Berger, claimed that executive privilege did not exist—he argued that the doctrine had no basis in the Constitution, which never expressly mentioned the term.[139] President Nixon claimed executive privilege in the Watergate affair, arguing that the privilege insulated him from turning over tapes that could constitute evidence of a criminal conspiracy. The Supreme Court in *United States v. Nixon*[140] rejected Nixon's extreme position, but recognized the president's need for confidential counsel.[141] The Court held that confidentiality cannot be absolute.[142] In the criminal context, assertion of the privilege must bow to the judiciary's constitutional role in assuring the accuracy and fairness of criminal prosecutions.[143]

A federal district judge appointed by President Bush cited *United States v. Nixon* in rejecting the administration's arguments.[144] The judge noted that Congress's powers under Article I, Section 8, of the Constitution clearly comprise not only the ability to legislate, but also the ability to oversee implementation of legislation. Congress's oversight responsibility requires the power to compel testimony, or at least the appearance of senior executive officials, with the possible exception of the president and vice president. As the Supreme Court put it, Congress's "power of inquiry—with process to enforce it—is an essential and appropriate auxiliary to the legislative function."[145] The district court opinion noted that lawyers advising President Reagan, justifying a decision to decline to honor congressional subpoenas, had acknowledged that if Congress wished to compel compliance, it could go to federal court to enforce those subpoenas as the Judiciary Committee had done regarding Bush officials.[146] Moreover, if Congress can't investigate a United States Attorney scandal, no other agency can do so.[147] The district court further noted that if civil suits for money damages are authorized against officials, and officials cannot claim absolute immunity from these lawsuits, it would seem odd to grant officials absolute immunity from testifying before Congress.[148] The district court also was skeptical about the OLC opinion relied on by the administration. OLC's Steven Bradbury, who had so eagerly embraced the administration's position on coercive interrogation of terror suspects, was equally eager to accommodate the administration's aversion to congressional questioning of White House officials. The district court discounted Bradbury's memo, which it caustically described as a "three-page . . . opinion . . . hastily issued on the same day that the President instructed Ms. Miers to invoke absolute immunity."[149]

The district court observed that a ruling favoring the president would allow the government to claim executive privilege with no constraints. This would elevate impunity to an art form, and make a mockery of checks and balances. As the court remarked, the "Executive cannot be the judge of its own privilege."[150] Bush administration officials, however, never believed that this elementary axiom applied to them.[151]

Conclusion

To officials in the grip of crisis, impunity always seems like a good thing. Officials like Bush, Cheney, and Addington did not start from the premise that they needed to engage in a deliberative process with other stakeholders. Instead, they started with the premise that their initial policy choices were correct, and reverse engineered the legal underpinning for those decisions. Some lawyers like Jack Goldsmith and Daniel Levin sought to temper the administration's positions and introduce that crucial deliberative component. While these lawyers had an impact, they often found themselves trapped in the detours that the Bush administration had devised. Sweeping interpretations of legal immunity, state secrets, and executive privilege heightened the atmosphere of impunity around the administration.

Centralizing Policy and Patronage

In 2002, William Mercer, who was then the United States Attorney from Montana and in 2006 became an acting Associate Attorney General, received an e-mail query from an official at "Main Justice" in Washington about a candidate for the Justice Department's Honors Program. The Honors Program, one of the nation's most prestigious programs for new law school graduates, hires based on merit, not political affiliation. The e-mail inquired whether the candidate was "someone we want at DOJ."[1] Mercer responded that "the guy is probably quite liberal." According to Mercer, the candidate was clerking for a judge who was "activist" and allegedly sympathetic to trial lawyers. For Mercer, the coup de grace was the candidate's law review article, which committed the unforgivable sin of recommending the "reintroduction of wolves" on public lands.

As this story about hiring demonstrates, the Bush administration sought to displace traditional criteria and processes, such as merit selection, to centralize justice policy. Both law and order ideology and unitary executive thought contributed to this move. The Bush administration, including officials like Ashcroft as well as their allies in the Republican Congress, wanted to exploit law and order as a political issue, and saw the opportunity after September 11 to do so. They viewed career officials and local representatives of federal authority like the United States Attorneys as out of step with the Bush agenda. In centralizing policy, the administration also targeted the courts, which the administration felt were soft on crime. In pursuing the goal of making established centers of power—such as career civil servants, the United States Attorneys, and federal and administrative judges—more compliant with Bush administration priorities, the administration also pushed politics and patronage further than any other modern administration.

Centralization and Local Control in the Federal Justice System

The federal justice system relies on equipoise between central and local control.[2] Central oversight is necessary to right misguided local priorities, as the

Justice Department showed in the 1960s when it ramped up its role in civil rights enforcement. The relentless quest for domination by Main Justice in Washington, however, can be counterproductive. Local federal officials, including United States Attorneys, are a valuable source of knowledge and experience about institutional culture, community sentiment, and governmental relationships. Ignoring this knowledge can stifle local initiatives, chill attention to context and fairness, and concentrate mediocrities in United States Attorneys' offices and the federal courts. Viewing United States Attorneys as mere subordinates and federal judges as subjects for intimidation damages the balance that preserves liberty and fairness in the federal system.

The Bush administration's push for central control began with Ashcroft, who believed with other law and order politicians that the courts and the federal bureaucracy were bastions of elitism that required a fundamental reorientation in perspective. As a senator, Ashcroft had taken the lead in fighting the appointment of liberal judges whom he perceived as less tough on law and order than he deemed fit. He opposed the nomination of a Seattle corporate lawyer, Margaret McKeown, who had been a member of a gender-bias task force, asserting that his goal was to "expose Mrs. McKeown and her ACLU friends for the liberal elitists that they are."[3] Ashcroft also put a hold on the nomination of an African American Missouri state court judge, Ronnie White, believing that Judge White, a distinguished jurist, was "pro-criminal."[4]

Ashcroft had a chip on his shoulder for the bureaucracy of the department, including both lawyers and nonlawyers. Ashcroft early in his autobiography recounted a parable about his baptism at Justice. He had received many flowers and potted plants from well-wishers upon his confirmation, and he wished to have them watered by the custodial staff. He particularly wanted the flowers to keep over the weekend. When the reply came back that the custodial staff had enough to do with merely keeping the offices clean, Ashcroft notes, "I couldn't believe that attitude."[5] Ashcroft extends the metaphor, noting that many people told him, "We've never done it that way, General Ashcroft." Ashcroft responded tartly that "I hope it won't be offensive to the department to improve." Ashcroft's insistence of the title of "General"[6] also showed his own imperious attitude. The word "General" in the title "Attorney General" is actually an *adjective*, describing the comprehensive nature of the Attorney General's responsibilities within the federal government at the time of its founding. Ashcroft chose to view it as a *noun*, as in "General Patton." Ashcroft's perspective on his job title revealed both an impatience with dissent and a disregard for history within the Justice Department.

Ashcroft also had no patience for lawyers, which is a problem for the government's chief attorney. According to Ashcroft, lawyers "are accustomed to contesting everything. The safest, easiest answer for most lawyers is, 'No.'"[7] It was no accident that Ashcroft's chief of staff, David Ayres, was not a lawyer. David Israelite, Ashcroft's deputy chief of staff, had acquired his principal experience for this job as political director of the Republican National Committee.[8] Ashcroft also invoked this distaste for lawyers in dismissing the Clinton administration's counterterrorism efforts, which in fact far exceeded the Bush administration's moves prior to September 11. Ashcroft argued before the 9/11 Commission that when government personnel charged with capturing bin Laden before 9/11 needed "clear, understandable guidance . . . they were given the language of lawyers. Even if they could have penetrated bin Laden's training camps, they would have needed a battery of attorneys to approve the capture."[9] This dismissive caricature of the role of lawyers dominated the tenures of both Ashcroft and his ill-fated successor, Alberto Gonzales.

Charging and the Ashcroft Memo

A key initiative launched by Ashcroft to minimize the role of local prosecutors and federal judges involved the consolidation of Washington's control over charging and sentencing decisions. For both Ashcroft and Gonzales, local discretion was simply an excuse for prosecutors and judges being "soft" on crime. By displacing this discretion with centralized control, they claimed to be injecting rationality and uniformity into the sometimes messy federal system. The dark side of this centralizing move was the intimidation of judges who believed that one size cannot fit all in sentencing defendants to prison, and the firing of United States Attorneys who urged sparing use of the death penalty.

Main Justice consolidated control with the so-called Ashcroft Memo,[10] which required that prosecutors charge a defendant with the most serious charge that the evidence allowed. On the surface, the memo seemed unobjectionable. After all, a prosecutor who possesses strong evidence that a suspect has committed murder should not be content to charge the defendant with littering. Many students of the criminal justice system, however, might argue that instructing the average prosecutor on aggressive charging is a bit like training a German Shepherd to bark—it's not really necessary.

Instead of encouraging aggressive prosecution, the memo betrayed a contempt for the context, prudence, and judgment that informs the seasoned prosecutor's work. Historically, prosecutors have exercised discretion that tempers the harshness of the criminal law based on factors such as the youth, health, or family situation of the defendant, or the treatment received by other defendants in similar cases. A prosecutor may take such concerns into account to build relationships with local communities, encourage cooperation in future investigations, and tailor charges to the expectations of local juries, who can react to a prosecutor's overcharging with an outright acquittal of a sympathetic defendant. For Ashcroft, who had built his political career on a law and order platform, such concerns muddied the water. Ashcroft wanted charging decisions to reflect the domestic equivalent of Bush's statement to other nations on terrorism—"You're either with us or against us." Ashcroft aimed this message not merely at criminals, but also at the federal prosecutors who have to traverse a blurred boundary between firmness and restraint in enforcing the criminal law.

Intimidating Judges

An even more troubling development involved the systematic intimidation of federal judges who had exercised their discretion to give a lesser sentence under federal sentencing guidelines. Federal sentencing rules often allow judges to downwardly depart when equity or other factors suggest the need. For example, a judge may feel that a defendant's sentence is inequitable if equally culpable participants in a criminal enterprise have received less prison time. Or the judge may feel that the defendant's age or ill health warrant a downward departure.

Ashcroft and his allies in the Congress believed that judges taking such factors into account were being soft on crime. In the attack on judges, which was co-led by the Justice Department and Republicans in Congress, legislation known as the Feeney Amendment mandated compilation of a "blacklist" of judges who had given more moderate sentences.[11] The Justice Department could use the list to blackball judges for elevation to appellate judgeships, or even to seek impeachment. Like other databases, this list could include rumor, innuendo, and distortions, with minimal opportunity for judges to correct the record. The net result was a chilling effect for members of an independent branch of government—interference so egregious that it attracted stern criticism from then Chief Justice William Rehnquist, no friend of an activist judiciary. Rehnquist, in his annual report on the federal courts, described the Feeney Amendment as an "unwarranted and ill-considered effort to intimidate individual judges in the performance of their judicial duties."[12]

Congressional immersion in the adjudication and disposition of specific cases marked a break with tradition and constitutional values. Congress has no role in the prosecution of individual cases. If Congress wishes to absolve someone, that interferes with both the prosecutor's obligation to go where the evidence leads and the president's pardon power. On the other hand, if the Congress wishes to target someone, that triggers the Constitution's bar on so-called bills of attainder. Congress has previously tried to target individuals. For example, during the Cold War, Congress tried to require that the government deny security clearances to specific individuals. During World War II, Congress pursued a vendetta against a number of presidential appointees, requiring that the government terminate the salaries of these individuals unless they were appointed to jobs requiring the advice and consent of the Senate. The Dies Committee in 1943 presaged the ugly McCarthyist turn of the postwar era, condemning thirty-nine government employees as "irresponsible, unrepresentative, crackpot, radical bureaucrats" and denizens of "Communist front organizations."[13] In voting to deny compensation to these specific individuals as part of a general appropriations bill that the president had little choice amid World War II but to sign into law, the Supreme Court had found that Congress was acting not as a legislative overseer, but as a modern "star chamber."[14] The Feeney Amendment was a similarly insidious attempt to target perceived opponents on the federal bench. It did not seek to deprive judges of a salary, and so was not an exact duplicate of the statute at issue in the World War II–era case mentioned above. In singling out specific government appointees in a way that could adversely affect their future government service, however, it revealed a similar impulse. The dynamic at work was classic law and order politics: executive officials and legislators triggered a political auction in which participants competed to condemn judges who had little opportunity to defend themselves and who must make decisions that are politically unpopular.

Unfortunately, the lawyer who drafted the Feeney Amendment lacked understanding of both the need for judicial independence and the basics of ethical propriety. Jay Apperson, a staffer with Representative Jim Sensenbrenner, improperly used Sensenbrenner's name in writing a letter demanding tougher sentencing for a drug defendant. After Epperson was forced to resign, four senior Department of Justice officials demanded that the United States Attorney for the District of Columbia give him a job.[15] Representative Tom Feeney of Florida, the sponsor of the amendment, subsequently confronted his own legal issues. A House body determined that Feeney had improperly participated in a trip to Scotland organized and paid for by convicted lobbyist Jack Abramoff.[16]

In one particularly egregious case of legislative intimidation, Republican members of Congress sought to bully a Reagan appointee to the bench who had also served as the Minnesota United States Attorney, James M. Rosenbaum. Rosenbaum had testified against a bill that would have raised sentences for those drug defendants judged to have had only a minimal role in the drug distribution network.[17] For his efforts to provide information to Congress, he was targeted with a vicious report by the House Judiciary Committee, chaired by Representative Sensenbrenner. The committee report accused Judge Rosenbaum of misconduct, including providing false and misleading information to Congress, because he had dared to order downward departures in a number of cases where defendants had been "small-fry" participants.[18]

On the sentencing front, courts pushed back. In *United States v. Booker,*[19] the Supreme Court held that the Sentencing Guidelines were merely advisory, and that a sentencing judge therefore had discretion to depart from them. By so ruling, the Court largely mooted out the demagoguery of the Feeney Amendment. The Court also declined to allow *juries* to find facts relevant to sentencing, arguing that such a move would transfer even more power to prosecutors to resolve cases through plea bargaining, since very few cases actually go to trial.[20] In requiring merely that judges be reasonable in their sentences,[21] the Court spoke volumes about judicial independence.

In a more recent case, the Court held that a sentencing court could remedy the inequity—often viewed as racial—between defendants convicted of possession to distribute crack versus powder cocaine.[22] In doing so, the Court affirmed that judges should have this discretion because they see the defendant and consider individual circumstances. Moreover, the Court noted that the Sentencing Commission itself, which drafted the Sentencing Guidelines, had deplored the crack cocaine differential. Here, too, the Court pointed the way to a collaborative effort starting at the local level to define best practices, including reducing the crack-powder disparity.[23]

Although the Court's decisions in *Booker* and its progeny diffused the attack on judges, this attack presaged the firing of nine United States Attorneys three years later. In the past, federal judges had a role in selecting interim United States Attorneys. Justice Department officials worked with a Judiciary Committee staff lawyer to insert an amendment in the Patriot Act reauthorization eliminating the courts' role and allowing the administration to name interim United States Attorneys who would stay in the post indefinitely. One rationale for this was administration anger at judicial resistance to the blacklisting in the Feeney Amendment.[24]

Another ominous initiative was the attempt by Ashcroft and Gonzales to promote use of the death penalty in federal cases. Here, Ashcroft and Gonzales clashed repeatedly with United States Attorneys, who were concerned about the disparities created by use of the death penalty in federal cases in areas such as San Francisco where local sentiment ran heavily against death. The United States Attorneys, such as Paul Charlton of Arizona, Margaret Chiara of Michigan, and Kevin Ryan of San Francisco, were not absolutist opponents of the death penalty, but they believed that a rigid pro-death penalty position would be both inequitable and impractical. Ashcroft and his successor Gonzales ignored these arguments, and retaliated against officials who voiced them.

Equity figures in this issue because a defendant's sentence should not hinge on whether he finds himself in a state or federal court. If community norms discourage the death penalty in state court, seeking it in federal court creates an anomaly. There may be times when state justice systems systematically undercharge defendants, as in cases of racial violence in the South a generation or more ago. Federal efforts should focus on eliminating those kinds of invidious disparities, as Attorney General Robert F. Kennedy did in the early 1960s, and not on promoting the death penalty for its own sake or as a political issue.

The Ashcroft death penalty policy ignored both this equitable argument and the pragmatic concerns of prosecutors. For example, Paul Charlton of Arizona did not wish to pursue the death penalty in one case unless the government was willing to recover the body of the victim, which was buried under tons of rubble. Charlton reasoned that a jury would want to see the body before imposing the death penalty.[25] Moreover, recovering the body would have sent a message that the government cared about victims, rather than sending a message that the government did not want to foot the bill for moving rocks. Charlton's stand made even more sense given the increasing reluctance of juries to impose the death sentence. Main Justice refused on cost grounds to recover the body, but directed that Charlton seek the death penalty anyway. Gonzales cited Charlton's disagreements on these issues in his justification for Charlton's dismissal, viewing them not as pragmatic reminders but as evidence of "insubordination."

There are other pragmatic reasons for deferring to local decisions. For example, nixing a death penalty deal will also sabotage a defendant's cooperation with prosecutors.[26] Without this cooperation, many cases simply cannot be made, including cases that send away dangerous individuals. In this fashion, intervention in death penalty decisions is counterproductive.

Moreover, a local federal prosecutor may decide not to prosecute a case at all because the prosecutor believes that state authorities can do as good a job—say, in a drug trafficking case—and that federal resources could be expended more efficiently in a different direction.[27] This occurs with respect to death penalty issues, as well. Often the state can deal effectively with a death-penalty-eligible case. In addition, capital cases require a far greater expenditure of time and resources, not just at trial but also on appeal and in collateral proceedings.

Another facet of the stress on the federal death penalty was the administration's attempt to up the ante on prosecution for killings of drug confederates. Typically, the government would have sought life imprisonment for such charges. In a number of cases, however, the Bush Justice Department sought to transform these cases into death penalty cases, including one case where the victim was another drug figure who had allegedly plotted to kill the defendant.[28] In this case, the federal judge presiding indicated that in his view, based on the past practices of juries in Brooklyn, there was "zero" chance the defendant would actually receive the death penalty. Moreover, the defendant recently offered to plead guilty and accept a sentence of fifty years, which would require that the defendant live until age eighty-seven to regain his freedom. In a continuation of the disregard for localized decision-making typical of the Bush administration, however, the Attorney General rejected the offer.[29]

Pursuit of the death penalty also triggers substantial opportunity costs. A prosecutor's office could do five serious prosecutions of traffickers for the time and effort involved in one death penalty case. Moreover, as noted, juries in non-death-penalty states often have significant reservations about the death penalty. Persuading jurors to vote for death may be a quixotic enterprise that alienates communities and reduces cooperation with law enforcement. In Brooklyn, for example, juries have rejected the death penalty in a substantial majority of cases where prosecutors have sought it. Overall, in New York, since 1988 federal prosecutors have sought the death penalty nineteen times; the jury has imposed a death sentence exactly once.[30]

Insistence on the federal death penalty can also alienate judges. Judges have to deal with finding a jury that will impose the death penalty, and with the delay that seems endemic to death penalty prosecutions. Judges lose control of their dockets when death penalty trials crowd out other important cases. In New York's Eastern District, a mini-revolt among judges ensued involving public criticism of the Department's stance. For these judges, Main Justice's death penalty agenda had become a circus, with the day-to-day work of dispensing justice in criminal cases reduced to a sideshow.[31]

Centralization and Leniency

While the Bush administration's penchant for centralization often coincided with a law and order agenda, it sometimes led to inappropriate pleas for leniency. Centralizing impunity is no better than centralizing rigidity. Here, too, Main Justice's drive to centralize led to a clash with a United States Attorney exercising judgment based on local knowledge.

In Missouri, Todd Graves, a Republican United States Attorney, wanted to prosecute a bully who had burned a cross on a family's lawn. The case arose because on a summer night in 1997, a group of men and teenagers enjoying their liquor grew angry that a mixed-race couple had just moved into their small town.[32] Declaring that "those kind of people" did not belong, the group burned a cross on the front lawn of the house occupied by Liza Costa and three young children. In an irony that was of small consolation to the victim, it turned out that Ms. Costa was not African American, but instead was of Portuguese descent. United States Attorney Graves knew the ringleader of the group, Dennis Popisil, who had a long arrest record. Popisil was convicted of a federal hate crime and sentenced to twelve years in prison. Graves was worried that the defendant would repeat the crime, and sought additional restrictions that would govern Popisil's conduct upon his release. After two years of negotiating, Graves succeeded in getting Popisil and a federal magistrate to approve an agreement that required that Popisil receive counseling and prevented him from engaging in public intoxication.

Here, however, the administration balked. For some reason, Main Justice decided that cross burning was not a serious matter, and that racial violence was not a priority. It directed Graves to arrive at a more lenient settlement. A senior official in the Justice Department, Bradley Schlozman, who would become head of the Civil Rights Division and also succeed Graves, traveled to Missouri to "mediate" between Graves and the defendant. Graves believed that backing off the agreement after such extended negotiations would harm the federal government's credibility with local law enforcement officials and with the federal magistrate[33]—a concern he raised in an e-mail to Main Justice. Ultimately, in an argument with Schlozman that Graves described as "very heated," Graves stuck to his guns. Senator Whitehouse of Rhode Island, a former United States Attorney and a member of the Senate Judiciary Committee, noted that "we have locally appointed United States attorneys . . . so that they will make exactly that kind of call."[34] Popisil is now going straight, has given up drinking, and is a friend of the Costa family. He says race counseling gave him a "different outlook."[35]

The attempted detour around the local United States Attorney caused resentment, and may have set a tone that eventually led Graves to resign. Two years later, Schlozman, who apparently had a memory that an elephant would envy, replaced Graves.[36] Graves was removed even though he was on the brink of trying a difficult case involving the insanity defense, in which a woman was murdered in a rural part of the state near where Graves was born, and the woman's baby was cut from her womb. Since Graves had developed an expertise in the insanity defense, he wanted to try the case, but the government wanted him to leave to make room for his old nemesis Schlozman.

Policy Centralization and the United States Attorney Firings

The urge to centralize policy also played a substantial role in the United States Attorney firings that resulted in the resignation of Attorney General Gonzales in 2007. Policy disagreements can be a legitimate basis for removing political appointees. The firings were notable, however, because generally issues of policy and performance seemed to be pretexts for decisions with other motivations. In another case, involving Paul Charlton of Arizona, the United States Attorney had a strong equitable argument for local discretion that Main Justice ignored.

Justice Department officials made the most elaborate case for policy differences driving a prosecutor's termination in the case of San Diego's Carol Lam. High-ranking Justice official William Moschella testified before a House Committee that Carol Lam of San Diego had been lax in bringing criminal prosecutions based on immigration. According to Moschella, Lam's "numbers . . . just didn't stack up."[37] There was only one problem with Moschella's testimony—it failed to accurately depict Lam's record.

First, Lam had brought big immigration cases that had more bang for the buck, including prosecution of corrupt Border Patrol officers. Such officials can let in thousands of undocumented aliens, so diligent prosecution of corrupt officials is a worthwhile investment of prosecutorial resources. Lam also sought to bring illegal re-entry cases involving serious criminals, such as child molesters, where prosecution could take criminals off the streets for years,[38] instead of prosecuting smugglers, who would get only months in jail under current guidelines. These were sensible choices obscured by a rush to judgment on statistics.

The administration's stress on routine immigration prosecutions also masked the significant opportunity costs caused by this shift in priorities. When federal prosecutors in border areas devote the bulk of their time to criminal prosecution of nonviolent aliens whose only crime is their attempt to re-enter the country,[39] prosecutors lose the opportunity to launch organized crime, narcotics, or fraud prosecutions.[40] Eventually immigration prosecutions become the tail wagging the dog, even though there is little evidence that such prosecutions deter aliens from seeking to re-enter the United States looking for work.[41]

Lam's firing did not even make sense on the administration's own terms. Lam had substantially improved even on the raw numbers front, as her superiors had requested. Six months before her firing, Moschella had noted in correspondence with Senator Diane Feinstein of California that Lam's immigration filings had gone up, and that she had devoted "substantial resources" to immigration cases.[42] It was misleading for Moschella to fail to note this when he mentioned a past deficiency in immigration prosecutions as a reason for Lam's dismissal.[43]

Sometimes local prosecutors wished to innovate by developing best practices in investigation, but Main Justice intervened, for suspect reasons, to frustrate this aspiration. In Arizona, for example, the United States Attorney, Paul Charlton, wished to implement a best practice—the videotaping of defendants' statements to the authorities. Charlton had a couple of rationales. First, Charlton believed that videotaping was a necessary innovation for ensuring that more locally based and democratic institutions, such as juries, have adequate confidence in the justice system.[44] After all, the credibility of law enforcement is its stock in trade—without credibility, law enforcement lacks the legitimacy it needs to gain citizen cooperation and effectively prosecute anyone. Videotaping also allows prosecutors and law enforcement officials to more effectively monitor interrogators, so that agents do not violate Fifth Amendment guarantees against coercive interrogations. In addition, enforcing these rules, according to centuries of jurisprudence in both English and American courts, promotes "getting it right"—making sure that interrogators get good information from suspects, instead of a story that a frightened defendant believes that the prosecutor wants to hear.

Charlton also was concerned about perceptions of inequity within the Native American community. In Arizona, the United States Attorney, not state prosecutors, has jurisdiction over crimes on Indian lands.[45] Centuries of genocide, abuse, and disregard of traditions by white Americans have spurred mistrust of Anglo law enforcement. Charlton looked at the law enforcement landscape in Arizona, where those being investigated by *state* authorities had the benefit of videotaped confessions. Mandating videotaping in federal prosecutions would ensure that the feds were just as protective of individual rights as state authorities. This would serve to promote goodwill in the Native American population, and mitigate mistrust.

Charlton's rationales, however, did not carry the day, because he ran into a foe at the national level that wished to minimize accountability: the FBI. Through director Robert Mueller, the FBI contended that this reform was impractical, and would interfere with anti-terror efforts.[46] While the FBI actually conducts far fewer interviews of suspects than do local police departments, the FBI's director conjured up illusory obstacles, asserting that "we interview thousands and thousands of people every day of the year," and expressing concern about the expense involved in transcribing interviews. The FBI argued that agents would be chilled by videotaping, and that jurors might not understand their methods. A Justice Department official expressed skepticism, finding it puzzling that letting jurors do their jobs would threaten the FBI. Unfortunately, this view did not prevail; when Charlton insisted on videotaping as a best practice, the Justice Department grouped him with the other United States Attorneys slated for firing.

Centralization and Attacks on Corporate Attorney-Client Relationships

A more ambiguous case of centralization occurred on the question of prosecutors' ability to inspect material covered by attorney-client privilege. Here, government agencies have legitimate enforcement and regulatory interests that emerged before the Bush administration; however, the administration overreached.

The issue emerged in the Bush administration's investigations of corporate wrongdoing after the Enron debacle. Prior to the Bush administration, other officials on occasion sought evidence protected by attorney-client privilege. For example, agencies investigating charges that the Westinghouse Corporation paid bribes to foreign officials reached a plea agreement with Westinghouse only after the company agreed to waive attorney-client privilege and disclose the contents of an independent investigation it had commissioned from outside lawyers.[47] Companies had long argued that government pressure to waive attorney-client privilege was a form of official blackmail, since prosecutors typically threatened to indict the company if it did not comply, and indictment could spell financial ruin.

In a series of memoranda, Bush Justice Department officials codified the waiver policy, encouraging prosecutors to request waivers more frequently.[48] Waivers and related efforts to stop corporations from advancing legal defense fees to indicted former executives made sense in individual cases where corporations knowingly sought to use attorneys to conceal information relevant to a plea agreement or paid executives to discourage cooperation with federal investigators. But the signals sent by the Bush administration exacerbated the natural aggressiveness of federal line prosecutors, who often are young and just developing the judgment possessed by more senior officials.[49] Seeking a waiver of privilege became not merely one technique to be used in appropriate cases, but virtually a routine procedure. After the 2006 election, the new Congress, with Senator Specter of Pennsylvania taking the lead, reacted unfavorably to this challenge to attorney-client privilege.[50] In response, the Justice Department announced a new policy directing prosecutors to refrain from seeking waivers of privilege.[51] Ongoing efforts to address the issue must vindicate the government's legitimate interest in acquiring information before it agrees to a plea, while ensuring that clients feel safe in conferring with their lawyers.

Bringing Politics to Merit-Based Hiring

The Bush administration also attempted to reshape the Justice Department by supplanting merit hiring with patronage. This sad story goes against a proud tradition in the office of the attorney general. In addition, it conflicts with law and policy freeing civil service hiring from politics that goes back over 120 years.

Throughout history, attorneys general have struggled with the need to be both a trusted adviser to the president and an independent voice for the rule of law.[52] The first Attorney General, Edmund Randolph, strove to give independent advice. Indeed, Randolph was so anxious to state both sides on an important matter—the creation of a national bank—that he wrote not one but *two* opinions—one supporting the measure and the other pointing out its flaws.[53] Some time later, Robert Jackson, the Attorney General for Franklin Roosevelt, deliberated extensively before rendering an opinion that supported the destroyer deal with Britain during World War II. Jackson issued an opinion after narrowly construing a federal statute, the Neutrality Act, that appeared to ban such assistance.[54] During Watergate, Elliot Richardson was appointed Attorney General after President Nixon's earlier appointees,

John Mitchell and Richard Kleindeinst, were forced to resign due to scandal. Richardson announced that because the legitimacy of the Justice Department is "handicapped by the suspicion of political influence, we cannot afford to have at the head of the Department—or in any of its key positions—a person who is perceived to be an active political partisan."[55] Richardson continued, "A citizen . . . who perceives an Attorney General wearing . . . [a] political hat is scarcely to be blamed for doubting whether . . . [the Attorney General] ever really takes it off."[56]

While the independence of the Attorney General is a matter of institutional culture and history, merit-based hiring for less-senior positions is a creature of both history and law. For over 120 years, the federal government has used merit-based criteria to hire candidates for civil service jobs. The premise of this idea, developed in response to the "spoils system" that corrupted federal hiring in the Republic's first century,[57] was to make merit the sole determinant of civil service hiring. Insisting on merit would ensure that federal workers had no partisan ax to grind, but rather focused on doing their job. Before the Pendleton Act of 1883, federal employees usually owed their jobs to patrons in Congress, who expected that their protégés would kick back a portion of their salaries to subsidize the patrons' political campaigns.[58] After the Pendleton Act's passage, merit-based hiring became increasingly established in tradition, culture, and law.

Laws and regulations in place today reflect this concern for removing political criteria from hiring for career positions. Justice Department rules and federal statutes prohibit the use of political criteria to select candidates for all but the most senior "political" positions. The department's regulations straightforwardly bar discrimination, not merely on the basis of race, religion, disability, sexual orientation, or gender, but also on the basis of "political affiliation."[59] The federal Civil Service Reform Act mandates "fair and equitable treatment" in personnel decisions "without regard to political affiliation."[60] Moreover, in 1974 the Supreme Court decided in *Arnett v. Kennedy*[61] that employees in government had a due process right to a hearing prior to termination.

Merit-based hiring does more than restrain the influence of politics and partisanship. More affirmatively, it serves to shape the organizational culture and character of officials at Justice and elsewhere. Forced to hire on the basis of merit, government will look to those who have the initiative, intellect, and judgment to be career attorneys. These attorneys interact with other government officials, including law enforcement agents. They make complex decisions about the scope of federal law, including criminal, environmental, and civil rights statutes. By focusing on merit, the government can attract people who can make judgments and forge effective working relationships, without the distractions of partisan politics.

Unfortunately, merit-based hiring clashed with the theory of the unitary presidency that drove the Bush administration. Theorists of the unitary presidency argue that the president must have unfettered power to remove federal employees, to shape her administration based on promises to the electorate, and to promptly eliminate incompetence and corruption.[62] These theorists often support merit-based hiring, however, believing that it promotes competent personnel management.[63] Unitary executive theorists would argue that with merit-based hiring, the executive has no incentive for partisan removals, since replacements will have to be selected on merit. But these thinkers fail to consider the message sent to career appointees when someone is summarily fired. The remaining officials will be chilled in the exercise of their duties, and their judgment will be affected, even if the president has some obligation to hire on merit to replace the official who departs. As a practical matter, the offending official has probably shown independence in taking action against a friend of the administration or declining to act against an adversary. The message conveyed to remaining officials, and to the person hired, is that this is not the way to "get along" in the department.

The political tilt was evident in Justice Department hiring from early in Ashcroft's tenure. Ashcroft repealed a policy that had given career Justice Department employees an opportunity to interview and opine on prospective new hires.[64] In the past, various Justice Department divisions, such as civil rights or environmental enforcement, had selected their lawyers, particularly for prestigious programs like the Honors Program. As of 2002, Ashcroft reversed this policy, concentrating hiring decisions about the Honors Program in the hands of political employees. This change in course, echoed in 2006 during the tenure of Alberto Gonzales, resulted in the rejection of many applications by qualified candidates suspected of being liberal, and the disproportionate hiring of those with conservative credentials, in violation of federal law.[65]

Bush officials introduced patronage hiring and job actions into a jewel of the Justice Department, the Civil Rights Division. Leading the charge was Bradley Schlozman,[66] who had acted as the Justice Department's point man in seeking lenient treatment of the cross-burning Missouri defendant against the wishes of fired United States Attorney Todd Graves. Schlozman told colleagues that he wanted to hire "real Americans"[67] for positions in the division, not "politburo members" or individuals with allegiance to a "psychopathic left-wing organization designed to overthrow the government."[68] He flagged job applicants with liberal credentials, such as work with Democratic members of Congress, and inquired whether other applicants were conservative enough.[69] Inquiring about one candidate for a civil service job, Schlozman asked, "How does he view the world, if you know what I mean?"[70] Referring to another candidate being interviewed, Schlozman described the applicant as "some lefty who we'll never hire."[71] Schlozman froze out seasoned female minority lawyers in the Civil Rights Division, giving plum cases to new recruits with conservative activist backgrounds, including membership in the Federalist Society.

Moreover, Schlozman engineered the improper transfer of career employees with excellent work evaluations and long-time records of service. For example, Schlozman transferred several members of the Appellate Section, whom he described as "disloyal," "against us," and "not on the team."[72] Outstanding career lawyers in the Employment Discrimination Section were transferred to the Civil Division. The chief of the Voting Right Section had his responsibilities stripped and allocated to other attorneys viewed as hewing to the views of political appointees. Deputy section chiefs were also transferred—a step never taken before. Meetings with political appointees were rare, and debate was discouraged—a detour from consulting the accumulated wisdom of career staff.[73] In some cases the work product of the division suffered, as members of different sections were ordered not to share their work with one another. Appellate lawyers, for example, would write briefs for appeals courts, but could not seek guidance and insight from the lawyers who had tried the cases in lower courts.[74] In addition, long-time employees who had incurred the wrath of political appointees were given assignments having nothing to do with their experience, such as defending immigration appeals, when federal courts were unanimous in criticizing and overturning the government's decisions in this area.[75] This led to alienation among career staff, who subsequently left, taking the institutional memory and competence of the Department with them.[76]

An even more powerful player in politicizing Justice Department hiring was Monica Goodling, who rose with alarming speed to a senior post at Justice under Attorney General Gonzales. Goodling acquired her powerful job at Justice with virtually no experience after graduation from law school at Regent University, founded in the 1990s by the televangelist Pat Robertson. Goodling was one of 150 graduates of Regent to find employment in the Bush administration, an astronomical number for such a new institution. After graduating from law school in 1999, Goodling worked from 1999 through 2002 with the Republican National Committee, where she apparently did "opposition research" involving digging up negative information on political opponents.[77] Goodling then joined the Department of Justice Office of Public Affairs, where she handled media relations.[78] Goodling had virtually no experience with the practice of law prior to assuming her senior position with the Justice Department. Her sole litigation experience was a few months spent with the United States Attorney's office in Virginia.[79] After this decidedly modest tour of duty, which compares with the two years or more that young lawyers often spend in a prosecutor's office, Goodling received the new and important job of deputy director of the Executive Office for United States Attorneys, where she supervised interaction between Main Justice and individual United States Attorneys' offices. Then Goodling moved to the office of the Attorney General in October 2005, where she was counsel and then senior counsel to the AG, in charge of hiring for the Justice Department.[80]

In job interviews, Goodling asked questions that were nakedly political. For example, she asked candidates about their "political philosophy," citing "Social Conservative," "Fiscal Conservative," and "Law & Order Republican" as options.[81] After interviewing one career candidate, she noted that the candidate was "pro-God in public life" and "pro marriage, anti–civil union."[82] She also asked candidates about their favorite public official.[83] Goodling was not always satisfied when job seekers named an official in the current administration. For example, one candidate said that he respected Secretary of State Condoleezza Rice. Goodling warned the applicant that Secretary Rice was "pro-choice."[84] Goodling also conducted Internet searches on career candidates to ferret out their political views: the search string she used included terms like "Florida recount," "spotted owl," "abortion," "homosexual," and "Kerry."[85]

These tactics had real-world consequences. Goodling succeeded in blocking an appointment to a career position on grounds that the candidate had not yet "proved himself" to the Republican Party.[86] Goodling opposed plans by an interim United States Attorney to hire an Assistant United States Attorney on the ground that the candidate was too "liberal."[87] There is also evidence that Goodling may have misled Congress about her involvement in these personnel matters, asserting that she discussed them with higher-ups when in fact she was given free rein and sought no guidance.[88] Indeed, there was evidence that Goodling sought to hold up career appointments on political or ideological grounds even after the firestorm erupted over the firing of United States Attorneys in early 2007.[89]

The push to inject politics into merit-based appointments was nowhere more apparent than in the hiring of immigration judges. Immigration judges have a distinctive role. As executive officials, they serve without the protection of lifetime tenure that the Constitution provides federal judges. They are part of the Department of Justice, and their job involves very high stakes. They decide asylum and Convention Against Torture cases, in which an individual may risk persecution or torture if the judge denies his plea. Officials in the administration such as Jan Williams, who served as White House liaison to the Justice Department, responded eagerly to a May 2005 message from the White House to "get creative" in finding positions for political supporters. Williams replied eagerly, "We pledge 7 slots within 40 days and 40 nights. Let the games begin!"[90] Williams began to match Bush volunteers with immigration judge slots, but later claimed that she did not realize that these were merit-based positions for which the use of political criteria violated the law.

The real-world consequences here were severe. Bush immigration judges tended to vote substantially more often than their colleagues to deny asylum. They often rejected claims that their colleagues would have accepted. Out of sixteen judges for whom comprehensive statistics were available, the Bush judges had a denial rate of 66.3 percent—6.6 percentage points greater than their peers. One judge denied asylum claims 88.1 percent of the time, 9.8 percentage points higher than the local average.[91] Political hiring accelerated the anti-immigrant bias that Ashcroft had hoped to hard wire into the Justice Department.

Ironically, the Bush administration in its waning days sought to promote its ideological positions and insulate patronage hires through the only device open to it after the resounding political repudiation of the November 2008 elections: the civil service system. After this brutal defeat, the Bush administration, in a practice known as burrowing, moved to convert *political* positions to *civil service* positions, to save the jobs of conservative political appointees. While other administrations have resorted to this strategy to protect loyalists, none were as aggressive as the Bush administration in undermining civil service protection throughout the rest of their time in office.[92]

Conclusion

Centralizing policy is not inherently lawless or unproductive—indeed, sometimes it's necessary. But the Bush administration used centralization of policy as a weapon in the service of law and order politics, as in the charging, sentencing, and death penalty areas. It distorted the mission of prestigious units like the Civil Rights Division, engaging in a slow-motion effort to undermine the legislation that promoted equal rights. The administration also showed contempt for the distinctive give-and-take that historically has marked relations between Main Justice and United States Attorneys, disregarding arguments about equity, and seeking undue leniency in the Missouri case of a convicted cross burner. In addition, it used policy centralization as a pretext for patronage decisions. Driven by a reading of the unitary executive theory, Bush administration loyalists like Monica Goodling violated laws that guaranteed merit-based hiring, trashing traditions reaching back over a century that had sought to remove civil service employment from the partisan tangle of politics. Here, as elsewhere, the theory seemed to allow a detour from cherished processes and values, and theorists failed to acknowledge or understand the forces that they would unleash once those sources of constraint evaporated.

5

Conspiracy's Discontents

Prevention and False Positives After September 11

After September 11, criminal law was in danger of being declared obsolete. Although the Justice Department had successfully prosecuted terrorists in the 1990s, Attorney General John Ashcroft claimed that the September 11 attacks required a new mind-set for law enforcement. The administration's fixation on measures such as indefinite detention, warrantless surveillance, and coercive interrogation made the criminal justice system seem leaden and labored. To compete on the new playing field, Ashcroft announced a paradigm shift to prevention. Ramped-up conspiracy prosecutions were the cornerstone of this strategy.

As a response to political violence, conspiracy charges often succeed more as public relations than as effective law enforcement. Conspiracy cases attract media attention. They also have a pragmatic premise that is intuitively appealing: punishing illegal agreements now will prevent even more serious wrongdoing in the future. In indulging this justification, the legal system makes a Faustian bargain. We give law enforcement greater power to prevent crime. Responsible officials will struggle to exercise that discretion wisely. Opportunistic or overzealous law enforcement officials will wield their power in ways that imperil democratic principles and increase the number of false positives—people wrongfully convicted.[1] The Justice Department's use of conspiracy after September 11 tilted toward the latter extreme.

The post-9/11 elevation of conspiracy to pride of place in the prevention arsenal[2] punished amorphous conduct and targeted vulnerable groups, including immigrants, Arabs, and South Asians. It was a convenient safe harbor for cases like that of Jose Padilla, the erstwhile alleged ringleader of a plot to bring in a "dirty bomb" on Al Qaeda's behalf, which originated in the shadow government of detention, surveillance, and torture. It also prompted ethical lapses among the lawyers in charge.

To illustrate these dangers, consider *United States v. Koubriti et al.*[3] The government arrested the defendants in Detroit shortly after September 11. The men had been staying in an apartment formerly rented by an individual sought by the government in connection with the attacks. In the apartment, authorities found a number of items of interest, including a drawing that appeared to be a sketch of an American air base in Turkey and a video that appeared to have been an effort to "case" sites in Las Vegas for possible attack. The government charged each of the defendants with conspiracy. Attorney General Ashcroft eagerly proclaimed that the defendants had received advance word of the 9/11 attacks. At the defendants' trial in the spring of 2003, the government's chief witness testified to incriminating statements made by the defendants about their plans. Ashcroft again spoke out publicly, thanking the witness for his valuable work.[4] A jury convicted two of the defendants of conspiracy.

In a nation legitimately concerned about the threat of renewed attacks, this story seems to vindicate the preventive rationale. Generally, we rely on criminal law to send strong messages about illegal conduct. The law will deter some people because of fear of punishment, and others because of the internalization of norms expressed in the criminal law. Suicide bombers, however, do not fit into this neat little paradigm. They embrace death, the legal system's most extreme punishment. Further, they reject the moral authority of the criminal law, which they view as a fig leaf for a corrupt and degenerate social order. Law enforcement turns to prevention because nothing else addresses the real threat at hand.

Unfortunately for the preventive ideal, very little about the *Koubriti* case turned out to be real. Before the trial, the government's own experts had discredited the prosecution's theory that the drawing depicted an American air base. Instead, the experts said, the drawing was more likely a crude map of the Middle East.[5] Experts cast similar doubt on the prosecution's theory about the Las Vegas video, viewing it as generic tourist footage. Even before the trial, the judge presiding over the case forced Ashcroft to retract his statement that the defendants had received advance notice of the September 11 attacks, as both prejudicial and unsupported by proof. Subsequently, the judge admonished Ashcroft for his laudatory comments during trial about the prosecution's chief witness.[6] The prosecutor in the case, however, failed to alert the defense to the views of his experts. Meanwhile, the informer Ashcroft praised so highly had, as it turned out, fabricated or exaggerated much of his testimony. After the defendants had spent well over a year in jail, pressure from defense lawyers and the court forced the government to acknowledge the warnings of its experts and the problems with its informant, and move to vacate the convictions.[7] The government also charged the prosecutor in the case with obstruction of justice.[8] *Koubriti* was a case study of conspiracy run amok.

Was the prosecutor one bad apple,[9] echoing the administration's story about errant guards practicing torture and humiliation on the night shift at Abu Ghraib? While *Koubriti* is an egregious case, the lessons for the place of conspiracy charges in the administration's preventive strategy are far broader in scope. To use conspiracy as a weapon against political violence, law must navigate through a minefield of risks. Failing to heed those risks can make conspiracy cases an exercise in political posturing. All too often, the Justice Department under Ashcroft and Gonzales fell into this trap. Before addressing those issues, a brief history of the premises and historic perils of conspiracy cases will sharpen our discussion.

Conspiracy History and Theory

Conspiracy "has been a favorite of prosecutors for centuries."[10] A prosecutor charging defendants with conspiracy to murder need not show that a murder was committed. Indeed, she need not prove that the defendants even made an attempt. A jury need only find an agreement among two or more people, sometimes joined by some overt act in furtherance of that agreement.

In the appropriate case, charging conspiracy serves legitimate law enforcement purposes. Consider the case of a group that plans to rob a bank, and purchases a gun or car to assist that effort. Acquiring a gun or a vehicle is a token of the group's earnestness. The group's agreement is also a precommitment device, with the eagerness of some members solidifying the resolve of the others.[11] In this case, law enforcement should not have to wait until the group actually attempts a bank robbery. Viewed from a broader perspective, however, resort to conspiracy doctrine creates substantial tensions with democratic values.

In a constitutional democracy, criminal law requires that the government prove that the defendant is responsible for a past misdeed. We do not want the government to be able to imprison an individual for a status that is uncontrollable, such as ethnicity, or for a factor that is viewed as crucial to democratic rights, such as the content of speech or thought.[12] The courts have in the modern area struck down statutes, such as vagrancy laws, that permitted the government to exercise such sweeping authority.[13] The law considers future risks only in specially bounded areas of law, such as commitment of persons with mental disabilities. Of course, there is some spillover between past responsibility and prevention—if the system imprisons a burglar for burglaries already committed, we tend to assume that the time in prison will also prevent burglaries from happening in the future. But this effect is incidental to adjudication of responsibility for a past wrong. Indeed, judges caution juries that their verdicts must be based on evidence demonstrating responsibility for a past offense, not on concern about future misconduct.

Conspiracy is different.

The heart of a criminal conspiracy charge is the intangible element of agreement.[14] Because of this intangible core, the government need only prove that the defendant participated in a "vaguely criminal scheme," rather than showing that the defendant committed concrete criminal acts.[15] Justice Jackson described conspiracy as "chameleon-like,"[16] focusing on an elusive "meeting of the minds" instead of on conduct.[17] As a result, jurors can convict when they perceive the defendant and his associates as possessing "a general disposition towards unlawful behavior."[18] Moreover, the doctrine of conspiracy encourages guilt by association: jurors who take a dislike to one defendant on trial may extend that dislike to the others accused.[19]

One factor that contributes to the amorphous nature of the agreement charged in conspiracy cases is that courts tend to interpret agreements broadly. This expansive construction frequently exceeds a particular defendant's own understanding and capacities. Once an agreement is in place, a defendant may be liable for acts in which she had no material role. In *Anderson v. Superior Court*,[20] the court held that the defendant, who had referred clients to a person performing abortions, was liable for abortions committed later on women whom she did not refer.[21]

Historically, conspiracy centered on offensive thought and speech, with action as an afterthought—in *Dennis v. United States*,[22] for example, the Supreme Court upheld the Smith Act, under which the government had charged the defendants with the crime of being members of the Communist Party. According to the government, by their very membership, the defendants conspired to "advocate and teach the duty and necessity of overthrowing and destroying the Government of the United States by force and violence." On the theory of conspiracy that *Dennis* represented, it was irrelevant that the defendants may have joined the Party for entirely separate reasons, including campaigning for racial justice[23]—a cause that mainstream political parties did not wholeheartedly embrace at that time. While subsequent case law on the First Amendment has overruled *Dennis*, the key here is, in Jackson's words, the "drift in the federal law of conspiracy [that] . . . is characteristic of the long evolution of that elastic, sprawling, and pervasive offense. Its history exemplifies the 'tendency of a principle to expand itself to the limit of its logic.'"[24] This drift in conspiracy law is gravitational in force, defying occasional judicial attempts to stem its momentum.

The overt act requirement in conspiracy is at best a modest hurdle for the government. The act need not be criminal in itself. It can be a daily or routine act, like making a purchase or traveling to a particular destination, that thousands of other people might do without incurring criminal liability.[25]

The legal system structures conspiracy doctrine in this way because of what cognitive psychologists call anchoring. In anchoring, people focus on one characteristic or event, and then make judgments that are consistent with that anchor.[26] Anchoring, like many other shortcuts in human judgment, can work in a "quick and dirty" way, but can also lead to serious mistakes. Mistakes occur when the anchor is either unreliable or insufficiently related to the ultimate judgment being made.

In conspiracy law and proof, one anchor is the arrest and charging of the defendants. The allegations against defendants are often extreme, particularly in terrorism cases. The human tendency is to treat the allegations as true, and then reason backward in time for evidence that will support the charges. Viewed in hindsight, a nebulous agreement appears more concrete, and routine or equivocal actions appear to further the agreement.[27] Only later, if at all, do people ask whether the charges are accurate.

Rules for conspiracy trials compound this problem. In most criminal cases rules seek to avoid errors that social scientists call "false positives"—finding someone guilty of a crime that she has not committed. In a democracy, the law cares more about avoiding false positives than about avoiding false negatives—people not detected or punished even though they *have* committed a crime. Confirming this principle, the Supreme Court in *In re. Winship* held that it is better to let a hundred guilty men go free than to wrongly imprison one who was innocent.[28] While many of the same rules, such as the government's burden of proving guilt beyond a reasonable doubt, also apply in conspiracy trials, the emphasis is different. More than other criminal cases, conspiracy trials seek to prevent guilty defendants from gaming the system. The result, however, is a greater risk of false positives.

To prevent conspiracy defendants from exploiting the secrecy that marks a successful plot, courts relax rules on the reliability and specificity of evidence. The prosecution can rely on hearsay that would otherwise be inadmissible.[29]

The government can also introduce statements made by coconspirators in the course of the alleged plot that the defendant did not know about or authorize. Participants do not need to know the details of an alleged plan, or know one another. They can resemble spokes in a wheel, acting without express coordination to achieve a common goal.[30] Moreover, their ends may overlap but need not be identical. In essence, as Justice Jackson noted, the government can present a "hodgepodge" that a defendant cannot hope to disprove in every particular.[31] Moreover, lest a jury seek more specific evidence, the court will usually instruct the jury that insisting on a "smoking gun" merely rewards the cunning conspirator.[32] The entire framework is a recipe for false positives. As senior federal judges acknowledged in a report more than seventy-five years ago, "The rules of evidence in conspiracy cases make them most difficult to try without prejudice to an innocent defendant."[33]

The risk of false positives in conspiracy cases is highest in cases of alleged political violence. Here, too, cognitive psychology enlightens our analysis. Cognitive psychologists have found that people tend to overestimate the likelihood of events that are vivid and emotionally salient.[34] Airplane crashes are a useful example: people fear airplane crashes far more than they fear car accidents, although the latter occur far more frequently and cause exponentially greater harm. Terrorist attacks are another example. Legitimate outrage at the targeting of civilians by terrorists can obscure the rarity of these attacks in the United States. The September 11 hijackings made many people reluctant to fly for months afterward, although at every moment in the awful aftermath getting into one's car for a drive to the supermarket was more risky.[35] Since terrorism in this country has an exceedingly low incidence of occurrence, separating the committed terrorist from the big talker is difficult. The terrorist and the poser may talk the same talk; in fact, the poser may be less guarded than the truly dangerous individual. While the best prosecutors seek to factor in this concern,[36] other officials trot out conspiracy charges to stoke the public's fear and make political points.

History demonstrates that officials often use conspiracy charges against political foes. Centuries ago, Sir Walter Raleigh was charged with conspiracy when he became a political threat.[37] Within the last 150 years, American authorities used conspiracy to suppress agitation by trade unionists and anarchists.[38] Labor conspiracy charges were a favorite tool for prosecutors and big business seeking to break strikes. More recently, consider the example of the Chicago Seven conspiracy trial, in which prosecutors put on trial political protesters at the 1968 Democratic Party Convention, including counterculture icons such as Bobby Seale of the Black Panthers and Tom Hayden of

Students for a Democratic Society. The 1960s conspiracy trial of Dr. Spock, the world-renowned author of books on baby care, for facilitating draft evasion reveals similar concerns. As in the Chicago Seven case, the courts eventually overturned the convictions.[39] But the government sent a message to political dissidents.

The government's reliance on informants and sting operations compounds the problem of false positives. Informants are sometimes necessary, but always risky. Usually, informants have unclean hands and private agendas.[40] They often sport track records of illegal conduct, and resort to cooperation with the government in the hopes of favorable treatment. Indeed, in some cases the kingpins of illegal operations are also the first to recognize the need to cooperate, giving up subordinates while masking or minimizing their own role. Some informers are attracted by other rewards and inducements, including the hundreds of thousands of dollars that the government has spent on informants after September 11. As a result, informants have an incentive to embellish or even fabricate their stories.[41] In one case, the defendant was mentally unstable, at one point setting himself on fire outside the White House in an effort to secure even more money.[42] Similarly, informants used in sting operations have an incentive to push, cajole, and browbeat their targets into more and more damaging statements and admissions, just as undercover agents have an incentive to get targets in drug prosecutions to buy or sell larger amounts of drugs, which will trigger stiffer sentences. A substantial number of post-9/11 conspiracy cases concerned young men targeted by stings in this way, who may have never come close to an illegal agreement without the informant's influence.

Both informants and sting operations tend to target people of a particular race or ethnic background. Although commentators and activists regularly clamor for police to run more stings on kids from the suburbs buying drugs, buy and bust stings are regularly run on residents of inner-city neighborhoods, who are disproportionately impoverished people of color. Sting operations have the same problem with selective targeting in the terrorism setting. It hardly seems likely that police running a sting operation to arrest members of potential sleeper cells will target a group of middle-aged mahjongg players from the suburbs. Instead, police and prosecutors will focus on institutions and residents of neighborhoods that are predominantly Muslim, Middle Eastern, or South Asian.

Prosecutors have an incentive to ignore the risks posed by reliance on informants. Senior government officials sometimes care more about making a splash with a high-profile arrest than about subsequent difficulties with the case, which typically receive less attention from the media. Moreover, prosecutors often buy into the tales spun by informers, just as Bush administration officials snapped up the exaggerated accounts of Saddam Hussein's WMD relayed by Iraqi exiles. Part of this symbiotic relationship between prosecutors and informants stems from instrumental motives—a prominent conspiracy prosecution can make a prosecutor's career. Moreover, prosecutors are often competitive, and a high-profile arrest brings the benefits of prestige and bragging rights. Prosecutors also want to take the initiative. Using informants and sting operations, prosecutors appear in control of the law enforcement agenda.[43] Without a portfolio of such projects, prosecutors cede the initiative to their adversaries on the other side of the law.

As with all portfolios, over-investing in informants and sting operations creates risks. The best prosecutors are effective gatekeepers, winnowing out unreliable informants and cutting losses when investigations yield little of value. Too often, however, prosecutors stick with cases that are going south, "doubling down" like an investor who is sure that a declining stock will rebound.[44] In sting operations, competitive prosecutors may experience disappointment when a subject seems to lose interest in the terrorist venture that the informant or undercover agent has proposed. For example, agents seeking to get a Bronx jazz bassist, Tarik Shah, to commit to terrorist activity had to play second fiddle to the target's interest in working out and making gigs.[45] A gatekeeping prosecutor would have taken the target's distraction as evidence that his occasionally extreme talk did not dovetail with an interest in action. Instead, the prosecutors in this case redoubled their efforts, eventually persuading their target to participate in a mock swearing-in ceremony for Al Qaeda and promising to provide martial arts training for the group. By getting Shah to take the bait, the government salvaged its investment. It obtained a guilty plea from Shah, who was apparently afraid of the jury's response to his swearing-in. Nevertheless, a gatekeeping prosecutor could reasonably ask whether the operation succeeded only in netting a false positive, who would not have acted without protracted efforts by law enforcement agents.

In addition to the problems posed by unreliable informants, invidious assumptions and prepackaged scripts may skew the path of an investigation. Pervasive narratives about the prevalence of terrorism within Islam or among Arabs and South Asians can skew prosecutorial decisions.[46] Here, too, the best prosecutors will acknowledge the influence of such images, and manage their cases accordingly. But less reflective prosecutors lack this insight.

Conspiracy and the Aftermath of September 11

In the wake of September 11, the preventive goals of conspiracy law became a signature of senior officials seeking strategic, political, and institutional advantage. As a matter of effective anti-terror strategy, the catastrophic losses of September 11 argued for a revision of the traditional American formula that accepted some false negatives to avoid false positives. In fact, the government needs an appropriately tailored flexibility in some areas to address the gravity of the risk posed by terrorism. Conspiracy cases should be part of this counterterrorist repertoire. The Bush administration's reliance on conspiracy cases, however, exceeded this prescription. While the motivation of these officials encompassed dismay at the attacks and an understandable desire to prevent future harm, their moves bolstered a monolithic model of law enforcement that undermined checks and balances.

Attorney General Ashcroft wasted no time in marginalizing the deliberative virtues extolled by predecessors such as Robert Jackson, an Attorney General under Franklin Roosevelt who as a Supreme Court justice developed a subtle critique of executive power. Ashcroft pointedly evoked Robert Kennedy, warning that the Justice Department would arrest potential terrorists for "spitting on the sidewalk," as Kennedy had cautioned racketeers.[47] This willingness to use trivial charges complemented the increase in conspiracy prosecutions. Unfortunately, Ashcroft's reference to Kennedy (whom he seems to have sincerely admired) concealed one essential difference between the situations facing the two men.

Kennedy's prey, including labor racketeers such as Jimmy Hoffa of the Teamsters union, engaged in corruption as a way of doing business. Their wrongdoing was open and notorious, at least in union circles. They had succeeded in avoiding accountability before Kennedy because they bribed, intimidated, or killed potential witnesses. Indeed, the successful racketeer burnishes his reputation precisely to instill fear and enrich himself and his associates. Because of these factors, the likelihood of Kennedy punishing the wrong people was small, and the problem of false positives did not afflict his efforts.[48] In contrast, as we have discussed, the base rates for political violence are very low, and American terrorists tend to keep to themselves.

Kennedy's strategy reflected these differences; indeed, Kennedy moved the government away from an area—the prosecution of subversives and Communists—where false positives were rife, taking on J. Edgar Hoover and the FBI in the process.[49] Unfortunately, Ashcroft ignored the telling discontinuities between the Bush administration's efforts and Kennedy's approach.

While prosecutors have a legitimate interest in keeping the public apprised about their activities, Ashcroft and Gonzales elevated public information about alleged conspiracies to the level of political theater. In the spring of 2002, Ashcroft took time out from a trip to Moscow to broadcast the news that the FBI had arrested U.S. citizen Jose Padilla at O'Hare Airport in Chicago in an alleged plot to acquire a "dirty bomb."[50] Ashcroft went public about another terrorism case, the *Koubriti* case from Detroit, claiming shortly after September 11 that the defendants had advance notice of the attacks.[51] Ashcroft also asserted that John Walker Lindh, the so-called "American Taliban," had engaged in a significant conspiracy against the United States,[52] and labeled Zacarias Moussaoui, who had engaged in flight training on Al Qaeda's behalf before September 11, as a coconspirator in the attacks.[53]

The promotion of Alberto Gonzales to Attorney General brought an acceleration of reliance on conspiracy. Gonzales had been heavily engaged in designing the president's overall legal strategy on terrorism, including the infamous torture memos justifying interrogation techniques that were prohibited under both international and domestic law. Gonzales continued the preventive focus of the Justice Department, announcing indictments at elaborate press conferences for investigations such as the Miami Seas of David case that gathered headlines for ominous charges involving plots against celebrated buildings such as the Sears Tower.

In each of these cases, the government had to struggle to support its initial public assertions. Padilla, for example, has never been charged with seeking a dirty bomb. In the Detroit case, the government ultimately had to move to throw out the convictions it had obtained because it had failed to disclose exculpatory evidence. Lindh pleaded guilty and is currently serving a twenty-year sentence, but the facts in his case clearly pointed away from any grand conspiracy. While Moussaoui was by his own admission in training to be a terrorist, the case for his participation in the September 11 plot was strained at best, and the government's request for the death penalty unfair in light of its refusal to provide access to detainees who could offer exculpatory information.[54]

In this climate, Ashcroft and Gonzales selected immediate subordinates who accepted their preventive vision or were marginalized and left in frustration. Many of Ashcroft's closest aides were actually political hands with minimal prosecutorial or litigation experience. Ashcroft's first Deputy Attorney General, Larry Thompson, was a competent professional who could not rein in Ashcroft's public comments, and left in 2003. James Comey, who succeeded him, had been a tough federal prosecutor in New York. Holding down a senior post at Justice, however, exposed Comey to the public relations imperatives that drove Ashcroft's choices. Comey participated in the Justice Department's public justification for the detention of Jose Padilla outside the criminal justice system, accusing Padilla of plotting to blow up U.S. apartment buildings just as the Supreme Court was considering Padilla's case.[55] While both Comey and Ashcroft drew a line in the sand on an early version of the president's warrantless surveillance program, there is no evidence that Comey disagreed with Justice's preventive stance in conspiracy cases. Indeed, as United States Attorney in New York, Comey had continued with a terrorism case that had been vigorously criticized by a federal judge— the case ultimately ended with an acquittal after Comey had left for the private sector.[56]

Gonzales selected Paul McNulty as Deputy Attorney General, after McNulty made a name for himself as the prosecutor who had supervised the prosecution of Lindh and Moussaoui, and had also conducted highly intrusive raids of Northern Virginia Muslim educational institutions, resulting in panic of staff, disruption of operations, and confiscation of thousands of documents and books.[57] While Lindh and Moussaoui basically fell into the government's lap, the Virginia raids yielded relatively modest results, centering on the convictions of a few young men for conspiring to fight against Indian forces in Kashmir, along with a Muslim scientist for encouraging them.[58] McNulty may have played a role in the United States Attorney firings, or may simply have been passive as the momentum for the firings accumulated. To his credit, he gave testimony to a Senate committee that indicated a patronage-related reason for the Arkansas firing, thus angering the White House and Gonzales—but whether he did this out of genuine concern or simply to minimize his role in the other firings is unclear.

Gonzales selected Michael A. Battle as chief of the Office of United States Attorneys, who in 2002 had prosecuted the Lackawanna Six, a tiny group of misfits and malcontents who had participated in an Afghanistan training camp before September 11. Each of them came back tired and disillusioned, with little appetite for jihad.[59] Indeed, this reaction has been virtually universal among the returning camp followers, who realized nearly to a man that to pursue jihad they would have to give up comforts that they took for granted as Americans. While it is appropriate to prohibit Americans from participating in such training, Battle insisted that the prosecution present the case as a breakthrough in antiterrorism efforts. After his promotion to the senior ranks at Justice, Battle delivered the news to a number of United States Attorneys that they had been fired.

These cases also played a significant role in political strategy. Karl Rove spoke regularly about his goal of solidifying a permanent Republican majority based on identifying Republicans with antiterrorism efforts. Rove's plan included a number of policy initiatives, including the war in Iraq and a focus on preventive efforts domestically. For example, President Bush and Rove pushed the creation of the Department of Homeland Security front and center in the 2002 campaign, accusing Democrats of being reluctant warriors. Homeland Security, established after the Republicans won a resounding victory in the 2002 congressional elections, has played a significant role in implementing the immigration provisions of the Patriot Act, which make material support of terrorism a deportable offense.

Conspiracy charges also played a significant role in the 2004 Senate race in the key state of Florida. Mel Martinez won the seat for Republicans in part because he attacked his opponent, Betty Castor, for her alleged failure to act, while she was a university administrator, against a professor, Sami Al-Arian, whom the Bush administration had charged with conspiracy to promote terror abroad.[60] While a jury ultimately acquitted Al-Arian of the most serious terrorism charges, Martinez's attacks cut into his opponent's base of support, and fueled his win. The attack succeeded even though the administration had earlier considered Al-Arian so respectable that he had been invited to attend a briefing at the White House with Karl Rove in 2001.[61]

How does this preventive focus compare with the record of the nine United States Attorneys that Gonzales dismissed in December 2006? For the most part, the fired United States Attorneys did not leap on board the conspiracy bandwagon. Doing a high-profile terrorism investigation may have inoculated them against their unceremonious dismissals, since few if any of the United States Attorneys who brought such cases were fired, and indeed those most prominent in bringing terrorism cases, including McNulty, Battle, and Comey, were promoted to senior positions within the department. Admittedly, geography and demography play a role in such decisions; a United States Attorney like Bud Cummins from Arkansas may simply have had fewer opportunities than a prosecutor from an urban district. Nor is it fair to say that the prosecutors who brought such cases made decisions to go forward for strictly political reasons. It is clear, however, that Ashcroft and Gonzales wanted to make prevention a signature issue of the Department in the post–September 11 environment, and that failing to join the surge did not advance one's career. Indeed, the determination of a number of the fired United States Attorneys, such as Carol Lam, to investigate allegations of conspiracy or other federal law violations against allies of the administration, including Republican officeholders and key constituencies such as the Border Patrol, may have served as a telling contrast to the absence of terrorism-related charges. Both trends contributed to the hardening of the view in Washington that the fired United States Attorneys were not "loyal Bushies," and were therefore expendable.

Statutory Foundations and Law Enforcement Performance Since September 11

In implementing their signature prevention approach, Ashcroft and later Gonzales turned to statutes that prohibit terrorist activity. These laws fit the preventive approach because they banned preliminary efforts to provide assistance (or "material support," in the statutory language). One law bans aid to government-designated foreign terrorist organizations such as Hamas.[62] Aid to any part of a designated organization triggers guilt under the statute, even if the donor intended the aid to go to nonviolent activities such as schools or hospitals. While turning off the spigot of financial support for groups like Hamas is a legitimate goal,[63] the statute provides prosecutors with a powerful weapon susceptible to abuse.

A related statute bars assistance to *any* terrorist activity, including activity by ad hoc groups or those not yet formally designated by the secretary of state.[64] The statutory definition of material support is sweeping, including not only cash or weapons, but also the defendant's providing himself as "personnel" in the "global jihad movement." To be found guilty under this law, a defendant must specifically intend to assist in terrorist acts. The terrorist acts envisioned, however, can be contingent in time, place, and context. For example, a defendant is liable if he provides photos of a building to any group to build a database that others may use in the future to plan terrorist acts. Since proof of the defendant's intent is key, prosecutors often rely on the defendant's communications with others. To acquire this evidence, prosecutors turn to informants, who encourage, manipulate, or even make up conversations with suspects.

The terrorism cases brought after September 11 against this legal background reflect an overall lack of prosecutorial judgment. In the most troubling cases, prosecutors and national security officials have used conspiracy charges to leverage the shadow government of detention and coercive interrogation established at Guantánamo Bay. The government has also exploited the amorphous nature of conspiracy by charging defendants with assistance to the "global jihad movement," not to specific plots. In addition, prosecutors have used conspiracy to target aspirants far removed from concrete plots and to resurrect stale cases involving conduct from the 1990s. Even where government investigation is appropriate, such as the recent cases involving plots against Fort Dix and JFK Airport, the use of informants to encourage and enable the defendants undercut the government's claims about the plots' seriousness. Indeed, the hype generated by these prosecutions also heightens the risk of government misconduct to avoid embarrassment from a failed case.

Conspiracy and Anti-terror Prosecution as an Extension of Detours in Government

The conspiracy and material support laws invoked by Ashcroft and Gonzales supplemented the detours that the administration had established after September 11. The government used the sweeping language of the material support laws to launder detentions that would otherwise have been impermissible. Consider the case of Jose Padilla.

Padilla is a U.S. citizen whom the government arrested at O'Hare Airport in Chicago and held for three and a half years as an enemy combatant. Over the course of Padilla's detention, first announced by Attorney General Ashcroft in the spring of 2002, the government used methods of interrogation and confinement that would be harsh even for a prisoner in a federal "supermax" security prison, including sensory deprivation. For much of this time, the government also refused to permit Padilla to meet with his attorneys. Justifying these extraordinary measures, the government told at least four distinct stories. These stories culminated not in a trip to Guantánamo or some "black site" operated by a friendly government abroad, but in a conspiracy conviction.

The first and most notorious government justification was the claim that high-ranking Al Qaeda operatives had tasked Padilla with the job of assembling a "dirty bomb" containing nuclear radiation. When it appeared that many of the statements demonstrating this story were obtained by torture, the government proceeded to plan B. According to this narrative, Padilla had intended to blow up apartment buildings, perhaps by leaving on the gas stove in an apartment. Deputy Attorney General James Comey, in what was probably his worst moment at Justice, detailed this justification in the spring of 2004, just as the Abu Ghraib scandal was gathering speed and the Supreme Court was considering Padilla's case.

After this story became difficult or inconvenient to prove, the government in 2005 (after the Supreme Court required more hearings from lower courts in the case) went to plan C—alleging that Padilla traveled to Afghanistan and sought to fight with the Taliban against the United States and its ally, the Northern Alliance. The government asserted this justification before the conservative Fourth Circuit federal appeals court, in a panel including Judge Michael Luttig, whose deferential views toward presidential authority had earned him consideration for the Supreme Court. Judge Luttig responded with an opinion upholding Padilla's continued detention.[65]

Finally, on the eve of Supreme Court review of the Fourth Circuit's decision in the fall of 2005, the government moved to plan D: conspiracy charges in federal court. It accused Padilla of conduct during the 1990s, including submission of an alleged Al Qaeda membership application form, to assist the "global jihad movement." Under these statutes, the government did not have to prove that Padilla traveled overseas to participate in a more specific plan, that he had sought a dirty bomb, or that he planned to blow up apartment buildings. The conspiracy charges rendered irrelevant the legal fight about Padilla's detention outside the civilian courts. Assessing the government's move, Judge Luttig inferred that the government had argued plan C to secure a favorable ruling from the Fourth Circuit, and had pivoted to plan D to avoid Supreme Court review.[66] For Luttig, who wrote in the anguished tone of a disappointed true believer, the pivot toward conspiracy damaged the government's credibility, by fostering the impression that Padilla's long detention had been a "mistake." Given the relatively modest evidence against Padilla in the criminal case, Padilla's conviction on conspiracy charges did not wholly erase this concern with the government's credibility.[67] It did, however, have the result of incapacitating Padilla for seventeen years in federal prison.[68] On balance, prosecutors acted appropriately in charging Padilla, whose track record of travel to Afghanistan does not fit the mold of a false positive. Nevertheless, the combination of Padilla's extensive detention without charges, the amorphous nature of the charges, and the modest evidence against him should raise concerns.

The utility of conspiracy and material support charges for legitimating the post–September 11 shadow government does not stop at Padilla's case. In several other cases, the government has used (or tried to use) conspiracy charges to convict and punish defendants who had been subject to abusive interrogations. These individuals included David Hicks, the Australian detained at Guantánamo for five years, whom the government handed over to Australia in early 2007 after Hicks pleaded guilty to material support.[69] Others included the student Abu Ali and Muhammed Salah, whom a jury apparently believed had been subject to abusive interrogation practices in Israeli captivity.[70]

Conspiracy legitimated the shadow government in another way, hinging on investigative and surveillance techniques. The material support case often involved evidence obtained through the Foreign Intelligence Surveillance Act (FISA), where applications for warrants go to a special court on vague allegations that the proposed subject is an "agent of a foreign power" (a category that includes terrorist organizations), instead of going to local judicial officers.[71] While FISA is constitutional, it lacks the local base or the concreteness of warrant procedures in the federal districts, and so raises concerns about accountability and monolithic government. The vast increase in FISA warrants since September 11 also fuels suspicion that conspiracy cases allowed the government to by-pass local gatekeepers.

The legitimation of shadow government also reaches into the plea negotiation stage. The government can threaten recalcitrant conspiracy defendants who are not U.S. citizens with a slow boat to Gitmo, where who knows what rigors await. Some evidence suggests that the government threatened defendant Iyman Faris with detention at Guantánamo before Faris pleaded guilty to conspiracy. While Faris's case suggests that he had visited an Al Qaeda training camp and even met with Osama bin Laden, his guilty plea is very thin on the issue of participation in concrete plots.

Faris acknowledged that he had assisted unnamed Al Qaeda members with extensions on plane tickets. He also acknowledged that he had visited the Brooklyn Bridge, to assess the feasibility of bringing down the famous structure by burning through its suspension cables with torches. Faris and the government disputed whether Faris had simply driven across the bridge, or had somehow examined it in greater detail. Both sides acknowledged, however, that Faris had reported back that the plan was not feasible. At trial, Faris could have argued that he had always known that the supposed plan would not work and that he informed others after driving over the bridge as millions do every year. In this case, as in a number of others involving thin facts and frail plots, the "difference maker" in agreeing to plead guilty rather than go to trial may have been the prospect of solitary confinement and coercive interrogation at Guantánamo Bay. Faced with the prospect of detention at Guantánamo, many defendants will plead guilty.[72] The appeals court that rejected Faris's argument only buttressed this concern with its blithe observation that "every guilty plea necessarily entails a choice among distasteful options."[73]

Conspiracy charges and the new anti-terror "material support" provisions have also played a crucial role in the course of the military tribunals established to try suspected terrorists at Guantánamo. The government charged Salim Ahmed Hamdan, Osama bin Laden's personal driver, with conspiracy to commit war crimes. While Justice Stevens asserted in his landmark opinion for the Court in *Hamdan* in June 2006 that the government lacked authority to charge Hamdan with conspiracy, precisely because the charge was so nebulous,[74] the Military Commissions Act passed by Congress to overrule *Hamdan* provides for various forms of liability very much like conspiracy, including material support to a group engaged in terrorist activity.

Recourse to conspiracy to provide material support in the military commission context raises substantial concerns about policy, fairness, and the integrity of legal proceedings. Generally, offenses against the law of war have focused on a few core areas, including violence against civilians, torture and cruel treatment of captives, and the unjustified use of force against nations or populations. Concentrating on these core areas ensures wide agreement within the international community that applies the law of war. Including more amorphous offenses, such as material support, threatens that international consensus.[75]

Charging crimes like material support in military commissions also raises fundamental questions of fair notice. In our system, an individual must have notice that conduct is criminal before the state can prosecute or punish him. The Bush administration charged detainees, including Hamdan and the Australian David Hicks, with providing material support, even though their alleged acts occurred *before* the MCA became law. When Hicks agreed to a plea bargain after spending almost five years in harsh confinement at Guantánamo, he admitted to conduct remarkably similar to the charges in *Koubriti* and other terrorism cases—"casing" buildings for possible future terrorist attacks. At first blush, therefore, the fundamental element of notice was missing.[76]

Conspiracy and material support charges in military commissions also encourage overreliance on informers and sting operations. The monitoring of informants and sting operations is difficult enough in a domestic legal system, where informants' private agendas frustrate efforts at quality control. In the international arena, developing accurate information is even more challenging. Informants' agendas proliferate, and contacts over time that build up trust give way to casual exchanges of information that no government can monitor for accuracy. In Afghanistan, for example, the United States relied on bounty hunters who received thousands of dollars and then disappeared into the maze of tribal existence. While some genuine terrorists were probably caught, it seems certain that the informants profiled their prey, handing over ethnic Arabs who stuck out from the native Afghan population. The whole slipshod process reinforced Justice O'Connor's concern in the *Hamdi* case that many detainees might be false positives—not hardened terrorists, but aid workers, journalists, or pilgrims in the wrong place at the wrong time.

Remaining Problems with Conspiracy:
Amorphous Prosecutions, Hype, and Stale Cases

Even charges that do not directly bolster the Bush administration's shadow government can be unfairly amorphous, exaggerated, or stale. Here, too, accusations of conspiracy and material support are convenient vessels. As an added temptation for the unreflective or opportunistic prosecutor, such charges do not send off the flares that mark obvious paradigm shifts, such as the detention of alleged enemy combatants.

Amorphous Prosecutions

For an example of a vague conspiracy prosecution, consider the case of Kifah Jayyousi, who was convicted in Miami with the erstwhile alleged "dirty bomber" Jose Padilla on charges of material support of terrorist activity. The charges against Jayyousi centered on his alleged recruitment of individuals like Padilla to attend terrorist training camps, and on his sending of supplies such as satellite phones to Chechnya. The recruitment charges were very general, since the evidence backing them up turned on Jayyousi's management of a regular publication that espoused Islamist ideas—activity that would typically be covered by the First Amendment. To make this into conspiracy, the government had to allege that the publication was merely a front for generating new training camp recruits. These "front" arguments were made before, during the McCarthy era; reviving them does not bode well for First Amendment freedoms.

Similarly, in Jayyousi's case the government was not able to prove where the satellite phones ended up in Chechnya, and whether they helped terrorist fighters or simply refugees from the violence there. Particularly since violence has occurred on both sides in the bitter Chechen conflict, proof that Jayyousi intended that the phones facilitate violence was thin. But conspiracy charges allowed the government to take its chances, with victory hinging less on concrete evidence and more on the jury's assessment of Jayyousi's "general disposition."

Hype

The advantages of conspiracy and material support charges have also helped the government convict a number of individuals whose connection to acts of violence was tenuous. In *United States v. Hayat*, the government prosecuted a young man who may have attended some kind of training camp in Pakistan, although the government never alleged that the camp was an Al Qaeda facility or identified its nature and location. The case was brought to the government by an informer, who was paid a six-figure amount for his work. In a recent case in Miami concerning a religious sect of Haitian Americans that an informant had allegedly persuaded to collect data on South Florida and Chicago buildings, the informant also had to regularly remind the leader of the sect about the group's responsibilities, as internecine squabbling within the group proved to be a distraction.[77]

This pattern also holds in the recent cases that attracted vast media attention, involving alleged plots to attack Fort Dix and JFK Airport respectively. In both of these cases, a number of the defendants expressed ambivalence when informants tried to "up the ante." In the Fort Dix case, for example, the defendants reacted negatively when the informant suggested that the group use rocket-propelled grenade launchers. Bona fide terrorists would have presumably leapt at the chance.[78] Even in the JFK case, where the alleged originator of the plan had worked at the airport, a number of the defendants expressed a concern about minimizing casualties, which seemed incongruous for committed terrorists.

Stale Claims

Conspiracy charges also give a tactical advantage to prosecutors because they perform a makeover on stale claims. Since even routine acts can further a conspiracy, prosecutors can lengthen the time that the conspiracy remained in effect by citing minor conduct far more recent than the core events of the alleged conspiracy. Consider here the prosecution's press conference at which John Ashcroft announced the indictment on conspiracy and racketeering charges of Muhammad Salah for allegedly providing financial aid to Hamas. Ashcroft touted the charges as demonstrating a "fifteen-year conspiracy."[79] In truth, the last significant events in the alleged conspiracy occurred in 1993.

In 1993, Salah was arrested on the West Bank and interrogated extensively by Israeli agents. After a lengthy interrogation that may have included techniques subsequently prohibited by Israeli courts, he was convicted and spent a number of years in jail in Israel. Because of acts only collaterally related to terrorism, including allegedly providing false answers in responses to a civil lawsuit, the government was able to argue in 2004 (and subsequently) that the conspiracy was ongoing, even though this claim exaggerated the conspiracy's nature and scope. Although the government had earlier designated Salah as a terrorist without a hearing and frozen his assets, he was finally acquitted of the principal terrorist charges in 2007. Since Salah was convicted of a felony based on his false answers, however, law enforcement authorities have been able to leverage this alleged early 1990s agreement into an ongoing hold on Salah.[80]

The Hazards of Conspiracy: Ethical Issues, Self-Fulfilling Prophecies, and Stereotypes Run Wild

While any exercise of power has risks, the hazards linked with conspiracy charges in national security cases should make the reflective prosecutor think twice. As law enforcement officials scramble to protect their investment in a shaky case, ethical lapses can proliferate. In addition, the law has not dealt adequately with the risk that juries will draw forbidden inferences based on the defendant's ethnicity or his political views. Finally, reliance on conspiracy prosecutions may be counterproductive in the long term, building resentment and despair in targeted communities.

Ethical Issues

The conspiracy cases reveal a litany of ethical lapses by government attorneys. Prosecutors have not only a constitutional duty to hand over evidence disproving guilt, but also an ethical duty to be honest with the court. The prosecutor's failure in *Koubriti* to hand over exculpatory evidence rebutting his claim that the drawings found in the defendants' apartment were "casing" material violated these crucial norms. Similarly, prosecutors are supposed to try their cases in the courtroom, not in the shifting winds of public opinion. This norm ensures that prosecutors develop the facts supporting their charges, instead of relying on an overheated jury pool. Attorney General Ashcroft's statements about the *Koubriti* case violated this standard. Deputy Attorney General Comey's public comments about Jose Padilla's plans, announced just before the Supreme Court decided the case, also violate the spirit of these norms.

Comey's comments on Padilla contrasted with his positive role in the internal dispute about the NSA spying program, and reinforce the interaction between detours and conspiracy charges. The government, at the time

Comey made his remarks, was still holding Padilla as an enemy combatant, so Comey may have reasoned that remarks made before Padilla was charged in a civilian court did not count. This reasoning seems strained, however, because unchallenged accusations contribute over time to a public image that can foster prejudice against a future criminal defendant. An anxious public may take unchallenged allegations as true, and the detained Padilla was in no position to respond.

Policy Problems and Self-Fulfilling Prophecies

The reliance on informers in the conspiracy cases creates other problems of policy and integrity. In a case like *Koubriti*, the informer turned out to be inaccurate and unreliable, spinning tales that his patrons in law enforcement wanted to hear. In other cases, too, citizens expecting integrity in government should wonder about testimony that was bought and paid for with ample cash, or informers seeking to stave off their own prosecution on drug and racketeering charges.

Other problems stem from the culture of informing nurtured by such law enforcement tactics. As commentators have noted, surveillance sometimes acts not as a deterrent, but as a catalyst for illegal behavior. Communities resent intrusive methods, and work collectively to thwart them.[81] Alienation and resentment become the coin of the realm in community discourse. In this environment, voices of moderation lose credibility. Moreover, when communities fear informers, discussion and debate go underground. Without the tempering effect of ventilating diverse views in the public square, groups preach only to the choir. Communities become more polarized. This polarization can produce more violence in the future. In a sense, reliance on informers to deal with the political violence robs Peter to pay Paul—it nets results today, but may build a more determined and dangerous terrorist tomorrow.

Stereotypes

The impact of conspiracy prosecutions on precious First Amendment freedoms also contributes to polarization. Courts have failed to adequately address this issue. Black-letter law allows the government to present a defendant's extreme political views as evidence of motive and agreement with coconspirators. But it is impossible to police the effect that such material has on a jury. The result is that a significant risk exists that defendants will be convicted because of their opinions, not their conduct.

This is not merely a problem in terrorism cases, of course. In many criminal cases, the possibility of juries being influenced by irrelevant or invidious factors exists. For example, it is possible that the ethnic identity of defendants in organized crime cases serves as a signal to the jury that the defendants are guilty—juries may be more willing to assume guilt if the defendant's last name ends with a vowel, despite any instruction that a judge might give to the contrary.[82] We know from our history that juries were often prejudiced against people of color.[83] But there is more reason to be concerned today about prejudice in the context of terrorism prosecutions.

First, changes in jury selection have helped ameliorate the problems in other areas. Government can no longer use preemptory challenges to keep African Americans off juries, for example. This means that an African American or Latino defendant in an urban area has a good chance of being judged by a jury of his peers. In contrast, the numbers of Arab or South Asian Americans or Muslim Americans are still so low that getting adequate representation in a jury pool is unlikely. Moreover, popular images of these groups as propagated in the media are so negative that many members of the jury pool from other backgrounds will experience some subtle prejudice.[84] Indeed, these images are so powerful that the prejudice may be unconscious[85]—all the more dangerous for being something that people will not recognize and acknowledge in the jury selection process.

Another problem is the asymmetry between the starkness of the opinions expressed and what the government actually has to prove in conspiracy cases. The government merely has to prove agreement and some overt act. Here, again, the problem of low base rates undermines the jury's deliberative role. The vast majority of people with extreme political opinions are no more likely than anyone else to act on them. Indeed, it is possible that those with extreme opinions vent their frustration through expressing those sentiments, thereby dissipating anger that might otherwise fester into violence. The calming effect of such venting in the public square is one pragmatic justification for democracy. In a conspiracy case, however, evidence of the large cohort of inactive people is either irrelevant to the charge of agreement or ineffective for the defense.

Even if it is unlikely that the defendants would have followed through with the plot, legally this does not rebut the prosecution's case. As a matter of law, the likelihood of follow-through is irrelevant. Mere agreement is enough, and the law says that moments of ambivalence do not rebut proof of a general underlying agreement. In any case, information about base rates of violence is less vivid and therefore less persuasive than the extreme opinions of *this* defendant, which the jury gets to hear. Here, as elsewhere, operating from individual cases instead of base rates can skew outcomes. A jury may also reason backward from the claimed object of the conspiracy to the proof of agreement. Suppose that the government has charged the defendants with conspiring to destroy JFK Airport, as a recent case alleges. Cognitive psychologists tell us that people tend to find proof more persuasive when the potential harm is horrific. Surrendering to this syndrome, the jury may adopt the government's preventive rationale, and reason that it is prudent to remove even a small risk of a major disaster. In this way, allegations of political violence turn our constitutional commitment to avoiding false positives on its head. "Better safe than sorry" no longer means voting to acquit to avoid imprisoning the innocent; instead, it means that prevention of harm justifies a guilty verdict even on thin evidence.

Affirmative defenses to conspiracy are nearly always futile. Our current law of entrapment requires that the defendant have no predisposition toward crime. Here, though, the defendant's opinions also play a role in confirming that the defendant has a predisposition. Moreover, the law of entrapment also permits a wide range of government enticement. One of the few cases where the courts found entrapment involved an informant's effort to persuade participants at a rehab clinic to engage in drug trafficking.[86] The Supreme Court condemned the government's effort to troll for drug suspects among people sincerely committed to kicking the habit. The modest standard set by this case, however, does not adequately regulate the more subtle government enticement at work in the political violence context.

Controlling Conspiracy

Despite these risks, in the hands of wise and effective prosecutors conspiracy charges can enhance public safety while respecting civil liberties. The legal system must encourage prosecutors to bring appropriate conspiracy cases while winnowing out cases that are ripe for abuse. This result requires a combination of internal, ethical, and judicial controls that enhance accountability and promote prosecutorial deliberation.

Internal and Ethical Criteria

Prosecutors should prioritize investigation of suspected terrorists with special indicia of risk. Criteria of this kind will minimize the use of precious law enforcement resources to pursue wannabes and big talkers. In addition, internal and ethical guidelines can require consideration of the opportunity costs of particular charging decisions.

Conspiracy investigations using informants and stings are appropriate when an individual has a pattern of appearances in reports of the illegal activities of others, under circumstances that strongly suggest advance knowledge or specific encouragement. In the pre–September 11 Abdel Rahman case, the government successfully prosecuted an extremist Brooklyn cleric known as the "blind Sheik."[87] Information available to the government suggested that Abdel Rahman had been a common thread in a group responsible for several high-profile acts of violence including the first World Trade Center bombing and the assassination of Rabbi Meir Kahane.[88] The jury convicted Abdel Rahman after hearing a tape of the Sheik specifically authorizing an informant to kill Egyptian president Hosni Mubarak during a visit by Mubarak to the United States.[89] The group's track record of violence reduced the risk of false positives that so often plagues conspiracy cases.

In a similar vein, ongoing illegality is an appropriate cue for law enforcement interest. If suspects are currently violating the law, they reveal the earnestness and commitment that characterize a successful conspiracy. In the Fort Dix case, the defendants, who were undocumented aliens, were seen firing guns in the now-infamous DVD that formed the basis for the first tip to law enforcement. Since undocumented aliens cannot lawfully possess guns under federal law,[90] this illegality was a sufficient basis for pushing forward with the investigation.

A suspect should receive priority for further investigation when he has special experience with the purported target of the attack. Experience increases the knowledge level of the suspect, and the possibility of a successful plot. It also enhances the likelihood that the suspect has a grudge or other motivation that may impel him toward consummation of the plot. Russell Defreitas, one of the defendants in the Kennedy Airport case, had long experience as an employee at JFK Airport.[91] While his plot to blow up gas tanks was still far-fetched, law enforcement officials could not wholly discount his experience.

The difficult deliberative calculus required of prosecutors could also benefit from further internal and ethical guidance on the interaction of conspiracy charges and issues of nationality, ethnicity, and religion. Guidelines in the United States Attorneys' Manual or elsewhere should require that prosecutors consider the long-term impact of investigative methods such as reliance on informers and sting operations, particularly in communities such as Arab or South Asian neighborhoods often targeted for terrorist investigations.[92]

In addition, the ethical rules that prosecutors must follow should require greater selectivity and more gatekeeping in targeting particular communities. Currently, the rules of ethics provide only modest guidance for prosecutors.[93] The American Bar Association's official comments to the rules, which aid their interpretation, articulate a shining vision of the prosecutor as a "minister of justice."[94] The rules themselves, however, do little to realize this ideal. More specific rules and more concrete enforcement will ensure that responses to crisis are both measured and effective.

In sum, prosecutorial deliberation is not a recipe for doing nothing. Indeed, a deliberative approach requires law enforcement officials to move quickly when the situation warrants. A more proactive strategy should focus on the reasonable possibility of violent acts or substantial funding of violence.

The Judicial Role

Courts also have a role to play as gatekeepers, making up for the lack of deliberation displayed by prosecutors. As always, a robust judicial role may clash with tactics that law enforcement and national security officials deem expedient. But courts can strike a balance that acknowledges security concerns while enhancing the government's accountability.

First, the courts should return to the wisdom of earlier conspiracy cases like *Kotteakos v. United States*[95] by requiring congruency between the scope of alleged agreements and the scope required under section 956. In the hub-and-spoke cases, the courts achieved this congruency by limiting the generality that the government could impute to specific transactions. When a defendant in one of the spokes agreed to engage in conduct with the goal of defrauding the government in a particular transaction, the courts limited the scope of agreement to that transaction. Courts refused to impute to this defendant each of the individual frauds generated by the many other spokes. Comparable specificity would promote fairness in the context of section 956.

A section 956 defendant like Padilla has allegedly committed what we can call an affiliative crime. His act was affiliative because it reflected solidarity with the general aims of Al Qaeda and other terrorist groups. As noted above, attendance at a camp is closely related to manifestations of solidarity that would clearly constitute protected speech, such as marching in a demonstration supporting Al Qaeda.[96] Some of the behavior at the camp, include chanting and posing for videos, is indistinguishable from such protected expressions of affiliation. The discrete act of applying to attend or even attending a terrorist training camp does not fit the broader agreement to commit violent acts that supports section 956 liability.[97]

Most important, attendance at a training camp is not a fungible good comparable to the provision of funding or equipment. Once provided, money or equipment may be used by a terrorist group for any purpose. But a person attending a training camp is not fungible in this sense. The individual must be trained, and has the opportunity to desert, defect, or become disaffected at any point.[98] In this sense, applying to or even attending a terrorist training camp possesses an element of uncertainty distinct from the conduct that could be properly charged under section 956.[99]

Beyond policing the scope of agreements punishable under section 956, courts should also be more robust in their gatekeeping function. In cases dealing with material support to designated terrorist groups such as Hamas, courts have struck down as vague or otherwise impermissible certain portions of the statutes. For example, courts have ruled that the use of the terms "training," "personnel," and "expert advice or assistance" encompass too much activity that the First Amendment protects, such as training a group in international law or nonviolent techniques.[100] According to courts, these terms provide insufficient guidance for individuals to discern the boundary between protected and prohibited acts, and therefore chill protected speech.[101]

Another important judicial innovation would require an emphasis on instructions to juries on the materiality of defendant's overt acts. In conspiracy cases, for example, the law could require not merely an act in furtherance of the conspiracy that might be casual or inadvertent, but rather an act that materially advances the goals of the conspiracy—that makes it more likely that the goals will be achieved. On this view, an alleged conspirator in a plot to blow up a subway station would commit a material overt act by purchasing ingredients such as fertilizer or dynamite that are needed for explosives. Other acts less proximate in time, such as a plane hijacker's taking plane trips with no other purpose than casing the airline's systems, could also be material overt acts. But acts with a more ambiguous interpretation, such as the assembly of diagrams of a site from generic online sources, would not be sufficient for 956 liability unless the government could show that the defendant or his coconspirators specifically intended to use the plans to destroy the site.[102]

Trial courts must also serve a gatekeeping function by excluding evidence that is inflammatory, irrelevant, and prejudicial to the defendant. For example, in *United States v. Al-Moayad*,[103] the trial court allowed the government to present video evidence and testimony about a terrorist attack as part of its case against an alleged Hamas fund-raiser. The terrorist attack described in this evidence, however, occurred *before* the acts that the defendant allegedly committed. Although Hamas's track record of violence was relevant to defendant's guilt, the graphic details of this particular attack were not.[104] In addition, the trial court permitted the government to introduce its trump card—video evidence and testimony about Osama bin Laden's visit to a training camp, again unrelated to the defendant.[105] To ensure that jury deliberations were untainted by such sensational and irrelevant evidence, a federal appeals court ordered a new trial.

Conclusion

The post–September 11 preventive paradigm ushered in an old dilemma: conspiracy's fragile balance between false positives and false negatives. Addressing the risk of political violence through conspiracy charges poses special risks, as history has revealed from Sir Walter Raleigh to the Chicago Seven trial. Unfortunately, the administration's policymakers—always impatient with a historical narrative that they did not initiate—ignored these risks. After September 11, conspiracy prosecutions laundered shadow government machinations such as extralegal detention and interrogation. The preventive paradigm thrived on hype, prioritizing stale cases and terrorist wannabe's. In the process, prosecutors too often let informants' agendas supplant prosecutorial judgment, and finessed obligations such as the duty to disclose exculpatory evidence and refrain from prejudicial pretrial publicity.

The government's broad interpretation of liability under section 956 in cases such as the prosecution of Jose Padilla accentuates conspiracy's perennial dilemma. By charging Padilla with conspiracy to murder, maim, and kidnap abroad by virtue of his application to attend a terrorist training camp, the government attributed plots and plans to Padilla that far exceeded the narrow scope of his alleged agreement. Padilla's conviction was surely expedient in light of the government's earlier assertions, never mentioned at trial, that Padilla had sought a "dirty bomb." But the expedience of the conviction only heightens the risk that the government will use section 956 conspiracy to target people because of who the government fears them to be. As Robert Jackson warned during an earlier time of crisis, that temptation is a central threat to the rule of law.[106]

Prosecutors should reject this temptation, while preserving conspiracy's virtues as a legitimate weapon against terrorists. Where suspects have prior knowledge of attacks and appear to be a common strand in a web of wrongdoing, as in the case of Sheik Abdel Rahman, the use of stings and informers is appropriate. This is also true where the suspects are already engaging in illegal conduct, as in the undocumented aliens taking target practice in the Fort Dix case, or have special knowledge or experience, as in the JFK arrests. The best prosecutors will use this powerful weapon when necessary, after deliberation about the always elusive balance between false positives and false negatives. To aid in this deliberation, ethics rules and Justice Department policy should require more deliberation about both the short- and long-term costs of conspiracy prosecutions to cooperation from targeted communities of Muslims, Arabs, and South Asians.

Courts play a necessary role as gatekeepers when prosecutors fail. In a case like Padilla's, courts should require congruency between the scope of the defendant's alleged agreement and the aim of murder, mayhem, or kidnapping required under section 956. Actual or attempted participation at a training camp abroad should be punishable not under section 956, but as lending material support to a designated terrorist group.[107] In addition, courts should make the overt act requirement more robust, to ensure that a conspiracy amounts to more than a wannabe's wish list.

Responsible prosecutors recognize that the wrongful conviction of an innocent person ultimately aids the terrorist cause. Terrorists wager that responses to threats will produce a crisis of legitimacy within democratic governments. Overreliance on conspiracy charges has generated such crises in the past, as the responses to labor and leftist agitation demonstrate. Courts and prudent prosecutors should learn from the excesses of the Bush administration, and implement reforms to guard against this risk.

Justice and Elections

In late October 2006, David Iglesias, United States Attorney for New Mexico, was at home when he received a disturbing phone call from his mentor, Senator Pete Domenici.[1] Domenici, known as "St. Pete" for his record of honesty and concern for the public good, had been largely responsible for getting Iglesias his position.[2] Domenici skipped the small talk and directly asked Iglesias about a pending prosecution in Iglesias's office concerning political corruption among Democrats, demanding to know if indictments in the case would be filed before the November election, the better to embarrass the Democrats and prop up the Republicans' sagging fortunes at the polls.[3] In asking about this investigation, Domenici was following up on a previous phone call from New Mexico congresswoman Heather Wilson, who had called Iglesias at a Washington hotel during a visit for a conference.[4] Iglesias, who was making sure he had his ducks in a row and was also reluctant to file a political case so close to the election, answered that the case would not be ready. Domenici replied, "I'm very sorry to hear that,"[5] and hung up.

A few short weeks later, in early December, after an election that saw Republicans lose majorities in the House and Senate, Iglesias got another call—this one from Mike Battle, a Justice Department official.[6] Battle informed Iglesias, who had consistently received strong performance evaluations, that the administration "wants to go a different way." In other words, Iglesias was fired.

The Iglesias episode became the epicenter of the furor over the firing of nine United States Attorneys. The episode revealed that for the Bush administration and the Justice Department, forging a political brand based on toughness in the war on terror was just the beginning. The terrorism issue also provided a rationale for the Bush faithful to target groups that could stand in the way of a permanent Republican majority, and to bypass rules that made political influences in criminal prosecution more difficult. The strategy was twofold: attack Democratic officeholders wherever possible, and place systemic barriers in the way of the emerging Democratic majority that included people of color, particularly Hispanics.

As in other Bush administration efforts, legal detours were essential. The administration tried to pressure prosecutors like Iglesias to ignore long-standing rules and traditions insulating federal prosecutors from politics. The administration also rejected the value of prosecutorial discretion, just as it had done in its attempts to centralize criminal justice policy, discussed in chapter 4. On some matters involving voting rights, the administration also received support from the courts, dominated by Republican appointees who, starting with *Bush v. Gore*, failed to strike the right balance between ensuring eligibility and inclusion in voting.

Vote Suppression and Vote Dilution: Partisan Trade-Offs

American law and politics has long addressed two problems: vote suppression and vote dilution. Democrats care about vote suppression—policies and practices that suppress turnout and hinder access to the ballot, typically for constituencies such as the poor and racial minorities that tend to vote Democratic. Republicans, on the other hand, have long been concerned about vote dilution—practices such as vote fraud that allow people to vote who are not eligible, and therefore dilute the value of the franchise for legal voters.

Both sides have legitimate points in their favor. But those concerned about vote suppression can marshal overwhelming evidence that goes back to the dawn of the republic, when only propertied white males could vote. In contrast, those concerned with vote dilution muster far less evidence, and rely far more on alarmism and anecdote. An artificial "balance" between suppression and dilution inflates the merit of dilution arguments. Measures to counter vote dilution have a dire consequence: they intimidate voters, thus exacerbating vote suppression. Ironically, this phenomenon helped install George W. Bush as president, as reflected in the Supreme Court's decision in *Bush v. Gore*.

For minority groups such as African Americans, the franchise was elusive until passage of the Voting Rights Act of 1964. Before then, formal and informal practices, particularly in the South, impaired ballot access. The Voting Rights Act gave federal officials a mandate to dismantle obstacles to voting in the South and elsewhere. In addition, the Supreme Court became far more willing to step in to strike down restrictive state laws and dubious apportionment schemes, declaring that the right to vote is fundamental. Before this regime, states and local governments had apportioned legislative representatives through often arbitrary schemes. For example, a city ordinance in Alabama changed municipal boundaries from a square to a twenty-eight-sided figure resembling an ink blot in a Rorschach test to exclude black residents.[7] The Voting Rights Act and the Supreme Court's heightened scrutiny of restrictive voting measures curbed such blatant discrimination.

With egregious discrimination ruled out of bounds, partisan interests that benefited from vote suppression focused on other methods clothed in the law and order mantle. Republicans have sought to portray Democrats and progressives as permitting felons[8] and undocumented immigrants to vote.[9] These felony disenfranchisement laws were applied in 2000 to block African Americans in Florida from voting, including those who merely shared a name with a convicted felon.[10]

The Supreme Court and Anti-Vote-Dilution Measures as Vote Suppression

In *Bush v. Gore*,[11] the Court responded to an exaggerated vote dilution concern by downgrading legitimate vote suppression concerns. In a state where thousands of voters struggled to follow sometimes confusing voting instructions, the Court held that the effort by Florida courts to ascertain the intent of each voter threatened to dilute the votes of those who had concededly complied with instructions. According to the majority, time was of the essence, requiring that the vote-counting process cease. But the majority conflated two issues: (1) arbitrariness of the vote-counting process in some Florida counties, and (2) the time available. The consequence was interference in state control over voting procedures.

If the Court had problems with the ad hoc nature of the recount procedures in certain Florida counties, it could have simply sent the matter back to the Florida courts for more specific guidance. Getting it right, rather than completing the process within an artificial time window, should have been the Court's priority. As Justice Stevens pointed out, the federal government, Congress in particular, had allowed Hawaii to choose electors appointed on January 4, 1961, well after the date set by Congress for the 1960 election.[12] While the majority was right that vote dilution can also be unconstitutional, the case addressing this issue dealt not with state attempts to discern a voter's intent, but rather with a formal scheme that systematically and in a clear pattern over time weighed the votes of certain groups more heavily than those of others.[13] In *Reynolds v. Sims*, which reflected the racial discrimination that afflicted voting in the South during the entire Jim Crow era, counties that had ten times the population of other counties had the same number of representatives. The Court rejected this flagrant inequity, observing that "the concept of 'we the people' under the Constitution visualizes no preferred class of voters but equality among those who meet the basic qualifications."[14]

A good-faith attempt to assess the intent of the voter with respect to ballots filled out by hand does not contravene this standard. The majority wrote a rule to this effect into the Constitution, however, and thereby paved the way for election of a candidate—George W. Bush—who had concededly received fewer popular votes nationwide. While the Supreme Court has in other respects pushed back against the Bush presidency, its later decision on the Indiana voter ID law bookended the Bush era, and again unduly discounted the adverse impact of anti-vote-dilution measures.

Voter identification laws are one way that conservatives have tried to stamp out vote fraud, although traditionally Democratic constituencies feel the effects of these supposedly neutral statutes. Here, as elsewhere, conservatives have used law and order ideology and rhetoric to accomplish their goals. Tom Tancredo, who as a member of Congress from Colorado pushed legislation to heighten immigration law enforcement, favored voter identification laws as a way of preventing undocumented aliens from voting.[15] Tancredo and others have conjured up the picture of thousands of undocumented aliens impersonating citizens at the polls. But the facts do not bear out this fear. Studies reveal that in Arizona, which enacted strict legislation in 2006, a grand total of *four* undocumented aliens actually voted in the last ten years out of millions of ballots cast. Experts on immigrant communities point out that these communities are often wary of government, and will not risk interaction with government authorities who may seek to deport them, even authorities as supposedly benign as election officials. The impact of this is clear on impoverished seniors who might vote Democratic. For example, consider Eva Steele, a senior with a disability living in a senior citizens' facility in Arizona. Steele, who uses a wheelchair and also has a son on active duty in the military, did not have a driver's license. She had no money to pay for the substitute ID that Arizona was offering for twelve dollars, and no transportation to pick it up.[16] The barriers built into the Arizona law would be relatively simple to overcome for a middle-class person with a car, but for Steele these were difficult barriers to hurdle.

The Supreme Court, unfortunately, has discounted the de facto disenfranchisement of people like Ms. Steele. In doing so, the Court failed to realize that vote restrictions—even those neutral on their face—in practice often deprive the poor and vulnerable of the right to vote. The Court's decision in *Crawford v. Marion County Election Bd.*[17] is a stark supplement to *Bush v. Gore*. Adjudicating the constitutionality of an Indiana law requiring a photo ID for voters,

Justice Stevens acknowledged that the requirement could be a serious burden for some groups of people, including the rural elderly. As Stevens conceded, those born out-of-state or abroad are also subject to this "special burden," because they may encounter great difficulty in securing a birth certificate. Justice Stevens was cavalier, however, in asserting that the rural elderly poor, with no access to public transportation, could rely on the kindness of friends or family to assist them. Stevens also dismissed the partisan genesis of the law, even while noting that the law seems to be a solution looking for a problem, since there is virtually no documentation of voter fraud in Indiana.[18]

Along with the supposedly neutral rules that the Court upheld in *Crawford*, conservatives have used other tactics that smack even more of opportunism. Republicans have focused for decades, for example, on compiling lists of prospective voters whose registration data, including their address, appears to be inconsistent or inaccurate. Once they develop these lists, they use them to challenge such voters who show up at the polls on Election Day.[19]

A related tactic is systematic intimidation of organizations seeking to register new voters. Of course, law enforcement authorities should combat vote fraud, which injures the cause of democracy. But election officials and experts agree that attempts to file fraudulent voter registration applications have little impact at the polls.[20] Exaggerations of this fear risk suppression of bona fide registration efforts.

The Republican campaign against organizations registering the poor and people of color also played a role in the removal of New Mexico United States Attorney David Iglesias. Republican operatives pressured Iglesias into forming an election task force.[21] After investigating more than a hundred incidents reported during the 2004 election, however, Iglesias, Main Justice in Washington, and the FBI agreed that no incidents warranted federal prosecution. New Mexico Republicans were outraged by this result, since they were concerned about a close election in 2006. Some complained to Main Justice and to the White House. One Republican stalwart told Iglesias that Republicans had wanted "splashy headlines" on voter fraud charges, and blamed Iglesias for being insufficiently aggressive.[22]

Politics and the Prosecutorial Function

While aggressive prosecution is often a virtue, in election cases it can be a vice. Prosecutors exercise sound judgment when they avoid interference in the political process. A distinguished United States Attorney in New York during the Nixon administration, Whitney North Seymour, made this point, asking, "Where does policy end and politics begin?" Seymour also cautioned that prosecutors had to be wary of "requests for improper political favors channeled through the White House."[23]

This aversion to politics goes to the heart of the prosecutorial function. Avoiding the taint of politics is essential to the prosecutor's integrity. The best prosecutors understand that avoiding even the appearance of entanglement in politics is a crucial institutional goal. Any whiff of political influence will undermine the credibility of the department, and cast into doubt the many prosecutions the department initiates that have nothing to do with politics. When, as Rhode Island's Senator Whitehouse said, the attorney general gives "the Vice President's staff a green light to muck around in sensitive Department of Justice affairs,"[24] those fundamental norms of professionalism have been turned on their head.

Of course, political concerns have intruded in previous administrations, although the best prosecutors have always resisted pressure from senior officials to play politics. Whitney North Seymour described a distressing phone call he received in 1972 from L. Patrick Gray, then the Deputy Attorney General, asking Seymour to interview a prominent political figure outside the United States Attorney's office to avoid embarrassment.[25] It turned out governor Nelson Rockefeller of New York had intervened on the witness's behalf with Attorney General John Mitchell. Seymour declined to cooperate, but one can imagine the pressure imposed on a Justice Department lawyer when informed that the Attorney General and Deputy Attorney General of the United States, and the governor of his home state, wanted him to "play ball."

Over time, federal prosecutors have developed rules of thumb to separate criminal cases and politics. Senator Whitehouse of Rhode Island, who had served as a United States Attorney, pointed out during the Senate investigation of the United States Attorney firings that federal policy in place prior to the Bush administration strongly discouraged announcing charges for a reasonable period of time prior to an election.[26] This prudent practice served to deter prosecutions that could skew an election outcome. In addition, federal guidelines limited the number of White House officials authorized to contact the Justice Department about a pending investigation. This practice also minimized political influence, helping to ensure that federal prosecutors would make decisions on the merits. The Bush White House and Justice Department ignored both of these rules.

Bush administration officials, including Karl Rove, White House Counsel Harriet Miers, and chief of staff to Attorney General Gonzales, Kyle Sampson, believed that serving the administration's political interests should figure prominently in the job evaluation of each United States Attorney. In Sampson's memorable phrase, the administration conducted a rolling survey to determine which ones were "loyal Bushies."[27] Political factors played some role in the dismissal or retention of a number of United States Attorneys. The clearest case involved David Iglesias of New Mexico, who had refused to play ball on requests by Senator Domenici and President Bush to target Democrats in New Mexico.

In dismissing Iglesias, the White House also sought to destroy his reputation. Performance evaluations, however, did not support this effort. Iglesias received positive triennial recommendations in 2002 and 2005. His 2005 evaluation stated that he "appropriately oversaw the day-to-day work of the senior management team, effectively addressed all management issues, and directed resources to accomplish the Department's and the United States Attorney's priorities."[28] In March 2005, Sampson identified Iglesias as a "strong" prosecutor who should keep his job.

In February 2007, the task of evaluating Iglesias at the Justice Department fell to the inexperienced and ultra-partisan Monica Goodling. Although Goodling had only a couple of months' experience in practicing law, she did not hesitate to savage Iglesias, describing him as an "underachiever" and "absentee landlord." According to Goodling, Iglesias was "in over his head." She also passed along Domenici's comment that Iglesias "doesn't move cases." William Moschella of the Justice Department told the Senate in March 2007 that an internal study identified "management issues" with Iglesias. The study, however, actually did not mention any such issues. McNulty and Mercer also testified that they did not know of facts to back up the "absentee landlord" characterization. Kyle Sampson said in March 2007 Senate testimony that Iglesias delegated too much—but Justice Department official David Margolis said he told Sampson this only after the decision was made to dismiss Iglesias.[29]

The actual reasons for Iglesias's firing were political. Sampson in March 2007 testimony acknowledged that Domenici's calls to Justice and the White House played a role. Attorney General Gonzales also testified that in the fall of 2006 Karl Rove had mentioned his concern about vote fraud in Albuquerque. Bush had expressed similar concerns.[30] In short, the White House and Main Justice decided to fire Iglesias for political reasons, and needlessly stained Iglesias's reputation in scrambling to justify their decision.

While Iglesias's case was the most egregious, the "loyal Bushies" who consolidated their power under Attorney General Gonzales pushed political agendas at every opportunity. In state after state, they demanded voter fraud investigations, stemming from the Republicans' decades-long anxiety about

Hispanics, poor people, and immigrants gaining political power. In Missouri, for example, the head of the Civil Rights Division, Bradley Schlozman, helped persuade his superiors that United States Attorney Todd Graves was dragging his feet on a voter fraud case involving ACORN. In fact, Graves, a loyal Republican, simply questioned the strength of the evidence.[31] Once Graves left his post, Schlozman took his place and pushed the case forward. In a departure from practice, Schlozman filed his charges just five days before the 2006 elections.[32] Schlozman took this action even though ACORN had fired the offending employees and informed election officials.[33]

In Washington State, John McKay refused to indict individuals for voter fraud in a manner that could have tipped a close gubernatorial election. He was also fired. The election was indeed close, involving multiple recounts.[34] McKay did not see the requisite proof of a crime. Like Iglesias and Graves, McKay acted as the gatekeeper that a prosecutor should be, bringing cases when the evidence justifies an indictment. But Washington Republicans viewed this gatekeeping function as an obstacle to political mobilization. Republicans, operating with the Florida 2000 playbook, seemed to feel that any close election required legal action, and that federal criminal investigation was a political tool.[35] They clothed their desire in the now-familiar overheated rhetoric about vote fraud, even though there was scant evidence of vote fraud in the election. Washington Republicans approached McKay, and his name ended up on the list being compiled by Kyle Sampson, Gonzales's chief of staff. Even more hurtfully, the Justice Department, including Deputy Attorney General Paul McNulty, asserted that McKay and the other United States Attorneys on the list were being forced to resign for "performance-based" reasons. This rankled the prosecutors, who in virtually all cases had received sterling evaluations shortly before.

After Iglesias was fired, he teamed up with the other fired United States Attorneys, who were already on the receiving end of spin from Justice Department officials suggesting that they were incompetent. The administration had antagonized the wrong people at the wrong time. With the Democrats back in control of the Senate, Patrick Leahy, chair of the Judiciary Committee, held hearings. Iglesias, whose exploits as a JAG lawyer had inspired the Tom Cruise movie *A Few Good Men*, fought back. He told the Judiciary Committee about the intimidation he had experienced from both Senator Domenici and Representative Wilson, as well as the curt handling he received from Main Justice.

Witnesses from the Justice Department only enhanced Iglesias's credibility. Gonzales's chief of staff, Kyle Sampson, testified that he had methodically kept Gonzales in the loop about the firings.[36] Gonzales resorted to the familiar strategy of situational amnesia. His testimony collected terms for memory failure the way some men collect ties.[37] This lack of candor cost Gonzales the trust of the Senate, and ultimately his job; he resigned in September 2007.

Prosecution of Political Cases and the Failure of Proportion

The Bush administration's bias also emerged in its decisions to prosecute public officials. The prosecution of public officials is one of the most delicate areas of federal prosecutorial responsibility. On the one hand, federal prosecutors have the independence to prosecute officeholders and other political players who have corrupted the system. As noted above, however, federal prosecution is also the "atomic bomb" of law enforcement; prosecutors should be wary of prosecutions where the conduct at issue is simply part of the give-and-take of politics, or where other means of enforcement, including prosecution by the state or discipline by an employer, may be sufficient. Prosecutors appointed by one party must also ensure that they are not demanding blemish-free conduct from political opponents, while winking at similar conduct from political friends. Too often, federal prosecutors in the Bush administration—the ones who were *not* fired—failed to meet this test.

Consider here a case that even luminaries in prior Republican administrations have bitterly criticized: the prosecution of Dr. Cyril Wecht, a nationally known forensic expert who came to prominence in the 1970s for disputing the "single-bullet" theory of president John F. Kennedy's assassination. Wecht had been charged with federal mail and wire fraud because he allegedly used his employer's equipment and employees to aid his own forensic consulting business. Another allegation in the indictment was that Wecht acted illegally in having deputy coroners drive him to the airport for private business trips.[38]

While these matters are a legitimate concern of Dr. Wecht's employer, the Pittsburgh (Allegheny Country) Medical Examiner's Office, they may not meet the proportionality criterion for sound exercise of prosecutorial discretion. Most employees conduct at least a modest level of private business at the office without any repercussions—making a call to one's spouse about who is going to pick up the kids is private business. Many professional employees spend a modest amount of time (or perhaps more) surfing the Web at work. Generally, we view such derelictions as the province of the employer, not federal prosecutors. We separate out such petty missteps from areas where prosecutors have a legitimate interest, such as taking money to alter official positions, or appropriating money from a public employer.

Richard Thornburgh, a former governor of Pennsylvania and United States Attorney General under Presidents Reagan and Bush, is a lawyer for Dr. Wecht, so he may have an interest. His criticism was notably public and robust, however, accusing the Justice Department before Congress of engaging in a politically motivated prosecution of Dr. Wecht, a Democrat.[39] Recently, a jury trial of Dr. Wecht ended in a mistrial; the government, instead of taking this as a message that its prosecution was misguided, immediately announced its intention to retry the case. FBI agents also interviewed the jury, another step that could be read as intimidation of jurors who had failed to "get with the program" and convict.

In Wecht's case and in the case of former Alabama governor Don Siegelman (discussed below), the prosecutors' lack of proportion spread to the presiding judge. In each of these cases, the trial court abandoned its neutral stance, becoming a cheerleader for the government. An appellate court approved the mistrial declared by the trial court in Wecht's case, but noted that the court had failed to follow ideal procedures, including questioning the foreperson of the jury and each juror, and then holding a hearing with counsel for the parties.[40] By failing to follow this course, the trial judge had missed the opportunity to discern whether the jury could have continued deliberating and reached an acquittal. The court also imposed a gag order, denying counsel the opportunity to speak. The appellate court noted, in an unusual observation, that its holding in no way required that Wecht stand trial again—as close as an appellate court can possibly come to saying that a retrial is not worth the candle. The court noted that the case had already consumed thirty months, and resulted in numerous appeals and motions. In case the government did not take the hint, the court also relieved the trial judge of further duties on the case, allegedly to achieve a "reduced level of rancor in the courtroom."[41] While the court had earlier denied a motion to recuse the judge, it now indicated a preference for a "less invested adjudicator to take over from here."[42]

Another example of overkill was the government's pursuit of Geoff Fieger, a Democratic activist and trial lawyer famed as the attorney for Dr. Jack Kevorkian. The government alleged that Fieger had used "straw donors" to exceed the individual limit on campaign contributions. This practice, which involves the actual donor giving money to others, which they in turn donate to the candidate, is probably illegal under federal election law, but is usually dealt with by the Federal Election Commission through civil fines.[43] Instead of handling the case civilly, the government sent eighty FBI agents to raid Fieger's office and interview putative donors that he had reimbursed.[44] As in the death penalty cases that the government has lost, the jury apparently believed that the government had overreached and acted without an appropriate sense of proportion, and that it had not proven the intent to deceive. As a result, it acquitted Fieger.

A similar concern about ramping up federal charges for matters that are usually handled in a less punitive setting is present in the case of former Alabama governor Don Siegelman. Here, too, prosecutors resolved these issues *against* Democrats but *in favor of* Republicans. Alabama Republicans had resented Siegelman's victory in Alabama in 1998, apparently believing that state government in Alabama was now a Republican preserve. Siegelman was under investigation for much of his term, and was narrowly defeated in a disputed election in 2002. Karl Rove had done extensive political consulting in Alabama, working toward making the Alabama Supreme Court a Republican stronghold.

After Siegelman's narrow defeat, a major Republican in the state with close ties to Karl Rove assured his political allies that Siegelman would not escape punishment, because "my girls" will take care of him. "My girls" included the Republican's spouse, Leura G. Canary, who was serving as United States Attorney at the time. Canary ultimately recused herself from the case, but not before crucial signals were sent that the case was a priority for the national party and Main Justice in Washington. Most disturbingly, evidence has emerged that despite her pledge, Canary did not in fact recuse herself.[45] Like New York Mets manager Bobby Valentine, who after being tossed out of the game returned to his team's dugout disguised in Groucho Marx glasses and moustache, Canary continued to weigh in heavily with memos to her staff.

The Siegelman case involved an allegation that is usually par for the course in the rough and tumble world of politics—that Siegelman had appointed a businessman, Richard Scrushy, to a government board in exchange for Scrushy's giving five hundred thousand dollars to retire debt on a state campaign for an education lottery. Prosecutors, whose main witnesses admitted to a vast spectrum of corrupt activities, argued that Siegelman was personally liable on the debt, and that therefore the gift was in essence a gift to Siegelman himself. Political officials, however, are rarely if ever actually obliged to pay money in these situations; in that sense, the debt was a "paper" one with little or no practical consequences for Siegelman. It seems doubtful that the case was about more than the routine conduct that happens all the time in politics. There was no allegation that Siegelman skewed policies to benefit Scrushy, or that Scrushy benefited in any specific way from the post on the board. Major campaign contributors to presidential candidates often become ambassadors if their candidate prevails. The exchange here seemed of that order—hardly worth prosecution if prosecutors had thoroughly read and understood Robert Jackson's warning that prosecutors targeting a single individual are often likely to find something, but that they may end up prosecuting the person rather than the crime.[46]

Moreover, recent disclosures on *60 Minutes* have indicated that the main witness against Siegelman, former aide Nick Bailey, met with prosecutors about seventy times and had to write out his testimony repeatedly to learn it. Generally, case law requires that the government, upon request of defense counsel, turn over such material. According to the defense, the government never handed over the notes. Since Bailey's testimony was central to Siegelman's conviction, this failure to provide the defense with information that could impeach Bailey's credibility could have been a major flaw in the case.[47] While a federal appellate court affirmed Siegelman's convictions on most counts,[48] a substantial bipartisan cohort of ex-prosecutors has continued to push for Siegelman's exoneration because of problems with the prosecution's conduct.[49]

In at least one case pursued by the Bush Justice Department, the prosecutor's charges did not even amount to a crime. Wisconsin state employee Georgia Thompson was convicted of federal mail and wire fraud for awarding a tie-break on a bid for public services to a local company. While the proprietor of the company was a contributor to the governor's campaign, the contributions were lawful and "properly disclosed."[50] Moreover, there was no allegation that awarding the contract to this particular bidder was a quid pro quo or that a kickback was involved.[51] Indeed, the company selected was also the low bidder on the contract.

In a highly unusual step, the Seventh Circuit Court of Appeals informed the prosecutor that the government lacked any basis for its charges. The court then declared Thompson innocent, and vacated her conviction.[52] Moreover, the opinion, scathingly critical of federal prosecutors, was written by one of the best-known conservatives on the federal bench, Judge Frank Easterbrook, former University of Chicago Law School professor. In language that would peel paint, Easterbrook excoriated the government, noting that a whole host of reasons for giving the tie-break to the winner were entirely legitimate, including favoring the low bidder and favoring a local company. As Easterbrook put it in a tart aside, "Recognition that driving down the cost of government is good politics for incumbents does not transgress any federal statute of which we are aware."[53] At its core, the federal indictment charged that Thompson was guilty of depriving her employer of her "honest services" because she failed to give sufficient credit to the interview performance of Adelman's main competitor. The appeals court said that, while Thompson may have been mistaken, not every mistake can be a violation of federal criminal law. Otherwise, the court warned, we would need a lot more jails.[54]

What is perhaps most disturbing about the case is that Steve Biskupic, the Wisconsin United States Attorney, had initially been targeted for dismissal. But he was taken off the list.[55] The ginned-up prosecution of Georgia Thompson may have been the price for keeping Biskupic in the job.[56]

Conclusion

After President Bush took office because of a decision by the Supreme Court that some have criticized as the most nakedly political in the nation's history, his Justice Department became the most political in at least a century. The Court's decision in *Bush v. Gore* augured the Court's embrace of a fixation with the largely fictitious problem of voter fraud and vote dilution. The Bush Justice Department pursued this problem to the exclusion of most others, running a detour past established notions of sound prosecutorial practice. The Justice Department rewrote the "book" on prosecutorial conduct to permit wider knowledge of pending prosecutions by White House insiders, and political prosecutions within a short time prior to elections. It targeted prosecutors like David Iglesias who refused to become attack dogs for political operatives. In the process, officials in the Bush Justice Department left grave doubts about the impartiality of justice.

7

Regulation of Business and the Flight from Accountability at Home and Abroad

A shower stall is not supposed to be a dangerous place. That reasonable assumption proved to be tragically incorrect, however, for S. Sgt. Ryan Maseth, an American soldier in Iraq. American service personnel in Iraq often use showers with electric pumps that must be properly grounded. Several years ago, an officer reported that the contractor in charge of shower pumps failed to properly maintain them. The contractor in question was Kellog Brown & Root (KBR), a former subsidiary of the oil services giant Halliburton, which Dick Cheney ran prior to becoming the most powerful vice president in American history. Because KBR failed to respond to the officer's report, S. Sgt. Maseth was electrocuted while taking a shower. The military first blamed the soldier himself, claiming that he must have had an electrical appliance with him as he bathed. Eventually, however, the military had to acknowledge that chronic poor maintenance was the culprit. The officer and other whistle-blowers in the government and industry were harassed for trying to ensure that KBR and other contractors in Iraq completed the work that they had promised to perform.[1]

The shower fatality is a metaphor not only for what went wrong with Iraq, but also for the Bush administration's entire approach to economic issues. The administration practiced corporate welfare for its friends, rewarding military contractors like Halliburton and its subsidiaries with huge, no-bid contracts, and engineering detours around safeguards such as competitive bidding. The Bush administration also used the huge American apparatus in Iraq as a patronage sinkhole, employing many eager office seekers whose sole qualification was unswerving loyalty to a social conservative agenda. At home, the Bush administration largely failed to do anything about emerging corporate abuses in areas such as predatory lending and excessive leverage in financial markets. Indeed, Bush administration officials sought to dis-

141

mantle the New Deal regulatory scheme, and were foiled in this attempt only by the 2008 economic meltdown, which pointed up the virtues of regulation. The Bush administration also worked with business to expand the preemption doctrine and narrow avenues for accountability launched by states and private plaintiffs. In environmental matters, the administration sought to make decisions about crucial issues such as global warming by rejecting international consensus, and also evading accountability in Congress and the courts.

Using Contractors to Facilitate Foreign Ventures

In foreign policy, the Bush administration's watchword was corporate welfare. Private contractors like Blackwater and Halliburton allowed the administration the freedom to act without accountability, and the administration returned the favor.

While excesses in wartime contracting have a long historical pedigree, governments have usually tried to deter egregious abuses. For example, both the executive branch and Congress responded vigorously to profiteering during World War II. The Truman Committee brought the Senator from Missouri to prominence, investigating allegations of fraud. Congress also passed legislation allowing the government to pursue unscrupulous defense contractors and recover excessive profits.[2] Similarly, during World War II the federal Office of Price Administration vigilantly monitored prices on the domestic front.

No such vigilance attended the Iraq conflict. The government viewed accountability for contractors as a hindrance, instead of an opportunity for greater efficiency. Consider the administration's approach to the Blackwater company's abuses in Iraq. Blackwater is a company of mercenaries formerly headed by Erik Prince, scion of a family with a long Republican pedigree. The administration found Prince and Blackwater to be convenient, since the United States did not have enough troops in Iraq to guard diplomats and address other security needs. So the administration, and in particular the State Department, gave Blackwater free rein.

Blackwater's employees, who often adopted a "cowboy" attitude toward doing their jobs, engaged in a long string of abuses. These episodes included killing the bodyguard of a leading Iraqi politician, firing into vehicles whose drivers declined to immediately follow instructions to vacate an oncoming lane of traffic, and, most notoriously, starting a lethal firefight that killed seventeen innocent Iraqis.[3] Blackwater developed its own foreign policy, evading review or accountability by the courts or the political branches. Here, as elsewhere, detours triggered agency costs, since Blackwater's interest in giving its employees leeway conflicted with the United States's long-term interest in persuading all legitimate Iraqi factions that it could be an "honest broker" of their differences.

Legal avenues for holding Blackwater accountable, however, have been minimal. The United States has made it difficult for the Iraqi courts to consider cases against Blackwater employees. Blackwater employees are technically civilians, and the Supreme Court has held that American civilians cannot be subject to military trial. Senators have proposed a bill that would create a new basis for civilian criminal liability for American civilian contractors who commit crimes abroad, and this innovation would be welcome. But the Bush White House was not supportive of this measure.[4] In addition, the government has failed to require adequate accounting from security contractors, so that no one really knows how much the United States has spent on these services, although informed estimates place the number at about six billion dollars.[5] The Pentagon continues to resist calls for better accounting from Blackwater and other companies.[6] Indeed, the administration's principal response to the warnings from the executive branch's principal watchdog on Iraq contracting abuses, the Inspector General for Iraqi Reconstruction, was collusion with congressional Republicans to eliminate the budget for the watchdog agency.[7]

Related contractor abuses in Iraq and Afghanistan have also received comparatively little scrutiny. In Iraq, studies by the military reveal that a Marine Corps office was slow in procuring adequately armored vehicles for U.S. troops, and persisted in ordering inadequately armored Humvees. In the meantime, 150 U.S. soldiers were killed and 1,500 seriously wounded by improvised explosive devices.[8]

The frustrating course of the Falluja water treatment project in Iraq illustrates the problems of contractor accountability. Originally budgeted at about thirty million dollars, the project will end up costing approximately one hundred million dollars. Work on the project, originally awarded to the Fluor Corporation, is already two years behind schedule. When completed, the project will serve only one-third of the homes planned. Moreover, even these homes may derive only limited benefits from the project, since homeowners will now need to make the connection to the system on their own. Many homeowners lacking the necessary skills or equipment may make this connection in the quickest way possible, by punching a hole through manhole walls, subjecting the entire system to a death by a thousand leaks. Even the U.S. ambassador has lamented that the project has "gone so far off track and for so long."[9]

American officials on the scene when contractors developed their way-ward habits were part of the problem, not the solution. During the first fif-teen months of the American occupation, officials of the Coalitional Pro-visional Authority (CPA), led by Bush's viceroy, Paul "Jerry" Bremer, held sway. Unfortunately, many CPA officials were, like Michael Brown at FEMA, patronage hires, picked for ideological or political reasons, not expertise in nation building. For many, fidelity to the administration's views on abor-tion rather than experience in public works explained their appointment.[10] As with Monica Goodling in the Justice Department, a White House liai-son made most of the decisions, in conjunction with Republican members of Congress, right-wing activists, and conservative policy groups. One "ideal candidate" for a CPA position had little or no background in Iraqi affairs, but had worked for the Republicans in Florida during the 2000 recount.[11] Other young patronage hires with family, religious, or social connections but no background in economics, finance, or public administration ended up man-aging Iraq's thirteen-billion-dollar budget.[12]

With officials on the scene unable or unwilling to make contractors accountable, accountability became the province of that perennially endan-gered species, the whistle-blower. Unfortunately, current federal statutes are inadequate to identify such fraud and abuse, and case law has further evis-cerated these statutory protections for whistle-blowers. Indeed, case law has failed to adapt to the challenges of United States involvement in Iraq, allow-ing the proliferation of unaccountable fraud and waste involving billions of dollars. Case law has also failed to recognize the distinctive public interest in encouraging whistle-blowing in Iraq.

Federal whistle-blowers seeking to target waste and abuse can use the federal False Claims Act (FCA),[13] which Congress enacted to combat fraud within the U.S. government. Under the statute, whistle-blowers can sue in the name of the United States, bringing what's called a *qui tam* action to recover money from individuals or companies that have made false claims to secure money that properly belongs to the taxpayers and to the public. Here, courts have used a number of technical doctrines to frustrate Con-gress's intent. Moreover, the Justice Department has often been passive, fail-ing to initiate or join in FCA actions. For example, the courts have applied the presentment requirement in the statute in a mechanical way to exempt money received based on implicit conditions of honesty and fair dealing. The result of this mechanical approach is that if government officials overseeing contractors were lax, contractors get off the hook. Plaintiffs should be able to press implied presentment theories, so that courts can entertain lawsuits based on the harm to the public. This change would align incentives more effectively for government officials, whose monitoring may be diluted by the prospect of subsequent employment with contractors.

Second, courts have held that money given to authorities controlled by the United States, such as the Coalition Provisional Authority (CPA) that ruled Iraq through 2004, has not been paid out by the U.S. government within the meaning of the statute.[14] If the public benefits from habits of honesty that carry over to all contracting work, such a rigid approach surely sends the wrong message. If anything, the CPA carried more of a United States imprimatur than domestic ventures. Legal remedies should encourage contractors to be honest in all their dealings in government-related work, rather than allowing them to pick and choose where they commit fraud.

Third, arbitration provisions are enforced by courts in ways that ignore public interests. An employee of a contractor abroad faces significant problems of lack of information in developing his case. Moreover, the public has an interest in uncovering waste, fraud, and abuse. When an employee has been retaliated against for whistle-blowing, the public has an interest in prompt and public vetting of the employee's claims.[15] Individuals in Iraq who took on the uncomfortable and sometimes perilous role of whistle-blower were often threatened, harassed, and placed in physical danger. For example, in an April 2008 hearing by the Senate Democratic Policy Committee, the senators heard testimony that an employee had been brought up on charges after complaining about looting by superiors.[16] The employee's transgression was that she had noticed that her subordinates were being forced to drink contaminated water, and brought them clean water from the contractor's special stock. Faced with such retaliation, courts have said that the arbitration process is adequate, even though most company-based arbitration processes are stacked against employees and consumers.[17]

Of equally great concern was the record of Blackwater and other U.S. contractors on issues of sexual harassment. Many women reported being harassed by Blackwater employees and superiors. For example, Mary Beth Kineston, an employee at Kellog Brown & Root (KBR), a subsidiary of Halliburton, claims that another driver in Iraq sexually assaulted her. She endured a second assault, as well. After complaining to KBR management, the company dismissed her.[18] But legal avenues for dealing with this abuse were few.

The lack of legal remedies is troubling because other government institutions cannot pick up the slack. Congress before 2006 was passive on the issue of contractor abuse, not holding hearings on this issue, because the Republican majority believed rightly that hearings would embarrass the administration. This situation has improved since January 2007, as Democrats in Congress such as Senator Byron Dorgan and Representative Henry Waxman sought to supply sharper oversight. Such oversight is of limited use, however, unless the executive branch pitches in. The United States has commenced few FCA actions on its own, and has moved slowly to seek to recoup monies from contractors who spent the public's funds too freely.

Domestic Economic Regulation

The Bush administration's regulation in the domestic arena revealed the same pattern of helping friends avoid accountability. For Bush officials, constraints in the economic and environmental realm were impediments, not opportunities for measures that were both disciplined *and* creative. Distaste for firm regulation finally caught up with the administration as the financial excesses of the subprime lending epidemic came home to roost.

An early sign of the administration's disdain for regulation was Attorney General Ashcroft's handling of the lawsuit against tobacco companies brought by the Clinton administration. Here, as in the United States Attorney scandal and other issues involving criminal justice, senior officials at the Justice Department overruled subordinates with more local knowledge. In the tobacco case, line attorneys had wanted to pursue a tough strategy against the tobacco companies. But they ran into a number of obstacles. First, the administration did not see itself as aligned with tort lawyers, whom it viewed as parasites stifling free enterprise. Second, the administration used negative images of trial lawyers[19] to drive fund-raising and generate support for Republican candidates.

Indeed, evidence exists that the administration was seeking not only to stiff trial lawyers, but also to reward friends in the tobacco industry who had donated millions to Republican candidates in the 2000 election, including almost one hundred thousand dollars in direct contributions to George W. Bush's presidential campaign.[20] Moreover, Ashcroft had opposed legislation on tobacco while a senator.[21] After he became attorney general, Ashcroft quickly signaled his lack of interest in pursuing the case by slashing funding. The case has since foundered. As one tobacco company foe said, officials have "done everything they can to make sure the settlement is weak by leaking all over the place that they think the case is weak."[22] The tobacco lawsuit was an early indication of the administration's standard operating procedure: decide whom you want to help or hurt, and then make up procedures suited to that objective.

The administration also displayed its antiregulatory zeal through its appointment of Harvey Pitt as chair of the Securities and Exchange Commission. Pitt for many years had represented the accounting industry, which had campaigned to limit remedies for poor performance of the auditing functions that make corporations transparent to investors.[23] Although Pitt pioneered some worthwhile strategies, such as added scrutiny for executives' stock options,[24] he was passive in dealing with the onrush of corporate scandals at the dawn of the millennium, including Enron and WorldCom. Pitt resigned after the 2002 elections, replaced for a time with William Donaldson, a widely respected securities industry veteran; Donaldson's impact was limited, however, in light of the administration's pronounced antiregulatory tilt. Moreover, as we shall see, Donaldson presided in 2004 over a crucial decision that spiked unwise subprime speculation by major investment banks.

In 2006, Christopher Cox, a conservative Republican congressman with an antiregulatory slant, replaced Donaldson at the SEC. Cox and secretary of the treasury Henry Paulson promoted a plan hatched by Hal Scott, a pro-business Harvard law professor, for a Trojan horse within the domestic business regulatory framework. The Scott task force generated a deregulatory agenda that Paulson embraced even as the subprime crisis gathered momentum.[25] Ignoring the ominous financial news, the task force contended that American business suffered competitively from undue regulation, leading potential issuers of new stock to select foreign exchanges. While this alarm about regulation seemed persuasive at first glance, it fell short as a plausible theory. One universally acknowledged securities law expert, professor John Coffee of Columbia Law School, opined that for the most part issuers on American exchanges enjoyed a "regulatory premium," since investors were willing to pay more for stock protected by the integrity of the U.S. regulatory apparatus.[26] The transparency yielded by regulation was a good thing for both issuers and investors, it turns out, much as democracy is good for both government and the governed. The Paulson proposals dismissed this premium, however, instead recommending a defanged SEC that could do little to set concrete rules, but could only scramble to contain catastrophes once they had started.

The task force report diligently signaled its antiregulatory bent. First, the task force recommended that the SEC subject its proposed regulations to an expanded regime of cost-benefit analysis, directed by economists and business analysts. The task force recommended this step although it conceded that the SEC *already* must perform a cost-benefit analysis.[27] Requiring further cost-benefit analysis would inevitably tilt regulation toward corporations and securities traders, whose complaints about undue regulation fueled the report.

The Paulson task force also was oblivious to the subprime storm in recommending that the SEC replace the clear guidance provided by accepted accounting standards with a far more nebulous requirement that companies' financial disclosures present a "true and fair" view of financial conditions.[28] The problem here is that truth and fairness are in the eye of the beholder, giving corporations far greater leeway to manipulate financial data and deceive both regulators and the public. Indeed, the task force acknowledged that the "principles-based" regime they urged would give companies "less guidance about expected behavior."[29] In the absence of clear rules, the task force urged that regulators provide more guidance when problems emerged. As the subprime collapse teaches us, however, waiting until problems emerge ensures that a government response will come too late. Moreover, the task force's proposal used bank regulation as an ideal. The task force noted with approval the "convergence" of securities and banking regulation fostered by legislation such as the Gramm-Leach-Bliley Act of 1999 that allowed financial entities to offer a broad panoply of services. In retrospect, however, permitting companies like Citigroup to become financial supermarkets impeded transparency and effective regulation, allowing those companies to take on far more risk than was prudent.[30] The task force report did not address these issues, or indicate that the already burgeoning subprime crisis might temper its antiregulatory tone.

To follow up on these proposals, the SEC proposed a change in rules that would allow international accounting bodies to set standards. International bodies are not accountable to Congress. As one observer said, the rules would have outsourced securities regulation.[31] In particular, the rules would have allowed companies much greater leeway in stating earnings, thereby reducing the transparency that investors require. The administration's devotion to such detours revealed that it never understood how regulation promotes the long-term health of the financial sector. As Rhode Island senator Jack Reed put it, "There are a lot of lost jobs on Wall Street not because of competitiveness issues but because our regulators have actually not been up to the task."[32]

Significant issues have also been raised at the SEC about undue influence exerted by regulated businesses and top Wall Street insiders. For example, one SEC lawyer, Gary Aguirre, was terminated after what SEC senior managers viewed as inappropriately aggressive conduct in an investigation of Pequot Capital Management. One component of the investigation involved allegations of insider trading. Insider trading investigations are a major part of the SEC's enforcement mission, involving inquiries into whether an individual profited from trading on information acquired through work at a corporation or contact with a corporate insider. Deterring insider trading is crucial to maintaining a level playing field in which small investors are not at a disadvantage. The SEC's Inspector General found that Aguirre was inappropriately terminated, and that a top SEC manager had improperly shared confidential information with the lawyer for a potential witness in the investigation, bypassing Aguirre.[33]

Aguirre followed a venerable strategy in an insider trading investigation: pinning down the witnesses as soon as possible, rather than letting them obtain coaching about how to talk to the investigators. But Aguirre's superior was apparently concerned about two factors: the "political clout" of the witness, John Mack, who was subsequently hired as CEO of Morgan Stanley, one of the nation's largest investment firms, and the "juice" of Mack's counsel, Mary Jo White, a former federal prosecutor. Aguirre was terminated in September 2005, after his superiors rejected his pleas to call in Mack sooner rather than later.[34] While there was some evidence that Aguirre's superiors merely wanted to have more information before taking Mack's testimony,[35] one could also conclude that Aguirre's superiors imposed obstacles to the examination that constituted a departure from agency practice. White in June had gone way over Aguirre's head to Linda Thomsen, the SEC's head of enforcement. Thomsen told White that there was "smoke" but "surely not fire" regarding Mack's role. But Thomsen had not been briefed by SEC staff, including Aguirre, before rendering this assessment to White. Both Thomsen and her deputy, Paul Berger, provided Morgan Stanley with material information about an ongoing investigation, in violation of SEC policy.[36]

Thomsen's action could have locked the SEC into a passive position regarding Mack, thereby undercutting the agency's ability to bring meritorious cases. It also created the impression that the SEC was giving Mack and his lawyer, White, preferential treatment. In addition, the information that the SEC had no "smoking gun" could help a potential target manipulate a defense to any future investigation, including encouraging the target to destroy relevant evidence, secure in the knowledge that the agency did not suspect him of wrongdoing. Further, routine access of prominent counsel to SEC senior management creates inequities in enforcement. Such inequities would be avoided at a diligent federal prosecutor's office, as White herself told the IG.

Mack's testimony was eventually taken, days after the statute of limitations for prosecuting him had expired.[37] Although Aguirre had received positive written evaluations from the SEC,[38] he was subsequently terminated. After the termination, the SEC prepared a supplemental evaluation with negative material justifying the termination—a step unheard of at the SEC,[39] and an echo of the shoddy treatment received by the nine fired United States Attorneys.

Antiregulatory Bias and the Subprime Collapse

The administration's antiregulatory bias was most clearly manifest in its too-little, too-late response to the subprime mortgage crisis. The subprime crisis was a classic instance of market failure, which cried out for timely, effective regulation. A market failure involves a breakdown in the enlightened self-interest that makes markets both profitable for participants and beneficial for the public. Although markets generally perform better than wholly state-owned economies, in certain situations markets fail to properly align private and public interests. In such situations, government must step in to fill the gap. The Bush administration had abundant evidence that a market failure of gigantic proportions was developing in the area of subprime loans. Nevertheless, the administration failed to take remedial action until the problem spiraled out of control.

A central aspect of the subprime debacle was the erosion of the relationship over time between lender and borrower. When lenders and borrowers develop a relationship, the lender has an incentive to ensure that the borrower is a good credit risk. The lender values the borrower's goodwill and repeat business more than making an extra buck in the short term. Moreover, the lender will usually try to reach an accommodation with a distressed borrower who has encountered tough times.[40] The practices that led to the subprime crisis destroyed this relationship, creating a gap between the public interest and the incentive structure for loan originators.

Loan originators are not the old-fashioned savings and loan associations depicted in movies like Frank Capra's *It's a Wonderful Life*. Instead of holding onto loans and building relationships, loan originators got paid up front through fees. They then sold the loans to entities that securitized the loans for sale to investors.[41] Loan originators had every incentive to charge higher fees to borrowers, even if those borrowers would be better off with a loan that cost less up front. In fact, a significant percentage of borrowers with more expensive subprime mortgages were eligible for less expensive fixed-rate loans.[42] Unscrupulous lenders often targeted the vulnerable, signing them up for loans at higher interest rates over the life of the loan, with a low "teaser rate" that reeled in unsophisticated borrowers.[43] When the rate charged to customers "ballooned" from the teaser rate to a market rate, customers started defaulting on payments.[44]

The SEC also contributed to the subprime mortgage meltdown. In April 2004, the SEC voted to respond to appeals from the biggest investment banks, including Lehman Brothers and Goldman Sachs, that the SEC reduce the amounts of cash the banks needed to keep on hand to guard against the effects of losses in securities trading. The big investment banks complained bitterly that they would lose market power because of unduly harsh Washington regulation.[45] At least one commissioner asked questions—Harvey Goldschmid, a professor at Columbia, commented that "if anything goes wrong, it's going to be an awful mess."[46] Goldschmid went along, however, convinced that the big banks would never do anything so risky that it would put their continued existence in doubt. The SEC approved the measure, which freed up billions of dollars that the banks then used to borrow even more money for investments in mortgage-backed securities.

The SEC might have helped to head off the subprime crisis by monitoring the big investment banks, who had all agreed to voluntary self-regulation in exchange for the lowered reserve requirements. Unfortunately, the self-regulation plan went nowhere. It was a low priority for the incoming SEC chair, Christopher Cox, who had arrived at the agency after a career as a corporate securities lawyer and an anti-regulation member of Congress from California. For a year and a half, starting at March 2007, as the subprime crisis accelerated, the self-regulation division lacked a director.[47] The Commission ignored warning signs about the riskiness of the subprime investments and the increased use of borrowing among these elite firms.[48] For example, the Commission staff knew that Bear Stearns, a major investment house, had too many mortgage securities in its portfolio and had borrowed too much to purchase these risky investments. At one point, Bear Stearns had at least thirty-three dollars of debt for every dollar in equity. But the SEC did nothing to persuade Bear Stearns to limit its risk.[49]

The rubber met the road when the real estate market began to cool off. At this point, borrowers found it difficult to refinance, and the bubble burst. Moreover, the entity that had purchased the loan from the originator found it difficult to accommodate the borrower's changed situation through forgiving some of the loan payments, since the securitization agreements usually barred such forbearance.[50] Some loan originators even reacted to the bubble's bursting in 2006 by using more high-pressure tactics to sign up more customers, to get more fees to pay their own debts and meet their profit goals.[51] The result was a collapse of confidence in securitized loan packages, a tide of foreclosures, and a massive credit squeeze.

The Bush administration knew about these problems early in the game, as did successive chairs of the Federal Reserve, Alan Greenspan and Ben Bernanke. An outspoken Federal Reserve governor, Edward Gramlich, had warned for over a decade about the dangers of subprime lending.[52] Other commentators flagged the problem in 2003.[53] But the Bush administration failed to take action. Just as loan originators seemed to think the gravy train would roll on forever, the Bush administration did not want to roil the markets through insisting on responsible regulation.

Greenspan's testimony before Congress in October 2008 also summed up the Bush administration's perspective: Greenspan described himself as shocked that a "very solid edifice" and a "critical pillar" of the market had collapsed. In a candid moment, Greenspan admitted that he had "made a mistake" in relying on the self-interest of financial entities as a means of protecting shareholders and the public.[54] Similarly, after the crisis hit, Christopher Cox confessed that the SEC's "metrics were inadequate."[55] But Cox had repeatedly failed to insist on getting more information from the banks, even though the 2004 agreement gave the SEC this authority. As Commissioner Goldschmid ruefully observed after the crisis hit, that agreement "gave [the SEC] . . . the ability to get information that would have been critical to sensible monitoring, and yet the SEC didn't oversee well enough."[56]

None of this should have been a shock to anyone schooled in the dynamics of market failure. Self-interest does not adequately police all markets all the time—that is why regulation is sometimes necessary. But Cox failed to heed the warning signs. At the Federal Reserve, both Greenspan and Bernanke failed to take regulatory action that Congress had authorized in the Home Ownership Equity Protection Act to reduce the stampede of subprime securitization and foreclosures.[57]

After the crisis hit, the administration contented itself with incremental measures. In February 2007, Chairman Bernanke dismissed worries about the emerging crisis, informing Congress that the housing downturn was not a "broad financial concern or a major factor in assessing the state of the economy."[58] Despite valiant warnings from Sheila Bair, chair of the Federal Deposit Insurance Corporation, the Federal Reserve failed to assume a broader regulatory posture.[59] The administration waited until December of that year to announce a minimalist plan. The plan offered relief only to borrowers still keeping up with payments under the low "teaser rate" for their adjustable-rate loan.[60] The plan did not assist homeowners whose required payments had already ballooned, or those who could not even keep up with payments under the lower introductory rate. The administration also declined to consider other bold, albeit controversial, initiatives, such as permitting federal bankruptcy judges to extend relief to homeowners. These initiatives would apparently have trenched too deeply on the prerogatives of lenders and holders of securities. As a result, the administration's approach failed to stem foreclosures, prop up the sinking real estate market, or ease concern about the worth of securitized mortgage packages. In large part, the administration's sins on this front were sins of omission. But these omissions paved the way for the crisis that hit in September 2008, devastating the American economy.

The Bush administration's response to the crisis also showed its distaste for accountability. After Congress authorized the Troubled Asset Relief Program (TARP), the government gave hundreds of billions of taxpayer dollars to financial institutions whose lack of prudence had contributed to the economic disaster. While TARP probably helped some institutions weather the storm, Treasury Secretary Paulson failed to insist that corporations specify how they planned to use the funds or account for their expenditures. Federal money helped pay for executive bonuses at insurance giant American International Group (AIG) and bailed out AIG's many counterparties in the risky credit default swap market. Banks also used federal money to finance the purchase of other banks and for other purposes that may never be fully documented. The chair of the Congressional Oversight Panel, professor Elizabeth Warren of Harvard, described Secretary Paulson's approach succinctly: "Take the money and do what you want with it."[61]

The Supreme Court and Regulation of Business

The Supreme Court has also moved to constrain the ability of securities plaintiffs to act as a check on publicly traded companies. The Court has recently imposed heightened pleading requirements on plaintiffs, who now have to plead with particularity securities law violations.[62] Pleading with particularity is difficult, because corporations that fail to disclose information to investors are by definition opaque. In the past, plaintiffs' lawyers relied on the discovery process to develop information that could flesh out their claims. If their claims get dismissed without access to discovery, they have to rely on the public record, which will be sparse in the most egregious cases.

In another case, *Tellabs v. Makor Issues & Rights, Ltd.*,[63] the Court held that investors must bear a high burden of proof in suing corporations for violations of the securities laws. The Court ruled that a plaintiff must not only present evidence showing that the corporation intended to deceive investors, but also prove that neutral rationales for the corporation's statements or omissions were *not* more convincing explanations. This holding turns the rationale for burdens of proof on its head. Typically, once the plaintiff comes forward with some evidence, we place the burden on the side with the most information, since courts reason that this party has superior ability to provide the court with accurate data. Placing the burden on the plaintiff is both unfair and inefficient, since it imposes the burden on the party with the *least* access to information.

In another defeat for investors, the Supreme Court held that the Securities Act did not encompass aiding and abetting liability.[64] The common law of fraud had for centuries recognized liability of this kind, to deter those who assisted in dishonest conduct and to compensate the victims.[65] The Court's decision blunted incentives for potential gatekeepers like lawyers and accountants to monitor and prevent their clients' wrongdoing.[66]

The Environment and Unsafe Products

The courts have had a more mixed record regarding the Bush administration's persistent attempts to shirk its roles as steward of the environment and guardian of consumer safety. In a landmark decision, the Supreme Court required that the Bush administration address climate change. But the Court has at least in part enhanced the doctrine of preemption, shutting down state lawsuits against corporations making unsafe products.

The Bush administration sought for years to deny both the fact of global warming and the need to do anything about it. Indeed, the administration's detour also entailed a detour around science itself. In *Massachusetts v. EPA*,[67] Justice Stevens tersely dispatched the Bush administration's peevish arguments against science in the first paragraph of this opinion, explaining that a "well-documented" increase in temperature around the world was caused by the emission of gases into the atmosphere that act like "the ceiling of a greenhouse," hindering the exit of reflected heat.[68] The Court noted Congress's clear track record of concern about the effects of global climate change.[69] It also found that the state plaintiffs had standing to sue, by virtue of their sovereign interest in protecting air quality for all their residents and minimizing the adverse health effects of poor air quality.[70] The Court then dismissed the agency's convoluted argument that it lacked the power to regulate since continued economic expansion in India and China would impede the elimination of global warming. The Court noted that a showing that regulation would "slow the pace of global emissions" was sufficient.[71] While the agency may have had other priorities, the Court stated unequivocally that the statute required the agency to order other priorities within the scheme that Congress had established.[72] The Court noted that although the president "has broad authority in foreign affairs, that authority does not extend to the refusal to execute domestic laws."[73]

The administration has also used the preemption doctrine to shut the door on state regulation, persuading the Court to hold that medical device makers could not be sued in state court if the FDA had approved the product.[74] This use of preemption ignores significant problems with federal regulatory bodies. It unduly discounts the phenomenon of regulatory capture, in which agencies gradually become dominated by the industries they regulate. It also downplays the problem of political pressure by officials who find regulation inconvenient, as in the Bush administration's position on climate change. Such political pressure was routine in the Bush administration, exemplified in the complaints of a substantial group of FDA staff scientists, who said that political appointees demanded that the scientists change their assessment of certain new products up for review before the agency.[75] When regulators are subject to such pressures, state lawsuits act as a useful counterweight. Unfortunately, the Supreme Court marginalized these concerns in its rush to streamline the regulatory process for medical devices.

The Bush administration also sought to promote the interests of its friends through "midnight" regulations passed in the last days of the administration. For example, the Department of the Interior in October 2008 was preparing a rule that would have made it easier for mining companies engaged in mountaintop mining—which involves blasting the top off a mountain to get at the coal seams below—to dump the debris from the explosion into nearby streams.[76] Rules in effect in October 2008 require that companies refrain from dumping debris within one hundred feet of any stream if the debris would harm water quality. Even so, mining companies have repeatedly violated the rule, resulting in the erasure of 1,600 miles of streams. The Bush administration in its closing hours sought to accelerate this process.

Organizational culture at the Interior Department also encouraged detours from established practices and supervision. In the Minerals Management Service (MMS), over a dozen officials engaged in what the Inspector General called a "culture of ethical failure."[77] The Ethics in Government Act mandates that federal officials avoid conflicts of interest with the companies they regulate. Congress enacted these restrictions to curb the "revolving door," in which government officials depart for the private sector to peddle the influence they gained while ostensibly serving the public.

The Inspector General noted that senior executives at MMS systematically violated these rules. For example, two senior officials shared proprietary government information with a former senior official who had started a company to obtain Interior Department contracts. One of the officials later joined the company. Always happy to be of service, the remaining official sweetened the contract and instructed her private sector colleague in how to justify the increase.[78] These officials and others also received gratuities on at least 135 occasions from the businesses they were supposed to regulate.[79] In addition, they engaged in a pattern of substance abuse and sexual promiscuity with subordinates and representatives of regulated industries.[80] The MMS crew saw nothing wrong with their approach. Indeed, they viewed ethics provisions as an inefficient obstacle to the way business should get done.

Conclusion

The bacchanalian exploits of the MMS employees are an apt metaphor for the legal perspective of the Bush administration. The Bush administration's machinations on the environment and security contractors, as well as its omissions on global warming and the subprime collapse, all reflected a cardinal flaw of detours: by bypassing constraint and relying on self-interest to shape behavior, detours did not liberate decision makers, but instead merely enthralled officials to their own narrow agendas. The sweetheart deals for contractors like Blackwater and Halliburton made it easier for Cheney, Rumsfeld, and other officials to do what they wanted. The interests of these decision makers, however, turned out to be only imperfectly aligned with the interests of the public. More dissent would have forced more deliberation, and possibly identified the dangerous flaws in the administration's assumptions. Similarly, the subprime debacle has shown that relying on the self-interest of loan originators was a poor surrogate for constraints that would have preserved the incentives for responsible lending built into traditional banker-customer relationships. The erosion of investor protection at the SEC compounded this risk. In each case self-interest led to poor policy, while constraints might have given policymakers a more useful repertoire of policy choices as well as the discipline to select most widely from the choices available. While detours may sometimes be necessary, the habit of rejecting constraint often leads to errors in decision making. That dangerous interaction between detours and disastrous decisions may be the most significant lesson of the Bush administration.

Afterword

Detours are addictive. Once the institutional momentum grows for their proliferation, introducing constraint becomes even more difficult. Moreover, the Bush administration was not without evidence on its side: no further attacks occurred on American soil after September 11, although analysts will dispute for decades the role of Bush administration policies in that achievement. Overall, the aftermath of the Bush administration has been a study in ambiguity and ambivalence. On the one hand, the financial collapse of 2008 cast the Bush administration's neglect of regulation in an unforgiving light. On national security, however, the aftereffects of Bush administration measures like the establishment of Guantánamo have impeded a clean break. These complications have ensued despite the landmark decision of the Supreme Court in *Boumediene v. Bush*[1] and the election of Barack Obama.

New revelations about financial wrongdoing highlighted the failures of the Bush administration and illustrate the task facing Obama. In December 2008, revelations surfaced about a giant Ponzi scheme run by Bernard Madoff, a Wall Street executive whose family revealed that he had bilked investors out of tens of billions of dollars. Madoff, who had started his machinations before the Bush administration took power, used money invested by later victims to pay off initial investors until his entire enterprise collapsed of its own weight. The SEC acknowledged that it had begun receiving "credible allegations" of fraud nine years earlier, but had repeatedly declined to conduct an investigation, instead relying on Madoff's own financial statements.[2] The SEC failed to act despite plentiful warning signs, including Madoff's suspiciously consistent returns amid roiled financial markets, and his employment of auditors from an obscure storefront firm.[3]

As the financial collapse gained momentum, the Supreme Court ruled on *Boumediene*. In its landmark decision, the Court affirmed the primacy of the rule of law by striking down portions of the Military Commissions Act (MCA) of 2006 that had stripped the federal courts of jurisdiction over writs of habeas corpus sought by Guantánamo detainees. The enactment of the

MCA relegated detainees to the truncated processes of the Combatant Status Review Tribunals (CSRT), where detainees had no legal representation and no access to either exculpatory evidence or evidence against them. The MCA provided for very narrow judicial review of CSRT determinations, with no opportunity to have the reviewing court consider new evidence from the detainee.

In striking down the MCA's limits on habeas for Guantánamo detainees, the *Boumediene* Court demolished the structure of impunity through geography that the administration's legal architects, such as David Addington and John Yoo, had painstakingly labored to establish since November 2001. Justice Kennedy, writing for the Court in the 5–4 decision, observed that the political branches cannot "switch the Constitution on or off at will."[4] Kennedy noted the evils of monolithic government, in which the political branches march in lockstep. He suggested that the separation of powers, with its grant of authority to the courts, helps to break up these dangerous concentrations of authority. According to Kennedy, the framers knew that "pendular swings to and away from individual liberty were endemic to undivided, uncontrolled power."[5] For Kennedy, lack of accountability did not follow from the detention of individuals outside the borders of the United States, or from conceptions of legal or technical sovereignty.[6] Instead, the Court held that habeas jurisdiction existed because the United States had de facto jurisdiction and control over Guantánamo, acquired through the extended lease the United States had signed with the Cuban government shortly after Cuba attained its independence in the Spanish-American War.[7]

Since the Guantánamo detainees had access to habeas, Congress could curb this access only by providing an adequate substitute, which the Court ruled that Congress had failed to do. According to the Court, the CSRT process did not safeguard fundamental rights, because of its failure to give detainees access to evidence or an opportunity to cite new evidence to the reviewing court.[8] As a result, the Court said, the MCA's limits on habeas were unconstitutional.

The Court's ruling in *Boumediene* signaled an end to detours around the time-honored American tradition of individualized adjudication of dangerousness. After *Boumediene*, federal judges began ruling on the individual cases of detainees. These cases were not cut-and-dried; as befits individualized adjudication, sometimes the government prevailed, and sometimes the detainee.[9] Notably, however, the courts conducted an independent examination of the evidence, declining to accept the government's say-so as a substitute for proof.

The twilight of Bush's presidency also brought an extraordinary acknowledgment from a senior official in charge of the military commissions about the abusive treatment of a detainee. "We tortured Qahtani," said Susan J. Crawford, who had served as "convening authority" for the military commissions, in charge of referring cases for prosecution. Crawford, who had also served in the Reagan and George H. W. Bush administrations, revealed deep concern about the combination of tactics used against Mohammed al-Qahtani, the alleged "twentieth hijacker" discussed in chapter 2. These tactics included sleep deprivation over forty-eight days of interrogations, as well as sexual humiliation. Interrogators forced Qahtani to wear a woman's bra, told him repeatedly that his mother and sister were whores, and required him to perform dog tricks. Qahtani had to be taken to the hospital twice during his lengthy interrogation for the condition known as bradycardia, in which the heart rate falls below sixty beats a minute. Qahtani's heart rate dropped at one point to thirty-five beats per minute—a condition that if allowed to persist can lead to death.[10] Crawford, a lifelong Republican, did not believe that Qahtani could be prosecuted in light of his treatment, which she said undermined the voluntariness and reliability of any statements he made to authorities about his alleged role as the twentieth hijacker.

Crawford may have been incorrect on the prospects for Qahtani's prosecution. Evidence of Qahtani's foiled entry into the United States at the Orlando Airport, with 9/11 straw boss Mohammad Atta caught on videotape waiting in vain for Qahtani's arrival, along with Qahtani's subsequent capture in Afghanistan, may permit a jury to infer his guilt.[11] In a possible precursor to a successful prosecution of Qahtani, the Obama administration obtained a guilty plea from Ali Saleh al-Marri, the last alleged "enemy combatant" detained within the United States.[12]

Crawford was not the only significant official from the Bush administration to go public with her criticism. In the first months of the Obama presidency, John Bellinger and Philip Zelikow, who had both served in senior positions under Secretary of State Condoleezza Rice, discussed the role they had played in battling Cheney and Addington on coercive interrogations. Zelikow testified before Congress on his fight against the "strained and indefensible" legal reasoning in the Office of Legal Counsel (OLC) memos. He described the CIA's interrogation program as a mistake, possibly one of disastrous proportions.[13] Bellinger had pushed for a similar position on behalf of Secretary Rice during Bush's second term.[14] Zelikow and Bellinger pooled their valiant efforts with those of Matthew Waxman, a young State and Defense Department policy planner who had clerked for Justice David Souter of the Supreme

Court and currently teaches at Columbia Law School.[15] They joined a number of government officials who during their service had questioned aspects of the interrogation program—a list including FBI director Robert Mueller, senior FBI lawyer Marion "Spike" Bowman,[16] and former OLC heads Jack Goldsmith and Daniel Levin. Demonstrating that the coercive interrogation issue transcended politics, Republican senators Lindsey Graham and John McCain also took stands against the interrogation program.

Obama's election marked a departure from the disposition toward detours that had marked the Bush administration. Obama advocated more regulation of financial markets. The new Attorney General, Eric Holder, was clear where Bush's Attorney General Michael Mukasey had been reticent, declaring forthrightly that waterboarding was torture.[17] This statement gave both legislators and the public confidence that the new administration was seeking to turn the page on the excesses of the Bush-Cheney era. Holder also indicated that the new administration would seek whenever possible to try detainees in U.S. courts.[18]

The Bush administration's use of Guantánamo as a law-free zone has proved to be like Humpty Dumpty in reverse: easy to assemble, but very difficult to take apart. The United States cannot return some detainees, like the Chinese Uighurs, to their countries of origin, because of the risk that the detainees will face torture. Other countries have been reluctant to accept detainees. Obama administration officials also faced a dilemma in dealing with detainees whose release could endanger Americans, but whose trial would be hindered by restrictions on admissible evidence, including hearsay. To deal with the problem, Obama announced in May 2008 that he would revive and revise the military commission system, adding procedural safeguards that would exclude evidence obtained through coercion, and ensure that the government disclosed adverse and exculpatory evidence to the detainee or the detainee's lawyer. These safeguards brought the military commissions closer to tribunals widely praised for their fairness: courts-martial under the Uniform Code of Military Justice and international war crimes tribunals.[19] Obama also announced that, subject to procedural safeguards, some detainees who had helped Al Qaeda would be held under the laws of war.[20]

While many on the Left condemned these moves, Obama's strategy combined an understanding of the difficulties inherited from his predecessor with a commitment to dialog and transparency that contrasted sharply with the predispositions of the Bush administration. As scholar Ben Wittes had predicted and Defense Secretary Robert Gates had discovered in making the transition from the Bush to Obama administrations, closing Guantánamo will be a challenging task.[21] The courts may reject some of Obama's solutions, particularly if detention under the laws of war extends beyond those providing substantial assistance to Al Qaeda or the Taliban.[22] The new administration's eagerness for dialog, however, enhanced the legitimacy and credibility of its proposals.

The Obama administration also deliberated on whether to investigate or prosecute Bush officials who may have engaged in war crimes. Prosecution would send a message to future administrations to avoid the Bush administration's detours, whatever the temptations of crises to come. In addition, prosecution would send a resounding message to the world that the United States was strong enough to support accountability for senior officials, and offer compensation or closure to individuals who were harmed by administration policies.

That said, prosecutions also have a distinct downside. Payback jurisprudence can promote volatility and polarization in government. It can descend into "Monday morning quarterbacking," second-guessing officials facing extraordinary challenges. Criminal prosecution could become a new staple of presidential transitions, just as investigation by independent counsels became a mainstay of American politics in the era culminating in the impeachment of President Clinton. Such mechanisms can distort the political sphere, skewing the principal means of accountability envisioned by the framers: free elections. Prosecution can also boomerang, chilling the lawful exercise of authority tomorrow by today's critics. Confronted with the threat of prosecution, risk aversion is the logical response. As Lincoln and Roosevelt demonstrated, however, government officials sometimes need to embrace risks, to avoid greater peril to the country. When members of the Obama administration face difficult questions, regarding, for example, the targeted killing of suspected terrorists in Pakistan, they should be able to resolve those questions on their merits, without the paralysis that accompanies exposure to legal sanctions.

Moreover, the Bush administration's architecture of impunity would present formidable obstacles to prosecution. Officials could cite the broad OLC opinions by John Yoo and others authorizing virtually any action undertaken pursuant to presidential directive.[23] Reliance on OLC opinions, with their tradition of definitive guidance, would be a powerful defense for any defendant. In addition, the Military Commissions Act (MCA) confers immunity on government officials regarding the treatment of detainees.[24] While neither the OLC opinions nor the MCA provision may constitute a complete bar to prosecution,[25] either could derail future investigations.

These concerns suggest that criminal prosecution should be less a goal in itself than a means to an end—a source of leverage for achieving greater transparency about the detours of the Bush-Cheney era. A commission established to find out the truth about interrogation and surveillance could offer immunity to officials who testified candidly. This would promote development of a record, which would allow future administrations, the media, and commentators to note the warning signs for excesses and sidestep these dangers. A comprehensive account of the Bush administration's detours would also signal almost as strongly as criminal prosecution the United States's determination to end this sorry chapter of its history.

Although a commission would be useful, the Obama administration and the Democratic Congress wasted no time in revealing a new commitment to transparency. Hearings by the Congress, which started after the 2006 elections, shed light on Bush administration detours in interrogation and contracting. Just as important, the Obama administration's release of the most graphic legal memos from OLC enhanced transparency, promoting vastly greater understanding of the ways in which the Bush administration manipulated the law.

The Obama administration's release of the interrogation memos also marked a departure from the Bush administration's detours. By releasing the memos, the Obama administration signaled its rejection of coercive tactics and its return to the rule of law. This signal allowed the new administration to begin the process of reclaiming the moral authority and "soft power" that the Bush administration relinquished. Of course, there is a trade-off: future detainees will also know that the United States no longer uses "walling" or the waterboard. But the success the FBI had with Ibn al-Libi and others using traditional methods of persistence, rapport building, and a permissible quotient of deceit suggests that the trade-off will not injure U.S. interests, particularly given the benefits in international goodwill that have accompanied this change.

Reconfiguring the government's oversight mechanisms would also aid transparency. For example, the inspectors general of the various departments and agencies generally performed well during the Bush administration, particularly the Justice Department's Inspector General, Glenn Fine. Fine provided a painstaking record of detours, missteps, and overreaching that will benefit all who wish to learn from this troubled time. There is one blind spot, however, in the Justice Department IG's perspective: the Inspector General cannot investigate the ethics of Justice Department lawyers. This task has been left to the Office of Professional Responsibility (OPR), which was dormant through much of the Bush presidency. Either the Justice Department Inspector General should be given this portfolio, or OPR should be strengthened.

Other reforms might center on Congress. Particularly when Congress and the president share a party affiliation, Congress encounters challenges in fulfilling its oversight responsibility. Practices that evolved over the last twenty years under presidents of both parties exacerbated these difficulties by limiting the notification that the executive had to provide to Congress of pending national security measures. Central Bush initiatives, such as the warrantless Terrorist Surveillance Program and the CIA's coercive interrogation regime, were disclosed only to the "Gang of Four"—the chairs and ranking members of the House and Senate Intelligence Committees. These legislators could not share this information with staff and colleagues. When they indicated that they had reservations about the programs, as Senator Jay Rockefeller did with the Terrorist Surveillance Program, administration officials discounted the questions. At the very least, notification should extend to senior members of each Intelligence Committee and a small, select group of trusted staff.[26] Expanding notification would supply some institutional counterweight to the executive branch, and promote deliberation that avoids mistakes like the CIA interrogation regime.

Although the Supreme Court provided a check on executive and legislative excesses after September 11, its pre-*Boumediene* approach to interpreting the Constitution could have been even more robust. Earlier decisions like *Rasul v. Bush*[27] were statutory in scope, permitting overrides by Congress. The override risk was magnified because until 2007 the president and Congress belonged to the same party.[28] Prodded by President Bush's message of fear, in 2006 the Republican Congress enacted the habeas-stripping provisions of the MCA, which the Court struck down in *Boumediene*.[29] As a result of the MCA, innocent detainees spent many more months languishing at Guantánamo. To send a stronger signal to President Bush and Congress, the Court should have squarely grounded decisions such as *Rasul* in constitutional principle.

In individual terrorism trials, moreover, courts must ensure integrity and fairness. Judges in all tribunals should exclude statements obtained through the use of coercive techniques like those approved by John Yoo and others at Bush's OLC. Moreover, judges should exclude evidence that is both inflammatory and irrelevant, such as the video of Osama bin Laden offered by the government in a case against a Hamas fund-raiser.[30]

But judicial gatekeeping must be pragmatic. To minimize the use of military commissions and detention under the laws of war, civilian courts need to provide greater flexibility to the government. For example, the exigencies of arresting suspects overseas often make the immediate provision of a lawyer impracticable. Government agents should be able to tailor Miranda warnings to the situation on the ground in a foreign country with a different legal system.[31] Similarly, searches abroad should not require a warrant, and should be evaluated under standards of reasonableness that reflect their challenging surroundings.[32] In addition, security concerns may sometimes require that judges deciding on the admissibility of evidence receive information about government sources and methods outside the presence of the defendant or his attorneys.[33] These changes acknowledge the government's interest in pursuing and deterring terrorists, while preserving the accountability at the heart of American law.[34]

Of course, some people never concede the virtues of accountability. Vice President Cheney, interviewed in December 2008, compared the Bush administration's approach to Lincoln's suspension of habeas corpus.[35] But Cheney missed three crucial differences with Lincoln's course. As discussed in chapter 1, Lincoln arguably had authorization from Congress to impose martial law, promptly went public with his decision, and asked Congress for its consent at the earliest possible opportunity. Ultimately, Lincoln's action, while still controversial, reflected a different temperament and approach to law than did the decisions of Bush and Cheney. Lincoln took action with reverence for law, determined to minimize harm to the legal fabric and our constitutional order, which he above all wished to preserve. Cheney and Bush, in contrast, viewed the checks and balances of constitutionalism as a nuisance, and placed all virtue in the person of the president. Their temperament and philosophy found more resonance with the first president that Cheney served, Richard Nixon, with his claim that, "when the President does it, that means it's not illegal."[36] Avoiding the detours around the law spawned by that arrogant outlook should be a primary goal for all future presidents.

Notes

INTRODUCTION

1. See Office of Legal Counsel, United States Dep't of Justice, Application of the Religious Freedom Restoration Act to the Award of a Grant Pursuant to the Juvenile Justice and Delinquency Prevention Act, June 29, 2007 (hereinafter Office of Legal Counsel, RFRA), available at http://usdoj.gov/olc/2007/worldvision.pdf.

2. Id., 4.

3. Id., 2.

4. See Omnibus Crime Control and Safe Streets Act of 1968, Pub. L. No. 90-3581, 82 Stat. 197, 42 U.S.C. sec. 3789d(c).

5. See Pub. L. No. 103-141, 107 Stat. 1488, codified at 42 U.S.C. sec. 2000bb to bb-4 (2000).

6. The RFRA overrules Employment Division v. Smith, 494 U.S. 872 (1990) (holding that the state could criminalize a religious group's use of peyote). OLC also compared the nondiscrimination provision to rules that everyone concedes violate the Constitution, such as denying unemployment compensation to an employee fired for refusing to work on the Sabbath. Sherbert v. Verner, 374 U.S. 398 (1963). Common sense would suggest that employees forced to choose between work on the Sabbath and holding a job would suffer a pervasive and extreme hardship, while religious organizations are free to seek other sources of funding for programs they voluntarily undertake. OLC, however, dismissed this distinction. See Office of Legal Counsel, RFRA, 11–13.

7. Office of Legal Counsel, RFRA, 21 n. 15.

8. See The Federalist No. 51 (James Madison).

9. See David J. Barron & Martin S. Lederman, The Commander in Chief at the Lowest Ebb—Framing the Problem, Doctrine, and Original Understanding, 121 Harv. L. Rev. 689, 720–27 (2008) (arguing that Congress retains the power to regulate certain elements of war strategy, including the spread of war to a neighboring country).

10. See Cass Sunstein, Beyond the Republican Revival, 97 Yale L.J. 1539 (1988).

11. See Boumediene v. Bush, 128 S. Ct. 2229, 2277 (2008).

12. See Youngstown Sheet and Tube Co. v. Sawyer, 343 U.S. 579, 635–38 (1952) (Jackson, J., concurring).

13. See ROBERT H. JACKSON, THAT MAN: AN INSIDER'S PORTRAIT OF FRANKLIN D. ROOSEVELT 93–103 (John Q. Barrett ed., 2003).

14. See Office of Legal Counsel, United States Dep't of Justice, Legal Authorities Supporting the Activities of the National Security Agency Described by the President, Jan. 19, 2006, available at http://www.usdoj.gov/olc/2006/nsa-white-paper.pdf.

CHAPTER 1

1. See DOUGLAS BRINKLEY, THE GREAT DELUGE: HURRICANE KATRINA, NEW ORLEANS, AND THE MISSISSIPPI GULF COAST 544 (2006).

2. Ironically, like radical ventures since the French Revolution, the Bush administration eventually consumed its own. A number of key officials in the Justice Department responsible for early shaping of either policy or ideology eventually resigned because they opposed some of the extreme unilateral positions taken by the administration or clashed with Vice President Cheney and his legal aide, David Addington. Those resigning included Attorney General John Ashcroft, Deputy Attorney General James Comey, and Assistant Attorney General Jack Goldsmith. See CHARLIE SAVAGE, TAKEOVER: THE RETURN OF THE IMPERIAL PRESIDENCY AND THE SUBVERSION OF AMERICAN DEMOCRACY 196–99 (2007); see also JACK GOLDSMITH, THE TERROR PRESIDENCY: LAW AND JUDGMENT INSIDE THE BUSH ADMINISTRATION 161–62 (2007) (discussing Goldsmith's resignation as head of the elite Justice Department Office of Legal Counsel).

3. ARTHUR M. SCHLESINGER JR., THE IMPERIAL PRESIDENCY (2004).

4. See SAVAGE, 21.

5. Id., 53–54.

6. See Report of the Congressional Committees Investigating the Iran-Contra Affair, with Supplemental, Minority, and Additional Views, S. Rep. No. 110-216, H. Rep. No. 100-433 (1987), at 457.

7. See JANE MAYER, THE DARK SIDE: THE INSIDE STORY OF HOW THE WAR ON TERROR TURNED INTO A WAR ON AMERICAN IDEALS 57 (2008).

8. United States v. Curtiss-Wright Export Corp., 299 U.S. 304 (1936).

9. Id., 320.

10. See U.S. CONST. art II, sec. 2, cl. 1.

11. See GOLDSMITH, 58–60.

12. JACK L. GOLDSMITH & ERIC A. POSNER, THE LIMITS OF INTERNATIONAL LAW (2005); cf. ERIC A. POSNER & ADRIAN VERMEULE, TERROR IN THE BALANCE: SECURITY, LIBERTY, AND THE COURTS 275 (2007) (arguing that legal constraints on national security decision making are usually counterproductive and institutionally flawed); JOHN YOO, WAR BY OTHER MEANS: AN INSIDER'S ACCOUNT OF THE WAR ON TERROR 106–8 (2006) (arguing that restrictions on wiretapping and data collection endanger national security).

13. While Goldsmith did not agree with Yoo that the president could flout Congress's clear intent, he was eager to read federal law as ambiguous, thereby giving the president greater discretion over matters such as the unilateral creation of military commissions. See GOLDSMITH, 136. In addition, Goldsmith was reluctant to read federal statutes as incorporating international law. Id.; cf. Curtis A. Bradley & Jack L. Goldsmith, Congressional Authorization and the War on Terrorism, 118 Harv. L. Rev. 2047 (2005). This move gave the president greater freedom to disregard international norms.

14. See STEPHEN G. CALABRESI & CHRISTOPHER S. YOO, THE UNITARY EXECUTIVE: PRESIDENTIAL POWER FROM WASHINGTON TO BUSH 7 (2008).

15. Calabresi also believed that Congress could mandate that the president *hire* career government employees based on merit. Once employed, however, the president could fire such employees for any reason. Some progressive scholars have also espoused more tempered variants of the unitary executive theory, arguing that command of the bureaucracy is necessary for a president elected on a platform of progressive change. See Elena Kagan, Presidential Administration, 114 Harv. L. Rev. 2245 (2001).

16. See SAVAGE, 9.

17. See JONATHAN SIMON, GOVERNING THROUGH CRIME: HOW THE WAR ON CRIME TRANSFORMED AMERICAN DEMOCRACY AND CREATED A CULTURE OF FEAR (2007). For a cogent analysis arguing that Simon's reading unduly discounts other factors that shape governance, see Mariano-Florentino Cuellar, The Political Economies of Criminal Justice (book review), 75 U. Chi. L. Rev. 941 (2008).

18. SIMON, 94–95.

19. Id., 95.

20. See William J. Stuntz, The Pathological Politics of Criminal Law, 100 Mich. L. Rev. 505 (2001). Because a defendant's possession of the drugs presented a prima facie case for guilt, confessions were often not necessary. Miranda warnings therefore had little impact.

21. 384 U.S. 436 (1966).

22. See Papachristou v. City of Jacksonville, 405 U.S. 156, 158–59 (1972) (discussing facts suggesting that police stopped the petitioners' car because it contained two racially mixed couples).

23. See Richard Dvorak, Cracking the Code: "De-coding" Colorblind Slurs During the Congressional Crack Cocaine Debates, 5 Mich. J. Race & L. 611 (2000); Richard Delgado & Jean Stefancic, Images of the Outsider in American Law and Culture: Can Free Expression Remedy Systemic Social Ills?, 77 Cornell L. Rev. 1258, 1284 (1992); cf. David Cole, Foreword: Discretion and Discrimination Reconsidered: A Response to the New Criminal Justice Scholarship, 87 Geo. L.J. 1059 (1999) (analyzing modern antigang ordinances, and arguing that they are unconstitutional). Complicating the analysis, while high-handed law enforcement can target members of subordinated groups, law enforcement indifference can consign subordinated groups to unsafe neighborhoods that impede political participation and personal growth. See Dan M. Kahan & Tracey L. Meares, The Coming Crisis of Criminal Procedure, 86 Geo. L.J. 1153 (1998); see also Anthony V. Alfieri, A Colloquium on Community Policing: Community Prosecutors, 90 Calif. L. Rev. 1465 (2002) (discussing complexities of race in interaction of subordinated communities, and prosecutors concerned with eliciting community input).

24. See D. Marvin Jones, "We're All Stuck Here For a While": Law and the Social Construction of the Black Male, 24 J. Contemp. L. 35, 58 (1998).

25. See Chae Chan Ping v. United States, 130 U.S. 581 (1889).

26. See Kevin R. Johnson, Protecting National Security Through More Liberal Admission of Immigrants, 2007 U. Chi. Legal Forum 157, 161–63 (arguing that more liberal immigration policy will result in more thorough accounting for total immigrant population, thereby enhancing security); cf. Linda Kelly, Preserving the Fundamental Right to Family Unity: Championing Notions of Social Contract and Community Ties in the Battle of Plenary Power Versus Aliens' Rights, 41 Vill. L. Rev. 725 (1996) (criticizing plenary power doctrine); David A. Martin, Preventive Detention: Immigration Law Lessons for the Enemy Combatant Debate, 18 Geo. Immigr. L.J. 305 (2004) (discussing relationship between immigration enforcement and national security).

27. See Chae Chan Ping v. United States, 130 U.S. 581, 606 (1889).

28. See 151 Cong. Rec. H454, Feb. 9, 2005 (remarks of Cong. James Sensenbrenner, R-Wis.), cited in DAVID NGARURI KENNEY & PHILIP G. SCHRAG, ASYLUM DENIED: A REFUGEE'S STRUGGLE FOR SAFETY IN AMERICA 3 (2008).

29. See James Dao, The New Administration: The Justice Department: Ashcroft Leaned Right, Then Center, N.Y. Times, Jan. 23, 2001.

30. See SIMON, 267.

31. See Missouri: Ashcroft Shreds Wheat's Record, The Hotline, Oct. 4, 1994 (LexisNexis news file).

32. Id.

33. See Jeffrey Toobin, Ashcroft's Ascent: How Far Will the Attorney General Go?, New Yorker, April 15, 2002, 50.

34. See Berger v. United States, 295 U.S. 78, 88 (1935).

35. See SIMON; MICHAEL WELCH, DETAINED: IMMIGRATION LAWS AND THE EXPANDING I.N.S. JAIL COMPLEX (2002).

36. See Nina Bernstein, Dependent on Jail, City of Immigrants Fills Cells with Its Own, N.Y. Times, Dec. 27, 2008, A1.

37. 295 U.S. 602 (1935).

38. Id. at 628.

39. Id.

40. See Morrison v. Olson, 487 U.S. 654 (1988) (upholding statute providing for judicial appointment of independent counsel to investigate claims of executive overreaching despite traditional location of prosecution function within the executive branch because of need for independence, limited scope of judicial authority over executive function, and limited nature of counsel's role).

41. United States v. Curtiss-Wright Export Corp., 299 U.S. 304 (1936).

42. Id. at 320.

43. See Stephen Dycus, Arthur L. Berney, William C. Banks & Peter Raven-Hansen, National Security Law 66 (4th ed. 2007), citing 10 Annals of Cong. 613–14.

44. See Youngstown Sheet and Tube Co. v. Sawyer, 343 U.S. 579 (1952).

45. Id. at 586 (citing Labor Management Relations Act of 1947, 61 Stat. 136, 152–56, 29 U.S.C. sec. 141, 171–80).

46. Id. at 650 (Jackson, J., concurring).

47. For a comprehensive analysis, see Barron & Lederman, 720–27; see also Stephen I. Vladeck, Congress, the Commander-in-Chief, and the Separation of Powers After Hamdan, 16 Transnat'l L. & Contemp. Probs. 933 (2007) (discussing Justice Clark's opinion in *Youngstown*).

48. See Youngstown Sheet and Tube Co. v. Sawyer, 343 U.S. at 635–38 (Jackson, J., concurring).

49. Id. at 635. Chief Justice Rehnquist, for example, described Jackson's opinion as the most useful source of wisdom available on the architecture of the separation of powers. See Dames & Moore v. Regan, 453 U.S. 654, 668 (1981); see also Medellin v. Texas, 128 S. Ct. 1346, 1368 (2008) (Chief Justice Roberts cited Justice Jackson's approach in writing for Court that the president lacked power to compel Texas courts to follow international court rulings).

50. One element of the administration's repertoire here was the use of presidential signing statements. Rather than veto a law he disagreed with, President Bush in hundreds of cases issued a signing statement explaining that he would comply with the law only to the extent that he saw fit, and that any attempt to curb his discretion to decline to comply would be unconstitutional. See SAVAGE, 228–41. Legal groups such as the American Bar Association have criticized this practice. Id. at 241–49.

51. See 18 U.S.C. 2340A.

52. See Pub. L. No. 107-40, 115 Stat. 224 (2001).

53. See David Cole, The Grand Inquisitors, N.Y. Rev. Bks., July 19, 2007, at 53, 55, citing BOB WOODWARD, BUSH AT WAR 42 (2002).

54. See Testimony of John Ashcroft, Hearing of United States Senate Judiciary Committee, Department of Justice and Terrorism, Dec. 6, 2001 (hereinafter Dec. 2001 Hearing).

55. See James Risen & Philip Shenon, U.S. Says It Halted Qaeda Plot to Use Radioactive Bomb, N.Y. Times, June 11, 2002, A1.

56. See JAMES F. SIMON, LINCOLN AND CHIEF JUSTICE TANEY: SLAVERY, SECESSION, AND THE PRESIDENT'S WAR POWERS 184–85 (2006); Paul Finkelman, Limiting Rights in Times of Crisis: Our Civil War Experience—A History Lesson for a Post-9/11 America, 2 Cardozo Pub. L. Pol'y & Ethics 25, 35 (2003).

57. See DANIEL FARBER, LINCOLN'S CONSTITUTION 162 (2003); Ex parte Field, 9 F. Cas. 1, 6–7 (C.C.D. Vt. 1862), citing the militia statute of 1795 (1 Stat. 424); cf. Stephen I. Vladeck, Note, Emergency Power and the Militia Acts, 114 Yale L.J. 149, 175–77 (2004) (discussing *Field*).

58. See Ex parte Quirin, 317 U.S. 1 (1942).

59. See Korematsu v. United States, 323 U.S. 314, 219 (1944).

60. See Peter Margulies, Judging Terror in the "Zone of Twilight": Exigency, Institutional Equity, and Procedure After September 11, 84 B.U. L. Rev. 383 (2004).

61. See Al-Marri v. Pucciarelli, 534 F.3d 213 (4th Cir. 2008), cert. granted, 2008 U.S. Lexis 8886 (2008).

62. See 50 U.S.C. sec. 1801-45 (2008). For a comprehensive discussion of the rationale for FISA, see United States v. Duggan, 743 F.2d 59 (2d Cir. 1984).

63. See Duggan, 743 F.2d at 73, citing S. Rep. 95-701, at 14–15. Prior to FISA's enactment, a number of courts had held that the president had inherent authority to use warrantless surveillance to collect "foreign intelligence information." See, for example, United States v. Truong Dinh Hung, 629 F.2d 908, 912–14 (4th Cir. 1980). The Supreme Court had expressly reserved this question when it held that the executive lacked authority to engage in warrantless surveillance in purely domestic investigations involving national security. See United States v. United States District Court (Keith, J.), 407 U.S. 297 (1972).

64. See SAVAGE, 115.

65. In some cases, entirely foreign communications were merely routed through U.S. servers. But these communications, on which the government probably could conduct surveillance without a warrant, are not readily distinguishable from other communications through the same servers that involve at least one U.S. person; hence, part of the dilemma.

66. See ERIC LICHTBLAU, BUSH'S LAW: THE REMAKING OF AMERICAN JUS-
TICE 154–55 (2008). A federal appellate court recently upheld warrantless surveillance of
persons reasonably believed by the executive to be agents of a foreign power outside the
United States. See In re. Directives Pursuant to Section 105B of the Foreign Intelligence
Surveillance Act (U.S. Foreign Intelligence Surveillance Ct. Rev. Aug. 22, 2008).

67. See SAVAGE, 115–16.

68. See CBS News, Face the Nation, Jan. 4, 2009.

69. See LICHTBLAU, 140–42.

70. See Cong. Rec., H6758, Oct. 12, 2001.

71. The statutory language formerly was "specific and articulable facts giving reasons
to believe that the person or entity to whom the information sought pertains is a foreign
power or an agent of a foreign power." See United States Dep't of Justice, Office of the
Inspector General, A Review of the Federal Bureau of Investigation's Use of National
Security Letters, March 2007 (hereinafter OIG NSL Report), at 23, available at http://www.
usdoj.gov/oig/special/s0703b/final.pdf.

72. Id. at 23.

73. Id. at 22.

74. See Niki Kuckes, The Democratic Prosecutor: Explaining the Constitutional Function of the Federal Grand Jury, 94 Geo. L.J. 1265 (2006).

75. See In re Sealed Case, 310 F.3d 717 (FISA Ct. Rev. 2002) (upholding Patriot Act
standard).

76. See OIG NSL Report, 48 (describing how NSLs helped the FBI generate new leads,
follow up on existing leads, and connect the dots in disparate terrorism investigations).

77. See SAVAGE, 114.

78. See OIG NSL Report, 37.

79. Id. at 72.

80. Id. at 77–78, 83. Congress carefully regulated access to educational records through
the Family Education Rights and Privacy Act of 1974 (FERPA), commonly known as the
Buckley Amendment, 20 U.S.C. sec. 1232g. Violations of this kind were not reported to
either the OIG or the FBI's Office of Professional Responsibility. See OIG NSL Report, 83.
The FBI also failed to offer definitive instructions to its agents about internal reporting of
infractions for more than five years after it received broader authority under the Patriot
Act. Id. at 85.

81. OIG NSL Report at 86.

82. Id. Typically, the FBI in such cases would subsequently issue an NSL to "cover" the
information previously obtained. Id.

83. Id. at 89.

84. Id. at 90.

85. United States Dep't of Justice, Office of the Inspector General, A Review of the
FBI's Use of National Security Letters: Assessment of Corrective Actions and Examination
of NSL Usage in 2006, March 2008, at 6, available at http://www.usdoj.gov/oig/special/
s0803b/final.pdf.

86. See Eric Lichtblau, F.B.I. Made "Blanket" Demands for Phone Records, N.Y. Times,
March 13, 2008, A22.

87. The FBI regularly failed to properly document its use of NSLs both internally and
in reports to Congress. See OIG NSL Report, 32–33.

88. See Cong. Rec., H8702, Nov. 13, 2002.

89. Id. at H8700.

90. Id.

91. Id.

92. Id.

93. Congresswoman Sheila Jackson Lee of Texas noted that the act did nothing to enhance coordination between the FBI and CIA, which was the prime cause of the failure to connect the dots in a way that might have averted September 11. Id. at H8707.

94. See Mike Allen, Bush Urges Bipartisan Relations: Democrats See Disconnect Between Rhetoric and GOP Actions, Wash. Post, Nov. 8, 2002, A12. Ironically, Democratic senator Joe Lieberman of Connecticut was the initial proponent of DHS. See Getting the Homeland Bill Done, N.Y. Times, Sept. 16, 2002, A16.

95. See Dara Kay Cohen, Mariano Florentino-Cuellar & Barry R. Weingast, Crisis Bureaucracy: Homeland Security and the Political Design of Legal Mandates, 59 Stan. L. Rev. 673, 725–26 (2006).

96. Id. at 727.

97. Id. at 725–28.

98. See Juliette Kayyem, Appointments That Disappoint, L.A. Times, Sept. 12, 2005, B11. Ironically, one Republican cast the elimination of collective bargaining provisions as a good government initiative, predicting that the new department would be a "model for how we can reform the entire system . . . [to] promote and reward excellence." See Cong. Rec. H8705-06, Nov. 13, 2002 (remarks of Rep. Weldon, R-Fla.).

99. See Cohen et al., 741. See also U.S. Rep. Thomas M. Davis (R-VA) Holds a Hearing on Disaster Response Information Sharing, FDCH Political Transcripts, March 30, 2006 (remarks of Rep. Henry Waxman, D-Ca.) (noting that President Bush and Secretary Chertoff were unaware for a day that the levees in New Orleans had been breached and that the breach had caused widespread flooding).

CHAPTER 2

1. See United States v. Greenpeace, Inc., 314 F. Supp. 2d 1252, 1255 (S.D. Fla. 2004).

2. The statute is now codified at 18 U.S.C. sec. 2279 (2008).

3. See United States v. Sullivan, 43 F. 602 (Cir. Ct. D. Ore. 1890).

4. See Steven Brown, The Rhode Island General Assembly in the Defense of Civil Liberties, 12 Roger Williams U. L. Rev. 361, 383–84 (2007).

5. See United States v. Greenpeace, Inc., 314 F. Supp. 2d 1252, 1264 (S.D. Fla. 2004).

6. Id.

7. Id.; see also Adam Liptak, Typical Greenpeace Protest Leads to an Unusual Prosecution, N.Y. Times, Oct. 11, 2003, A9.

8. See FREDERICK A. O. SCHWARZ JR. & AZIZ Z. HUQ, UNCHECKED AND UNBALANCED: PRESIDENTIAL POWER IN A TIME OF TERROR (2007).

9. While some object to the term "alien," I use it because of its long history in this context, and because using other terms like "migrant" or "noncitizen" can be cumbersome and confusing for the reader.

10. See JANE MAYER, THE DARK SIDE: THE INSIDE STORY OF HOW THE WAR ON TERROR TURNED INTO A WAR ON AMERICAN IDEALS 23 (2008).

11. See Korematsu v. United States, 323 U.S. 214 (1944) (upholding the legislation and government order requiring Japanese Americans to report to government facilities for evacuation); cf. Ex parte Endo, 323 U.S. 283, 294 (1944) (holding that the government lacked statutory authority to detain concededly loyal Japanese Americans; *Endo* decision heralded the end of the internment program); ERIC L. MULLER, AMERICAN INQUISI-TION: THE HUNT FOR JAPANESE AMERICAN DISLOYALTY IN WORLD WAR II 16–18 (2007) (analyzing government stereotypes of Japanese Americans); Joseph Margu-lies, Evaluating Crisis Government, 40 Crim. L. Bulletin 627, 638–39 (2004) (discussing other World War II–era restrictions targeting Asian Americans and Pacific Islanders, including imposition of martial law in Hawaii).

12. See PETER IRONS, JUSTICE AT WAR 249–50 (1983); Peter Margulies, When to Push the Envelope: Legal Ethics, the Rule of Law, and National Security Strategy, 30 Fordham Int'l L.J. 642, 652–54 (2007).

13. See Timothy J. McNulty, Black Liberal Struggles in Missouri Race, Chi. Trib., Oct. 29, 1994, at 1.

14. See DAVID COLE & JULES LOBEL, LESS SAFE, LESS FREE: WHY AMER-ICA IS LOSING THE WAR ON TERROR 30–31 (2007); DAVID COLE, ENEMY ALIENS (2003); Susan M. Akram & Kevin R. Johnson, Race, Civil Rights, and Immigration Law After September 11, 2001: The Targeting of Arabs and Muslims, 58 N.Y.U. Ann. Survey Am. L. 295 (2002); Letti Volpp, The Citizen and the Ter-rorist, 49 UCLA L. Rev. 1575 (2002) (describing the marginalization of particular communities after September 11); Peter Margulies, Uncertain Arrivals: Immigration, Terror, and Democracy After September 11," Utah L. Rev. 481, 495–99 (2002) (same); cf. Muneer Ahmad, A Rage Shared by Law: Post–September 11 Racial Violence as Crimes of Passion, 92 Calif. L. Rev. 1261 (2004) (discussing violence against Muslims and those, like Sikhs, suspected of being Muslim, committed by individuals after September 11).

15. See Dec. 2001 Hearing.

16. Office of the Inspector General, United States Dep't of Justice, Review of the Treat-ment of Aliens Held on Immigration Charges in Connection with the Investigation of the September 11 Attacks, April 2003 (hereinafter OIG Sept. 11 Report), at 10.

17. Id. at 12.

18. Id. at 16.

19. Id. at 14.

20. Id. at 17.

21. Id. at 35.

22. Id. at 41.

23. See Declaration of James Reynolds, Chief of the Terrorism and Violent Crime Section, Crim. Div., U.S. Dep't of Justice, Jan. 11, 2002, Center for Nat'l Sec. Studies v. United States Dep't of Justice, 01-civ-2500 (D.D.C. filed Dec. 6, 2001), cited in OIG Sept. 11 Report, 41.

24. Id. at 41–42.

25. See Turkmen v. Ashcroft, 2006 U.S. Dist. Lexis 39170 (E.D.N.Y. June 14, 2006), at 6.

26. Id. at 13.

27. Id. at 13–14.

28. Id. at 16.

29. Id. at 17.

30. Id.; cf. Iqbal v. Hasty, 490 F.3d 143 (2d Cir. 2008), rev'd sub nom. Ashcroft v. Iqbal, 129 S. Ct. 1937 (2009) (listing the plaintiffs' allegations of mistreatment after their detention).

31. Id. at 147. For more on the alien registration program, see Rajah v. Mukasey, 544 F.3d 427 (2d Cir. 2008) (upholding legality of the program).

32. See Eric Lichtblau, Thousands From Muslim Nations Were Investigated Before '04 Election, Data Show, N.Y. Times, Oct. 31, 2008, A17.

33. Id.

34. See 8 U.S.C. sec. 1182(a)(3)(iv)(VI)(2008).

35. Humanitarian Law Project v. Reno, 205 F.3d 1130, 1135 (9th Cir. 2000), cert. den. sub nom Humanitarian Law Project v. Ashcroft, 532 U.S. 904 (2001) (upholding statute, while holding that certain terms were vague as applied).

36. See James J. Carafano, Brian W. Walsh, J. Kelly Ryan & Paul S. Rosenzweig, Thwarting Terrorists While Protecting Innocents: The Material Support and Related Provisions of the Immigration and Nationality Act, Heritage Foundation Reports, Jan. 31, 2008.

37. After pressure from Congress and humanitarian groups over a period of years, the administration has begun to grant waivers in some cases involving duress. See Carafano et al.

38. 23 I. & N. Dec. 572 (2003).

39. Id. at 579.

40. Id. at 580.

41. Pramatarov v. Gonzales, 454 F.3d 764 (7th Cir. 2006).

42. See Eric Lichtblau & Lisa Getter, Seeking Speedier Deportations, Ashcroft Plans Judicial Reforms, L.A. Times, Feb. 7, 2002, A24. For an excellent discussion of the problems created by Ashcroft's "reforms," see Michele Benedetto, Crisis on the Immigration Bench: An Ethical Perspective, 73 Brooklyn L. Rev. 467 (2008); cf. Jaya Ramji-Nogales, Andrew I. Schoenholtz & Philip G. Schrag, Refugee Roulette: Disparities in Asylum Adjudication, 60 Stan. L. Rev. 295 (2007).

43. Benslimane v. Gonzales, 430 F.3d 828, 829 (7th Cir. 2005).

44. 424 F.3d 608, 610 (7th Cir. 2005).

45. Id. at 609.

46. Id. at 610.

47. Id.

48. Id. at 611.The Court of Appeals ordered the Board of Immigration Appeals to reconsider its decision. Id.

49. For a review of the continuing challenges in this area, see Linda Kelly Hill, Holding the Due Process Line for Asylum, 36 Hofstra L. Rev. 85 (2007); Stephen H. Legomsky, Deportation and the War on Independence, 91 Cornell L. Rev. 369 (2006).

50. ICE, which is now part of the Department of Homeland Security (DHS), succeeded the INS when Congress created DHS.

51. See Julia Preston, Case of Mother Torn from Baby Reflects Immigration Quandary, N.Y. Times, Nov. 17, 2007, A1.

52. See Sherryl Zounes, Children Without Parents: An Unintended Consequence of ICE's Worksite Enforcement Operations, 21 Geo. Immigr. L.J. 511, 512 (2007); Lori A. Nessel, Families at Risk: How Errant Enforcement and Restrictionist Immigration Policies Threaten the Immigrant Family in the European Union and the United States, 36 Hofstra L. Rev. 1271, 1282–84 (2008).

53. See Julia Preston, An Interpreter Speaking Up for Migrants, N.Y. Times, July 11, 2008, A1.

54. 129 S. Ct. 1886 (2009).

55. See Nina Bernstein, Cellmate Sued Detention Center Where Immigrant Died, N.Y. Times, Aug. 20, 2008, B4.

56. ICE in December 2008 decided to stop sending additional detainees to the Rhode Island facility. See Nina Bernstein, Detention Center Facing Inquiry Will Get No More Immigrant Detainees, N.Y. Times, Dec. 6, 2008, A17.

57. See Senate Homeland Security and Government Affairs Committee, Nomination of Paul A. Schneider to be Deputy Secretary, U.S. Dep't of Homeland Security, May 14, 2008.

58. See MIGRATION POLICY INSTITUTE, COLLATERAL DAMAGE: AN EXAMINATION OF ICE'S FUGITIVE OPERATIONS PROGRAM 5–6 (2009), available at http://www.migrationpolicy.org/pubs/NFOP_Feb09.pdf.

59. Id. at 10–13.

60. BENJAMIN WITTES, LAW AND THE LONG WAR: THE FUTURE OF JUSTICE IN THE AGE OF TERROR 95 (2008); MURAT KURNAZ, FIVE YEARS OF MY LIFE: AN INNOCENT MAN IN GUANTÁNAMO 249 (2007).

61. Internal government documents observed that the United States had "no definite . . . evidence" against Kurnaz and that German authorities had confirmed an absence of Al Qaeda links. WITTES, 95.

62. Id. at 126.

63. See Mark Denbeaux & Joshua Denbeaux, No-Hearing Hearings—CSRT: The Modern Habeas Corpus?, available at http://law.shu.edu/publications/guantanamoReports/final_no_hearing_hearings_report.pdf.

64. Id.

65. See Scott Horton, The Great Guantánamo Puppet Theater, Harper's Mag., Feb. 21, 2008, available at http://harpers.org/archive/2008/02/hbc-90002460, cited in Ruling on Motion to Dismiss (Unlawful Influence), United States v. Hamdan, D-026 (Guantánamo Military Commission May 9, 2008) (Allred, J.), op. at 6, available at http://www.nimj.org/documents/Hamdan%20Hartmann%20Ruling.pdf; Colin Freeze, Politics Interfering with Justice at Gitmo, Colonel Says, Globe and Mail, Dec. 12, 2007, A13 (also citing Nathan Whitling, lawyer for detainee Omar Khadr, as asserting that "prosecuting Omar in order to advance someone's political agenda and to assist with election campaigns constitutes an egregious abuse of process, justifying a dismissal of the case"). For a more recent criticism of the pressures put on prosecutors in the military commission system, see Darrel J. Vandeveld, Outlook, Wash. Post, Jan. 18, 2009. On the military commissions generally, see Neal K. Katyal & Laurence H. Tribe, Waging War, Deciding Guilt: Trying the Military Tribunals, 111 Yale L.J. 1259 (2002).

66. See United States v. Hamdan, D-026 (Guantánamo Military Commission May 9, 2008) (Allred, J.).

67. For discussion of this dynamic, see WITTES, 74–79; Peter Margulies, The Detainee's Dilemma: The Virtues and Vices of Advocacy Strategies in the War on Terror, 57 Buff. L. Rev. 347 (2009).

68. See Neil A. Lewis & Eric Schmitt, Cuba Detentions May Last Years, N.Y. Times, Feb. 13, 2004, A1.

69. See WITTES, 74–79; William Glaberson & Margot Williams, Next President Will Face Test on Detainees, N.Y. Times, Nov. 3, 2008, at A1.

70. See Parhat v. Gates, 532 F.3d 834, 848 (D.C. Cir. 2008).

71. Id. at 848–49 (citing LEWIS CARROLL, THE HUNTING OF THE SNARK 3 [1876]). While the government could not establish that the detainees in this case were enemy combatants, the case also demonstrated the difficulties involved in reducing the Guantánamo detainee population. The detainees in the case were Uighurs—ethnic Turks and Chinese nationals who cannot be returned to China because they could face persecution or torture there. See Kiyemba v. Obama, 555 F.3d 1022, 1024 (D.C. Cir. 2009). In addition, although the government conceded in subsequent litigation that the Uighurs were not enemy combatants, ambiguity remained on whether the Uighurs, who were captured in Afghanistan, had been training to fight the Chinese government, which would also qualify as "terrorist activity" under U.S. immigration law. Id. at 1029 n. 14.

72. See MAYER, 129–34; COLE & LOBEL, 23–25.

73. See Dep't of Homeland Security, Office of Inspector General, The Removal of a Canadian Citizen to Syria, March 2008, available at http://ccrjustice.org/files/Office_of_Inspector_General_Report_6.08.pdf.

74. See MAYER, 132.

75. See Scott Shane, On Torture, 2 Messages, and a High Political Cost, N.Y. Times, Oct. 30, 2007, A18.

76. See Richard B. Zabel & James J. Benjamin Jr., Human Rights First, In Pursuit of Justice: Prosecuting Terrorism Cases in the Federal Courts, May 2008, available at http://www.humanrightsfirst.org/pdf/090723-LS-in-pursuit-justice-09-update.pdf (analyzing terrorism cases brought in federal courts and arguing that civilian courts have generally been up to the task of prosecuting suspected terrorists).

77. See R. v. Warickshall, 1 Leach 263, 168 Eng. Rep. 234 (K.B. 1783).

78. See Bram v. United States, 168 U.S. 532 (1897). For a useful summary of the Anglo-American case law, see Steven Penney, Theories of Confession Admissibility: A Historical View, 25 Am. J. Crim. L. 309 (1998).

79. See Miranda v. Arizona, 384 U.S. 436 (1966). For a historical discussion of American policy on interrogation at home and abroad, see John T. Parry, Torture Nation, Torture Law, 97 Geo. L.J. 1001 (2009).

80. See Rochin v. California, 342 U.S. 165, 172 (1952).

81. See 18 U.S.C. 2340A.

82. See U.N. Convention Against Torture and Other Cruel, Inhuman or Degrading Treatment or Punishment, art. 1, Dec. 10, 1984, S. Treaty Doc. 100-20 (1988), 1465 U.N.T.S. 85.

83. See Henry Shue, Torture, in TORTURE: A COLLECTION 47, 55 (Sanford Levinson ed., 2004).

84. See Committee on Armed Services, United States Senate, Inquiry into the Treatment of Detainees in U.S. Custody, 110th Cong., 2d Sess., Nov. 2008 (hereinafter Senate Armed Services Full Report), 16–17 (reporting that in 2002 then national security adviser

Condoleezza Rice asked Attorney General Ashcroft to personally vouch for legality of interrogation program); BARTON GELLMAN, ANGLER: THE CHENEY VICE PRESI-DENCY 177–78 (2008) (discussing in-depth briefings of president and advisers by then CIA director George Tenet, which featured detailed descriptions and sometimes photographs of particular techniques).

85. See MAYER, 105–6.

86. See Senate Armed Services Full Report, 173 n. 1333.

87. Id. at 48.

88. Id. at 17–24.

89. Id. at 48.

90. Id. at 28.

91. Id. at 229 (quoting a JPRA psychologist who noted in 2004 that the SERE training was designed to build resistance, not obtain information, and was "by definition ineffective interrogator conduct").

92. See Scott Shane, 2 Suspects Waterboarded 266 Times, N.Y. Times, April 21, 2009.

93. Bybee is now a federal appellate judge.

94. See Jay Bybee, Assistant Attorney General, Office of Legal Counsel, Memorandum for John Rizzo, Acting General Counsel of the Central Intelligence Agency, Interrogation of Al Qaeda Operative, Aug. 1, 2002, at 4. American tribunals have held that even more intrusive variants on this technique are illegal. In one variant, known as the "water cure," used by U.S. forces against Filipino rebels after the Spanish-American War, interrogators forced open the subject's mouth with a round stick and poured water down the subject's mouth and nose. See Parry, 5 n. 17; see also United States v. Lee, 744 F.2d 1124, 1127 (5th Cir. 1984) (rejecting Texas sheriff's appeal that was based on trial court's refusal to sever cases involving allegations of "water torture"); see also 154 Cong. Rec. S948–49, Feb. 13, 2008 (remarks of Senator Whitehouse, D-R.I.) (discussing history of waterboarding); Evan Wallach, Drop by Drop: Forgetting the History of Water Torture in U.S. Courts, 45 Colum. J. Transnat'l L. 468, 478–88, 502–04 (2007) (discussing case law).

95. A later memo purported, with the same dispassionate tone, to establish guidelines for the frequency of waterboarding. It stipulated that waterboarding would be approved for a thirty-day period, to be used on no more than five days during that time, with no more than two sessions within any twenty-hour period. In any given session, interrogators could not exceed six applications of water lasting ten seconds or longer, with no single application of water to exceed forty seconds. All applications of water within a twenty-four-hour period could not total more than twelve minutes. Steven G. Bradbury, Office of Legal Counsel, U.S. Dep't of Justice, Memorandum for John A. Rizzo, Senior Deputy General Counsel, Central Intelligence Agency, Application of 18 U.S.C. sections 2340–2340a to Certain Techniques That May be Used in the Interrogation of a High Value Al Qaeda Detainee, May 10, 2005 (hereinafter 2340 Memo), 16. In practice, interrogators had already exceeded many of these guidelines by several orders of magnitude. See Shane, 2 Suspects Waterboarded 266 Times.

96. See 2340 Memo, 15. Interrogators also threatened another detainee with a power drill and a handgun, and conducted a mock execution. See Inspector General, Central Intelligence Agency, Special Review: Counterterrorism Detention and Interrogation Activities, September 2001–October 2003 (May 2004), at 70, available at http://graphics8.nytimes.com/packages/pdf/politics/20090825-DETAIN/2004CIAIG.pdf.

97. The interrogator would fit the detainee with a c-collar around the neck to prevent whiplash. See Steven G. Bradbury, Memorandum for John A. Rizzo, Senior Deputy General Counsel, Central Intelligence Agency, Re: Application of United States Obligations Under Article 16 of the Convention Against Torture to Certain Techniques that May Be Used in the Interrogation of High Value Al Qaeda Detainees, May 30, 2005 (hereinafter CAT Memo), at 14.

98. Id. at 14 n. 11.

99. Id. at 14.

100. See Steven Bradbury, Office of Legal Counsel, U.S. Dep't of Justice, Memorandum for John A. Rizzo, Senior Deputy General Counsel, Central Intelligence Agency, Application of 18 U.S.C. sec. 2340–2340A to the Combined Use of Certain Techniques in the Interrogation of High Value Al Qaeda Detainees, May 10, 2005 (hereinafter Combinations Memo), available at http://luxmedia.vo.llnwd.net/o10/clients/aclu/olc_5102005_bradbury_20pg.pdf.

101. See 2340 Memo, 11.

102. Id. at 12.

103. See Scott Shane, Illusions Fueled Rough Handling of Qaeda Figure, N.Y. Times, April 18, A1.

104. U.S. Senate Armed Services Committee, Inquiry into the Treatment of Detainees in U.S. Custody, Executive Summary, Dec. 2008 (hereinafter Senate Armed Services Executive Summary), xxiii.

105. See Senate Armed Services Full Report, 176.

106. See Senate Armed Services Executive Summary, xxiii. Health care personnel indirectly facilitated this and similar techniques, by monitoring the detainees and informing interrogators when medical reasons dictated suspending the techniques, and when the subject had recovered sufficiently for the interrogation to resume. See INTERNATIONAL COMMITTEE OF THE RED CROSS, ICRC REPORT ON THE TREATMENT OF FOURTEEN "HIGH VALUE DETAINEES" IN CIA CUSTODY 21–23 (Feb. 2007), available at http://www.nybooks.com/icrc-report.pdf; see also Mark Danner, The Red Cross Torture Report: What It Means, N.Y. Rev. Books, April 30, 2009, at 48 (analyzing ICR Report); cf. M. Gregg Bloche & Jonathan H. Marks, When Doctors Go to War, 352(1) N.E. J. Med. 3 (Jan. 6, 2005) (discussing issues of medical ethics raised by facilitation of interrogation by health care professionals); David Luban, Torture and the Professions, Crim. Justice Ethics (Summer–Fall 2007), at 2 (same).

107. Senate Armed Services Full Report, 186.

108. Id. at 168–69.

109. Id. at 167–68 (quoting an e-mail by a counterintelligence officer, Capt. William Ponce, who advised that the "gloves are coming off gentlemen . . . casualties are mounting").

110. See PHILIPPE SANDS, TORTURE TEAM: RUMSFELD'S MEMO AND THE BETRAYAL OF AMERICAN VALUES 6, 10–13 (2008).

111. See SANDS, 5; Mayer; David S. Cloud, Concerns Led to Revisions, Rumsfeld Says, N.Y. Times, Feb. 22, 2006, A16 (noting Rumsfeld's subsequent observation regarding the comment that "maybe it shouldn't have gone out, but it did, I wrote it and life goes on").

112. For a balanced view from a scholar who served as counselor to the State Department under Condoleezza Rice and executive director of the 9/11 Commission, see Philip

Zelikow, A Dubious C.I.A. Shortcut, N.Y. Times, April 24, 2009, A27 (suggesting that intelligence reports derived from interrogations using "enhanced" techniques were "a critical part of the intelligence flow, but rarely—if ever—affected a 'ticking bomb' situation").

113. See Scott Shane, Interrogations' Effectiveness May Prove Elusive, N.Y. Times, April 23, 2009, A14.

114. See Peter Wallsten & Greg Miller, A Nuanced Defense of Stance on Torture; Obama Says Moral Concerns Trump Tactics' Possible Gains, L.A. Times, April 30, 2009, A18.

115. See Peter Margulies, Detention of Material Witnesses, Exigency, and the Rule of Law, 40 Crim. L. Bull. 599 (2004); cf. Bacon v. United States, 449 F.2d 933 (9th Cir. 1971) (holding that federal statute authorized detention of material witnesses in grand jury investigations).

116. See Margulies, Detention of Material Witnesses, at 604–5 (discussing case of Maher Hawash, whom the government detained for five weeks to investigate his travel to China with coconspirators seeking to aid the Taliban and Al Qaeda). Hawash eventually pleaded guilty and agreed to cooperate with the government; he was sentenced to a term of seven to ten years in prison. See Noelle Crombie, Portland 7 Figure Gets 7 Years, The Oregonian, Feb. 10, 2004, at A1.

117. See Office of the Inspector General, U.S. Dep't of Justice, A Review of the FBI's Handling of the Brandon Mayfield Case, Jan. 2006, available at http://www.usdoj.gov/oig/special/s0601/PDF_list.htm; cf. LICHTBLAU, 65–74.

118. Id. at 65–66.

119. The government eventually gave Mayfield over one million dollars for his ordeal.

120. 349 F.3d 42 (2d Cir. 2003); cf. Peter Margulies, Above Contempt? Regulating Government Overreaching in Terrorism Cases, 34 Sw. U. L. Rev. 449, 471–72 (2005).

121. See Ray Rivera & Matthew Sweeney, Acquaintance of 2 Hijackers Is Acquitted, N.Y. Times, Nov. 18, 2006, B1.

122. See Jim Dwyer, City Police Spied Broadly Before G.O.P. Convention, N.Y. Times, March 25, 2007.

123. See Karen DeYoung, Officials: Pentagon Probed Finances; Citizens' Records Culled in Expanded Intelligence Efforts, Wash. Post, Jan. 14, 2007, A12. Cf. Linda E. Fisher, Guilt by Expressive Association: Political Profiling, Surveillance and the Privacy of Groups, 46 Ariz. L. Rev. 621 (2004) (discussing criteria for investigations).

124. See The Attorney General's Guidelines for Domestic FBI Operations, n.d., available at http://www.usdoj.gov/ag/readingroom/guidelines.pdf.

125. See id. at 17, 20 (no need for "any particular factual predication").

126. See Office of the Inspector General, U.S. Dep't of Justice, The Federal Bureau of Investigation's Terrorist Watchlist Nomination Practices, May 2009 (hereinafter OIG Terrorist Watchlist Report), at 27, available at http://www.usdoj.gov/oig/reports/FBI/a0925/final.pdf.

127. Id. at 24.

128. Id. at 15.

129. Id. at 17.

130. See Eric Lichtblau, Terror List Wrongly Includes 24,000, While Some Actual Suspects Escaped It, N.Y. Times, May 7, 2009.

131. See OIG Terrorist Watchlist Report, 38.

132. Id. at 40–41.

133. Targeting also occurred on the state level. Consider the curious case of University of Colorado professor Ward Churchill. In an essay written after September 11, Churchill labeled the victims of the attacks "little Eichmans." In claiming that the victims were mere cogs in America's financial empire, Churchill badly misread the work of the political thinker Hannah Arendt, who had coined the phrase "banality of evil." See HANNAH ARENDT, EICHMANN IN JERUSALEM: A REPORT ON THE BANALITY OF EVIL 291–92 (Penguin Books rev. ed. 1994). Churchill's screed equated the economic activity of the financial workers in the World Trade Center with the mass murder supervised by Arendt's subject, who had coordinated the Holocaust. Cf. Richard Delgado, Shooting the Messenger (book review), 30 Am. Indian L. Rev. 477, 482–83 (2005–6) (critiquing the crudeness of some of Churchill's comparisons, while arguing that some of Churchill's arguments about American misdeeds were accurate). Churchill's misreading of Arendt richly merited the reception that Louis Brandeis urged for offensive remarks: "more speech." See Whitney v. California, 274 U.S. 357, 377 (1927) (Brandeis, J., concurring). The University of Colorado, however, did not take this time-honored route. Instead, it terminated Churchill. If universities were free to terminate scholars for insensitivity, academic freedom would soon be history. Although the university claimed that it had also uncovered evidence of plagiarism on Churchill's part, a jury found that Churchill's September 11 essay had prompted his termination. See Kirk Johnson & Katherine Q. Seelye, Author of Sept. 11 Essay Was Wrongly Fired, Jury Says, N.Y. Times, April 3, 2009, A19 (reporting that the jury found that Ward's plagiarism allegations were a pretext for his firing based on outrage regarding his essay; the jury awarded one dollar in damages to Churchill).

134. See Dec. 2001 Hearing.

135. See JOSEPH MARGULIES, GUANTÁNAMO AND THE ABUSE OF PRESIDENTIAL POWER (2006); CLIVE STAFFORD SMITH, EIGHT O'CLOCK FERRY TO THE WINDWARD SIDE (2007); Muneer Ahmad, Resisting Guantánamo: Rights at the Brink of Dehumanization, 103 Nw. U.L. Rev. (forthcoming 2009), available at http://ssrn.com/abstract=1268422; Mark Denbeaux & Christina Boyd-Nafstad, The Attorney-Client Relationship in Guantánamo Bay, 30 Fordham Int'l L.J. 491 (2007); Martha Rayner, Roadblocks to Effective Representation of Uncharged, Indefinitely Imprisoned Clients at Guantánamo Bay Military Base, 30 Fordham Int'l L.J. 485 (2007); Brendan M. Driscoll, Note, The Guantánamo Protective Order, 30 Fordham Int'l L.J. 873, 887 n. 64 (2007) (noting efforts by CCR to recruit pro bono counsel for detainees, including attorneys from major law firms).

136. See SMITH.

137. See David Luban, Lawfare and Legal Ethics in Guantánamo, 60 Stan. L. Rev. 1981, 1989–2006 (2008).

138. See JONATHAN MAHLER, THE CHALLENGE: HAMDAN V. RUMSFELD AND THE FIGHT OVER PRESIDENTIAL POWER (2008).

139. See Hamdan v. Rumsfeld, 548 U.S. 557 (2006).

140. For a balanced account of the Radack episode, see David McGowan, Politics, Office Politics, and Legal Ethics: A Case Study in the Strategy of Judgment, 20 Geo. J. Legal Ethics 1057 (2007).

141. See MAYER, 73.

142. See Naftali Bendavid, No Evidence Lindh Killed Agent; Prison Riot Victim Cited in Indictment, Chi. Trib., April 2, 2002, at 7.

143. The agents' questioning may actually have been appropriate, since case law then and now suggests that agents need not tell a suspect held abroad that an attorney is available when the logistical challenges of foreign legal systems often frustrate this goal. See United States v. bin Laden, 132 F. Supp. 2d 168, 188–91 (S.D.N.Y. 2001) (setting standard), modified by United States v. Odeh, 552 F.3d 177 (2d Cir. 2008) (granting government additional flexibility). These cases do not address a case like Lindh's, where the government may have known before questioning the suspect that his family had retained an attorney to represent him. But Lindh's waiver of his right to counsel may still have been valid if agents gave him the same Miranda warning given to ordinary criminal suspects in the United States, informing them that they have the right to an attorney. The case law does not establish that law enforcement officers must provide additional information, such as the identities of possible legal counsel. See United States v. bin Laden; United States v. Odeh. On this aspect of Lindh's case, which remains cloudy, see Jane Mayer, Lost in the Jihad; Why Did the Government's Case Against John Walker Lindh Collapse?, New Yorker, March 10, 2003, 50. Lindh pleaded guilty to supplying services to the Taliban, and received a sentence of twenty years. See United States v. Lindh, 227 F. Supp. 2d 565 (E.D. Va. 2002). Possibly because of the intense anger and trauma over September 11 that lingered throughout Lindh's prosecution, Lindh's sentence exceeded the sentences of others prosecuted later whose crimes may well have been more severe. For this reason, one can argue that the interests of justice would be served by commutation of a portion of Lindh's sentence. See Peter Margulies, Beyond Absolutism: Legal Institutions in the War on Terror, 60 U. Miami L. Rev. 309, 329 (2006).

144. Radack was apparently mistaken about this, since her correspondence was in the case file. Radack disputes this, although she has not claimed that she viewed the file. See Eric Lichtblau, Aftereffects: The Justice Department: Dispute over Legal Advice Costs a Job and Complicates a Nomination, N.Y. Times, May 22, 2003, A1.

145. See SAVAGE, 108.

146. Id. at 107.

147. See Mayer. The Justice Department also was heavy-handed in its investigation of a DOJ attorney, Thomas M. Tamm, who has acknowledged acting as the source for *New York Times* reporters who wrote about the TSP. See Michael Isikoff, The Fed Who Blew the Whistle, Newsweek, Dec. 22, 2008, 40, 48 (describing a 2007 search of Tamm's Maryland home conducted in front of Tamm's family by eighteen FBI agents).

148. See United States v. Abdel Rahman, 189 F.3d 88 (2d Cir. 1999).

149. See United States v. Sattar, 395 F. Supp. 2d 79 (S.D.N.Y. 2005).

150. Peter Margulies, The Virtues and Vices of Solidarity: Regulating the Roles of Lawyers for Clients Accused of Terrorist Activity, 62 Md. L. Rev. 173 (2003).

151. See United States v. Sattar, 395 F. Supp. 2d 79 (S.D.N.Y. 2005); see also Douglas Jehl, Islamic Militants Taunt Cairo, Demanding Break With Israel, N.Y. Times, Nov. 21, 1997 (the group claiming responsibility for attack that claimed lives of seventy tourists in Luxor, Egypt, sought release of Sheik Abdel Rahman, and volunteered that it might halt terror operations "for a while").

152. The government had obtained information about Stewart's violation of the SAMs through a FISA wiretap.

153. See Julia Preston, Lawyer Is Guilty of Aiding Terrorists, N.Y. Times, Feb. 11, 2005, at A1.

154. See Margulies, Virtues and Vices of Solidarity.

155. Legal academics and others with a range of views on Stewart's conviction wrote to the judge urging moderation in Stewart's sentencing. See Peter Margulies et al., Letter re: Lynne Stewart Sentencing, July 26, 2005 (copy on file with the author).

156. See Julia Preston, Sheik's Lawyer, Facing 30 Years, Gets 28 Months, to Dismay of U.S., N.Y. Times, Oct. 17, 2006, at 1.

157. See Kathleen Clark, Government Lawyers and Confidentiality Norms, 85 Wash. U. L. Rev. 1033, 1092–93 (2007); Rosa Brooks, The Good, the Bad, and the Prosecuted, L.A. Times, May 25, 2007, A33; Tim Golden, Naming Names at Gitmo, N.Y. Times, Oct. 21, 2007, sec. 6 (magazine), at 78.

158. See Jim Rutenberg, Trial Spotlights Cheney's Power as an Infighter, N.Y. Times, Feb. 20, 2007, at A1; see also SAVAGE, at 165.

159. See MAYER, 187.

CHAPTER 3

1. See Scott Shane, Nominee Describes Harsh Interrogation as Repugnant, N.Y. Times, Oct. 31, 2007, A16. The afterword discusses the difficult issues involved in prosecution of those who ordered the interrogations or carried out the orders. See Peter Margulies, True Believers at Law: National Security Agendas, the Regulation of Lawyers, and the Separation of Powers, 68 Maryland L. Rev. 1, 54–56 (2008) (noting virtue of prosecution as form of accountability, but cautioning that criminal prosecutions may chill future policymakers and increase partisan rancor).

2. See Jay S. Bybee, Assistant Attorney General, Office of Legal Counsel, U.S. Dep't of Justice, Memorandum for Alberto R. Gonzales, Standards of Conduct for Interrogation Under 18 U.S.C. sec. 2340–2340A, Aug. 1, 2002, in THE TORTURE PAPERS: THE ROAD TO ABU GHRAIB 172 (Karen J. Greenberg & Joshua L. Dratel eds. 2005) (hereinafter Bybee Memo); John C. Yoo, Deputy Assistant Attorney General, Memorandum for William J. Haynes II, General Counsel of the Department of Defense, Military Interrogation of Alien Unlawful Combatants Held Outside the United States, March 14, 2003 (hereinafter Yoo Memo), available at http://www.aclu.org/pdfs/safefree/yoo_army_torture_memo.pdf.

3. See GELLMANN, 96–99.

4. See JOSEPH S. NYE JR., THE PARADOX OF AMERICAN POWER: WHY THE WORLD'S ONLY SUPERPOWER CAN'T GO IT ALONE 35 (2002) (arguing that a preemptive approach by the United States will result in the loss of "important opportunities for cooperation in the solution of global problems such as terrorism"); Harold Honju Koh, On American Exceptionalism, 55 Stan. L. Rev. 1479 (2003).

5. See Jose Alvarez, Torturing the Law, 37 Case W. Res. J. Int'l L. 175, 215–21 (2006).

6. 182 U.S. 244 (1901); for criticism of the Insular Cases for justifying American imperialism, see Ediberto Roman & Theron Simmons, Membership Denied: Subordination and Subjugation Under United States Expansionism, 39 San Diego L. Rev. 437 (2002). For a general analysis, see GERALD L. NEUMAN, STRANGERS TO THE CONSTITUTION: IMMIGRANTS, BORDERS, AND FUNDAMENTAL LAW (1996).

7. 339 U.S. 763 (1950).

8. 494 U.S. 259 (1990).

9. See Geneva Convention Relative to the Treatment of Prisoners of War, 6 U.S.T. 3517.

10. See John Yoo & Robert J. Delahunty, U.S. Department of Justice, Office of Legal Counsel, Application of Treaties and Laws to Al Qaeda and Taliban Detainees, Jan. 9, 2002, in THE TORTURE PAPERS, 48–52.

11. Id., 50, 59.

12. See Geneva Convention Relative to the Treatment of Prisoners of War, art. 3, Aug. 12, 1949, 6 U.S.T. 3316, 75 U.N.T.S. 135. For a thoughtful discussion of detention policies by a former Bush administration official who sought a more balanced approach during his time in Washington, see Matthew C. Waxman, Detention as Targeting: Standards of Certainty and Detention of Suspected Terrorists, 108 Colum. L. Rev. 1365 (2008).

13. See Yoo & Delahunty, Application of Treaties and Laws to Al Qaeda and Taliban Detainees, 46–47. Afghanistan could have been embroiled in a civil war between the Taliban and pro-U.S. indigenous forces. But the administration's lawyers' argument that Afghanistan was a "failed state" without a functional government, id. at 47, 53–59, led to their conclusion that the indigenous conflict was not a contest between a party to the Geneva Conventions and a rebel group.

14. See Alberto R. Gonzales, Memorandum for the President: Decision re: Application of the Geneva Convention on Prisoners of War to the Conflict with Al Qaeda and the Taliban, in THE TORTURE PAPERS, at 118, 119.

15. See Yoo & Delahunty, Application of Treaties to al Qaeda, 47.

16. See MAYER, 260.

17. Id.

18. 542 U.S. 507 (2004).

19. See Hamdi v. Rumsfeld, 542 U.S. 507, 536 (2004).

20. Id., 530.

21. Id. O'Connor acknowledged, however, that the government required some flexibility regarding the difficult issues posed by the war on terror. O'Connor noted, for example, that the Non-Detention Act, 18 U.S.C. sec. 4001(a), a statute passed over thirty years ago to counter the threat of mass detentions like the Japanese American internment, did not preclude the detention of an individual apprehended at or near the theater of war (e.g., Afghanistan). See 542 U.S. at 517. To reach this result, the Court considered that detention in various forms has always been a fixture in the law of war. Moreover, the Court relied on Congress's enactment shortly after September 11 of the Authorization for the Use of Military Force (AUMF), which gave the president power to take action that was necessary and appropriate to deter and prevent future terrorist attacks by Al Qaeda. Id. at 517–18; see also Bradley & Goldsmith (discussing AUMF).

22. See Joel Brinkley & Eric Lichtblau, U.S. Releases Saudi-American It Had Captured in Afghanistan, N.Y Times, Oct. 11, 2004, A15.

23. 548 U.S. 557 (2006).

24. See Youngstown Sheet and Tube Co. v. Sawyer, 343 U.S. 579, 635 n. 2 (1952) (Jackson, J., concurring).

25. 548 U.S. at 631, citing 6 U.S.T, at 3320 (art. 3). Justice Stevens also found that Common Article 3 of the Geneva Convention protected members of Al Qaeda. This conclusion did not hinge on any hope that members of Al Qaeda would reciprocate toward Americans for receipt of decent treatment. Rather, Stevens concluded that the language

of Common Article 3, which includes conflicts "not of an international character," meant exactly what it said—it included conflicts not between nations, such as conflicts between a nation and a transnational organization such as Al Qaeda. Further, Justice Stevens wrote, the drafters and signatories of Common Article 3 wished the provision to have a very broad scope, to establish a floor for treatment. 548 U.S. at 626–34.

26. 548 U.S. at 609. Stevens's explicit reference was to war crimes committed by Henry Wirz, the commandant of the Confederacy's notorious Andersonville prison during the Civil War. Id.

27. See Patrick F. Philbin & John C. Yoo, U.S. Dep't of Justice, Office of Legal Counsel, Possible Habeas Jurisdiction over Aliens Held in Guantánamo Bay, Cuba, in THE TORTURE PAPERS, 31–32. Perhaps due to the influence of Philbin, who later parted company with the administration, this memo acknowledges arguments against the administration's position—arguments that the Supreme Court ultimately accepted.

28. Id., 31.

29. See Pub. L. No. 109-366, 120 Stat. 2600, codified inter alia at 10 U.S.C. sec. 948h.

30. See Sheryl Gay Stolberg, President Moves 14 Held in Secret to Guantánamo, N.Y. Times, Sept. 7, 2006 (quoting President Bush as asserting that, "as soon as Congress acts to authorize the military commissions I have proposed, the men . . . [who] orchestrated the deaths of nearly 3,000 Americans on Sept. 11, 2001 can face justice").

31. See 10 U.S.C. sec. 948r (2008) (providing that a statement obtained through coercion short of torture can be admitted if it is reliable and its admission is in the interests of justice); cf. Peter Margulies, The Military Commissions Act, Coerced Confessions, and the Role of the Courts, 25(2) Crim. Justice Ethics 2 (Summer–Fall 2006) (arguing that military judges should reject coerced evidence as inherently unreliable); Peter Margulies & Laura Corbin, Reliability and the Interests of Justice: Interpreting the Military Commissions Act of 2006 to Deter Coercive Interrogations, 12 Roger Williams U. L. Rev. 750 (2007) (same).

32. For a useful discussion of outstanding issues regarding Guantánamo, see Gregory S. McNeal, Beyond Guantánamo, Obstacles and Options, 103 Nw. U. L. Rev. Colloquy 29 (2008).

33. See Scott Shane & David Johnston, U.S. Acts to Avert Tactic Expected in Qaeda Trial, N.Y. Times, Feb. 13, 2008, A16.

34. See GOLDSMITH.

35. See Mark Mazzetti & Scott Shane, Notes Show Confusion on Interrogation Methods, N.Y. Times, June 18, 2008, A14.

36. See GOLDSMITH, 22–23.

37. See Bybee Memo. For commentary, see HAROLD BRUFF, BAD ADVICE: BUSH'S LAWYERS IN THE WAR ON TERROR (2009); DAVID LUBAN, The Torture Lawyers of Washington, in LEGAL ETHICS AND HUMAN DIGNITY 162, 176–80, 200–202 (2007); SCHWARZ & HUQ, 187–99; Stephen Gillers, Legal Ethics: A Debate, in THE TORTURE DEBATE IN AMERICA 236, 237–38 (Karen J. Greenberg ed., 2006); Kathleen Clark, Ethical Issues Raised by the OLC Torture Memorandum, 1 J. Nat'l Sec. L. & Pol'y 455 (2005); Margulies, True Believers; Sudha Setty, No More Secret Laws: How Transparency of Executive Branch Legal Policy Doesn't Let the Terrorists Win, 57 Kansas L. Rev. 579 (2009); W. Bradley Wendel, Legal Ethics and the Separation of Law and Morals, 91 Cornell L. Rev. 67, 80–85 (2005) (critiquing torture memos); W. Bradley Wendel, Professionalism as Interpretation, 99 Nw. U. L. Rev. 1167 (2005) (same).

38. See 18 U.S.C. 2340A.

39. See Alvarez, 215–21.

40. See 8 U.S.C. 1369.

41. Ordering priorities in this fashion implicitly discounts the risk that routine illness on the part of undocumented people, left untreated, would spread to the documented population. That judgment is faulty, in my view, and illustrates the distortions in the politics of undocumented immigration, which I discuss elsewhere in this volume.

42. See Yoo Memo, 11–18.

43. 744 F.2d 1124 (5th Cir. 1984).

44. Haynes had apparently cut Mora out of the initial process for drafting the memo. See MAYER, 221.

45. Id. at 229.

46. See Yoo Memo.

47. See Senate Armed Services Full Report, 132.

48. Id., 131.

49. See U.S. Senate Armed Services Committee, Origins of Aggressive Interrogation Techniques, Fed. News Service, June 17, 2008 (hereinafter Haynes Testimony).

50. For example, the Working Group Report notes, "As the Supreme Court has long recognized, and as we will explain further below, the President enjoys complete discretion in the exercise of his Commander-in-Chief authority." See Working Group Report on Detainee Interrogations in the Global War on Terrorism: Assessment of Legal, Historical, Policy, and Operational Considerations, March 6, 2003, in TORTURE PAPERS, 241, 255; see also Working Group Report, April 4, 2003 (hereinafter April 2003 Report), id. at 286, 303 (reproducing above passage). Identical language appears in the Bybee Memo. See id. at 202. Other crucial passages in the Working Group Report reproduce Yoo's March 2003 maiming memo virtually verbatim. Compare April 2003 Report, id. at 303 ("In the area of foreign affairs, and war powers in particular, the avoidance canon [requiring interpretation of statutes to uphold "complete discretion" of president] has special force"), with Yoo Memo, 12 (identical passage except for lack of comma after "foreign affairs"). In other situations, the Working Group Report's author changed only enough words to create an obvious paraphrase of Yoo's memo. Compare April 2003 Report, id. at 303 ("In order to respect the President's inherent constitutional authority to manage a military campaign . . . [federal criminal statutes] must be construed as inapplicable to interrogations undertaken pursuant to his Commander-in-Chief authority"), with Yoo Memo, 13 ("In order to respect the President's inherent constitutional authority to direct a military campaign against Al Qaeda and its allies, general criminal laws must be construed as not applying to interrogations undertaken pursuant to his Commander-in-Chief authority"). Cf. Clark, 470.

51. See Kent v. Dulles, 357 U.S. 116 (1958), discussed in Bradley & Goldsmith, 2103–4.

52. See GOLDSMITH, 152.

53. Id. at 156.

54. Goldsmith is not wholly lacking in insight on this score. See id. (arguing that view, initially expressed in October 2003, was legally appropriate, but musing whether it contributed to abuses at Abu Ghraib).

55. See Draft Memorandum from Jack L. Goldsmith, Assistant Attorney General, to Alberto R. Gonzales, Counsel to the President, Re: The Permissibility of Relocating

Certain "Protected Persons" from Occupied Iraq, March 19, 2004 (hereinafter Goldsmith Draft Memo), available at http://www.humanrightsfirst.org/us_law/etn/gonzales/memos_dir/memo_20040319_Golds_Gonz.pdf (last visited Aug. 29, 2009).

56. For a well-supported view opposed to Goldsmith, see JORDAN J. PAUST, BEYOND THE LAW: THE BUSH ADMINISTRATION'S UNLAWFUL RESPONSES IN THE "WAR" ON TERROR 163 n. 148 (2007).

57. See Vienna Convention on the Law of Treaties, 1155 U.N.T.S. 331, art. 31(1), (3) (b)–(c); cf. LUBAN, at 184–88 (critiquing Article 49 draft opinion). Goldsmith acted ethically by disclosing contrary sources of authority within his memo. Moreover, Goldsmith was diligent in finding that the Geneva Conventions protected Iraqi nationals, and in urging U.S. authorities in Iraq to carefully document the illegal immigration status of transferees. See Goldsmith Draft Memo, at 8 n. 9. But Goldsmith failed to recognize that an occupying power has influence over the occupied country's government, which may result in changes in the immigration status of disfavored groups. Indeed, during the Nazi occupation, compliant governments in France, Hungary, and Croatia stripped Jews of their citizenship, making them illegal aliens. An occupier's careful documentation of this status should not mitigate the violation of international law. Cf. David Weissbrodt & Amy Bergquist, Extraordinary Rendition and the Humanitarian Law of War and Occupation, 47 Va. J. Int'l L. 295, 322–25 (2007) (discussing historical background of Article 49).

58. See GOLDSMITH, 153.

59. See Sec'y of Defense, Memorandum for the Commander, U.S. Southern Command, in TORTURE PAPERS, 360, 361.

60. Id. at 362.

61. Id. at 365.

62. Id. at 360.

63. See GOLDSMITH, 153. Nor did Goldsmith consider the implications of the secretary of defense's authority to permit additional techniques upon request. See Sec'y of Defense, Memorandum for the Commander, 360.

64. See GOLDSMITH, 149–50.

65. Id. at 151.

66. Id. at 150. Goldsmith also said that he viewed unnecessarily broad legal advice as inviting unduly aggressive implementation. Id. He has not resolved the apparent conflict between his observation that Yoo's memos encouraged interrogators to overreach, and his insistence that the administration did not actually violate the law.

67. Id. at 165. Goldsmith does not expressly discuss these techniques, although they were described in OLC's August 2002 Techniques Memo, to which Goldsmith had access, and were widely known by the time that Goldsmith's memoir was published in September 2007.

68. Goldsmith credits OLC colleague Patrick Philbin and Deputy Attorney General James Comey, as well as Attorney General Ashcroft, with supporting his decision. See id. at 159–60.

69. Id. at 71 (emphasis in original). Goldsmith, along with his OLC colleague Philbin, had joined Attorney General Ashcroft, Deputy Attorney General Comey, and FBI Director Mueller in forcing changes in the TSP's operation and legal underpinnings. White House counsel Alberto Gonzales and White House chief of staff Andy Card visited Ashcroft, who had been hospitalized for severe pancreatitis, demanding that he approve

a sweeping version of the surveillance program. From his sickbed, Ashcroft mustered the strength to resist their entreaties and side with his colleagues. See LICHTBLAU, 179–84.

70. See GOLDSMITH, 161.

71. Id. at 162.

72. See Klostermann v. Cuomo, 463 N.E.2d 588 (N.Y. 1984) (holding that claims of people with mental disabilities to community services and housing were justiciable). I should disclose here that I worked with Levin in the 1980s on this litigation. Levin was then, and I assume continues to be, guided by ideals of professional craft and an innate sense of decency.

73. See Memorandum from Daniel Levin, Acting Assistant Attorney General, to James B. Comey, Deputy Attorney General, Dec. 30, 2004 (hereinafter Levin Memo), available at http://www.humanrightsfirst.org/us_law/etn/pdf/levin-memo-123004.pdf.

74. See Levin Memo, n. 8.

75. See MAYER, 298–99; Scott Shane, A Firsthand Experience Before Decision on Torture, N.Y. Times, Nov. 7, 2007, A22.

76. MAYER, 299.

77. U.S. Senate Armed Services Committee, Executive Summary, xxv. Whether the relationship between issuance of the Levin Memo and reduction in confirmed reports of abuse is causal, correlational, or coincidental awaits more investigation.

78. MAYER, 308.

79. Id.

80. 2340 Memo, 16.

81. For more discussion of this famous scene, see Andrew Horwitz, Taking the Cop Out of Copping a Plea: Eradicating Police Prosecution of Criminal Cases, 40 Ariz. L. Rev. 1305, 1327 n. 104 (1998).

82. See 2340 Memo, 16.

83. Bradbury observed that in any event a qualified physician would be on hand to perform a tracheotomy. Id.

84. Id., 15. Bradbury noted that interrogators used saline solution to avoid grave medical complications caused by reduced levels of sodium in the blood.

85. Id., 13.

86. See Shane, 2 Suspects Waterboarded 266 Times. Bradbury conceded in his memo that these episodes had been "numerous." See 2340 Memo, 16.

87. On the internment litigation, see Margulies, When to Push the Envelope, 652–54, and other sources cited in chapter 2.

88. See Bloche & Marks (arguing that the participation of medical personnel in regime of coercive interrogation violates the Hippocratic oath and principles of medical ethics).

89. See Combinations Memo; see also MAYER, 309; Scott Shane, David Johnston & James Risen, Secret U.S. Endorsement of Severe Interrogations, N.Y. Times, Oct. 4, 2007, A1.

90. See Combinations Memo, 18.

91. See U.S. Dep't of Justice, Office of Legislative Affairs, Letter to Hon. Ron Wyden, March 6, 2008, available at http://graphics8.nytimes.com/packages/pdf/washington/20080427-INTEL/letter4.pdf.

92. Id., 2.

93. See CAT Memo, 28–33, citing, inter alia, Rochin v. California, 342 U.S. 165 (1952).

94. See Country of Sacramento v. Lewis, 523 U.S. 833, 850 (1998). For a more recent case in which several justices asserted that the Constitution bars coercive interrogation in the domestic realm, regardless of whether the government seeks to introduce information from that interrogation in a criminal trial, see, for example, Chavez v. Martinez, 538 U.S. 760, 796 (2003) (Kennedy, J., concurring in part and dissenting in part) (in case in which police persisted in questioning an individual receiving emergency medical treatment for a serious gunshot wound, noting that the "Constitution does not countenance the official imposition of severe pain or pressure for purposes of interrogation"). In highly exigent circumstances, an interrogator might use coercion short of torture to obtain information that would prevent an imminent attack. The Bush administration's excesses have taught us, however, that officials should never authorize such conduct *ex ante*, that is, before the fact. See GELLMAN, 187; Margulies, Beyond Absolutism, 309, 317–18. If an interrogator resorts to coercion, he should be prepared to face the legal consequences. Those deciding on consequences should consider the context of the interrogation.

95. International Criminal Tribunal for Yugoslavia, Case No. IT-95-14/1-T, Trial Chamber Judgment, P 19, June 25, 1999, available at http://www.un.org/icty/aleksovski/trialc/judgement/ale-tj990625e.pdf.

96. Id., para. 53.

97. See Political Risks, Wash. Post, March 11, 2007, B4 (discussing conviction and subsequent pardon on Elliott Abrams, a Reagan administration official who returned to government in the Bush administration).

98. See United States v. Kennedy, 372 F.3d 686, 693–95 (4th Cir. 2004).

99. See United States v. Greer, 158 F.3d 228, 235–41 (5th Cir. 1998) (holding that the district court could enhance sentence because the defendant's feigning of mental incompetency constituted obstruction of justice under Sentencing Guidelines); United States v. Batista, 483 F.3d 193, 197–98 (3d Cir. 2007) (same); United States v. Murray, 65 F.3d 1161, 1165–66 (4th Cir. 1995) (holding that defendant's false claim of failure of memory triggered obstruction of justice sentence enhancement); United States v. Escobedo-Torres, 146 Fed. Appx. 736, 740 (5th Cir. 2005) (same).

100. Haynes was identified by Goldsmith as a friend. See GOLDSMITH, 153–54. Goldsmith argued that Haynes, even after receiving Yoo's March 2003 "maiming memo," sought to cabin the techniques used by Pentagon interrogators. Id. at 154. Haynes also testified that he "made sure" during December 2002 and January 2003 that Rumsfeld and the Chair of the Joint Chiefs of Staff were "aware of this continuing concern." He told the Committee that he "went back, from time to time, to the secretary, and ultimately convinced him that we needed to take another look at what he had . . . approved" (in Dec. 2002). Haynes also pointed out that the April 2003 approved techniques were different from the December 2002 approved techniques. See Haynes Testimony.

101. Id.; cf. SANDS, 56–71 (discussing Beaver's memo).

102. When asked by Senator Lindsey Graham (R-S.C.) whether he had seen the Bybee Memo before Secretary Rumsfeld approved the interrogation techniques, Haynes answered, "I don't know when I became aware of that, Senator . . . I don't remember that." See Haynes Testimony. One possible explanation here is that the Bybee Memo and other documents were not directed to Haynes, but to other officials. See Haynes Testimony (questioning by Senator Jeff Sessions, R-Ala.). Haynes eventually conceded that he was aware of concerns from military lawyers. He then implicitly marginalized those concerns

as stemming from a "law enforcement" paradigm out of touch with the realities of the global war on terror. Haynes also told Levin that he did not intervene to short-circuit a review of legal standards governing interrogation conducted by then Captain (now Admiral) Jane Dalton on behalf of the Joint Chiefs of Staff.

103. Haynes told Senator Graham that Rumsfeld had only authorized the use of muzzled dogs around the perimeter of the interrogation, while the Schmidt-Furlow Report described the use of an unmuzzled, growling dog as fully authorized. See Army Regulation 15-6: Final Report: Investigation into FBI Allegations of Detainee Abuse at Guantánamo Bay, Cuba Detention Facility, at 14, available at http://www.defenselink.mil/news/Jul2005/d20050714report.pdf.

104. See Haynes Testimony. Another administration official, Douglas Feith, former undersecretary of defense, echoed this point in his testimony before a House committee. As Feith put it, "Removal of clothing is different than naked." "Really?," a skeptical Congressman Nadler responded. See Hearing of the Constitution, Civil Rights, and Civil Liberties Subcommittee of the House Judiciary Committee, From the Department of Justice to Guantánamo Bay: Administration Lawyers and Administration Interrogation Rules, Part III, June 26, 2008. According to both Haynes and Feith, blame for the forced nudity suffered by some detainees lies solely with individual interrogators.

105. See GOLDSMITH, 122–23.

106. See Office of Legal Counsel, U.S. Dep't of Justice, Potential Legal Constraints Applicable to Interrogations of Persons Captured by U.S. Forces in Afghanistan, Feb. 26, 2002, in TORTURE PAPERS, 144.

107. See MAYER, 229.

108. It turned out that al-Qahtani possessed no actionable intelligence of this kind, but was only useful in confirming intelligence already possessed by the government. Id. at 211.

109. See Hearing of the Constitution, Civil Rights and Civil Liberties Subcommittee of the House Committee on the Judiciary, From the Department of Justice to Guantánamo Bay: Administration Lawyers and Administration Interrogation Rules, Part II, June 18, 2008 (hereinafter House Hearing).

110. Id.

111. Id.

112. Id.

113. See MAYER, 307 (describing the White House's keen interest in Levin's drafting of the footnote). Goldsmith also saw the footnote as a clean bill of health for the actual techniques authorized by the administration. See GOLDSMITH, 164–65. Levin acknowledged that his drafting of the footnote was imprecise. See House Hearing.

114. See MAYER, 215–16; see also United States Dep't of Justice, Office of the Inspector General, A Review of the FBI's Involvement in and Observations of Detainee Interrogations in Guantánamo Bay, Afghanistan, and Iraq, May 2008 (hereinafter OIG Detainee Interrogation), available at http://www.usdoj.gov/oig/special/s0805/final.pdf.

115. See Eric Lichtblau & Scott Shane, Report Details Dissent on Guantánamo Tactics, N.Y. Times, May 21, 2008, A21.

116. See OIG Detainee Interrogation, ii–iii n. 4.

117. Judge Brinkema in Virginia, presiding over the Zacarias Moussaoui conspiracy case, had issued orders that involved the tapes. See Mark Mazzetti & Scott Shane, C.I.A. Destroyed Tapes as Judge Sought Interrogation Data, N.Y. Times, Feb. 7, 2008, A8. The

Brinkema order was in connection with a criminal investigation, raising the specter of obstruction of justice. A judge in New York had also issued an order that appeared to request the material as part of a Freedom of Information Act (FOIA) lawsuit. The Court noted that the CIA Information Act, 50 U.S.C. sec. 431(c)(3), required that materials, even those of an operational nature, be available for review "concerning . . . the specific subject matter of an investigation" by Congress, the Justice Department, and the CIA inspector general. See ACLU v. Dep't of Defense, 351 F. Supp. 2d 265 (S.D.N.Y. 2005).

118. See Mark Mazzetti & Scott Shane, Bush Lawyers Discussed the Fate of C.I.A. Tapes, N.Y. Times, Dec. 19, 2007, at A1. In 2008, Attorney General Mukasey appointed a special prosecutor to investigate the destruction of the tapes. See Scott Shane, Prosecutor to Review Handling of C.I.A. Tapes, N.Y. Times, Feb. 10, 2008, A23.

119. See Robert M. Chesney, State Secrets and the Limits of National Security Litigation, 75 Geo. Wash. L. Rev. 1249 (2007).

120. 345 U.S. 1 (1953).

121. See DYCUS et al., 1043.

122. See Al-Haramain Islamic Found., Inc. v. Bush, 507 F.3d 1190 (9th Cir. 2007), remanded sub nom In re: NSA Telecommunications Records Litig., 564 F. Supp. 2d 1109 (N.D. Ca. 2008) (holding that provisions of FISA preempt state secret privilege). The administration also pushed successfully for legislation immunizing telecommunications carriers that had cooperated with the government regarding the TSP. See 50 U.S.C. sec. 1885, 1885a (2008). In April 2009, a federal appeals court cut back on the state secrets privilege, declining to dismiss a lawsuit claiming that an American company had assisted in the extraordinary rendition of a terror suspect. See Mohamed v. Jeppesen Dataplan, Inc., 563 F. 3d 992 (9th Cir. 2009).

123. S. 2533.

124. See Pub. L. No. 96-456, 94 Stat. 2025 (1980), codified at 18 U.S.C. app. 3.

125. See Arar v. Ashcroft, 532 F.3d 157 (2d Cir. 2008); see also James Barron, U.S. Appeals Court to Rehear Case of Deported Canadian, N.Y. Times, Aug. 15, 2008, at 4 (reporting that Second Circuit will rehear case en banc).

126. 403 U.S. 388 (1971).

127. See Arar v. Ashcroft, en banc oral argument (2d Cir. Dec. 9, 2009).

128. See U.S. Const., art. I, sec. 6, cl. 1; see also Eastland v. United States Servicemen's Fund, 421 U.S. 491 (1975) (interpreting speech and debate clause).

129. See Imbler v. Pachtman, 424 U.S. 409 (1976).

130. See Harlow v. Fitzgerald, 457 U.S. 800, 818 (1982).

131. 520 U.S. 259 (1997).

132. Id. at 271.

133. See Ashcroft v. Iqbal, 129 S. Ct. 1937 (2009).

134. See Edward Hegstrom, Foreign Student Tells of Beatings by Inmates in Mississippi Cell, Hous. Chron., Sept. 29, 2001, A31; cf. Richard A. Serrano, Many Held in Terror Probe Report Rights Being Abused, L.A. Times, Oct. 15, 2001, at 1; William Carlsen, Rights Violations, Abuses Alleged by Detainees: Beatings, Lack of Legal Representation Cited, S.F. Chron., Oct. 19, 2001, A12.

135. See also Bell Atlantic Co. v. Twombly, 550 U.S. 544 (2007) (announcing specific pleading requirement in antitrust case); cf. A. Benjamin Spencer, Plausibility Pleading, 49 B.C. L. Rev. 431 (2008) (criticizing Twombly as imposing unfair expectations on plaintiffs and impeding search for justice).

136. Indeed, the district judge in *Iqbal* had already stayed discovery pertaining to senior officials.

137. See chapter 4 for a discussion of the Graves firing, and chapter 6 for more detail on the Iglesias firing.

138. See Committee on the Judiciary v. Miers, 558 F. Supp. 2d 53, 57 (D.D.C. 2008). Documents obtained by congressional investigators subsequently revealed that Rove had played a key role in the firing of Iglesias. See Eric Lichtblau & Eric Lipton, E-Mail Reveals Rove's Key Role in '06 Dismissals, N.Y. Times, Aug. 12, 2009, at A1.

139. See RAOUL BERGER, EXECUTIVE PRIVILEGE: A CONSTITUTIONAL MYTH (1974).

140. 418 U.S. 683 (1974).

141. As the Court explained, "Human experience teaches that those who expect public dissemination of their remarks may well temper candor with a concern for appearances and for their own interests to the detriment of the decisionmaking process." Id. at 705.

142. Id. at 706.

143. Id. at 697–707.

144. See Committee on the Judiciary v. Miers, 558 F. Supp. 2d 53 (D.D.C. 2008).

145. Id. at 75, citing McGrain v. Daugherty, 273 U.S. 135, 174 (1927).

146. See *Miers*, 558 F. Supp. 2d at 76, citing Office of Legal Counsel, United States Dep't of Justice, Prosecution for Contempt of Congress of an Executive Branch Official Who Has Asserted a Claim of Executive Privilege, 8 U.S. Op. Off. Legal Counsel 101, 137 (1984) (Congress can seek information through civil proceeding in federal court); see also Charles Cooper, OLC: Response to Congressional Requests for Information Regarding Decisions Made Under the Independent Counsel Act, 10 U.S. Op. Off. Legal Counsel 68 (1986).

147. See *Miers*, 558 F. Supp.2d at 77–78.

148. Id. at 100, citing Harlow v. Fitzgerald, 457 U.S. 800, 808–9 (1982).

149. Id. at 104. While the Bradbury memo relied on an OLC opinion issued during the Nixon administration by then Assistant Attorney General William Rehnquist, the *Miers* Court noted that Rehnquist acknowledged that his own views were "tentative and sketchy" and later revoked those views in testimony before Congress.

150. Id. at 106.

151. President Bush's commutation of the prison sentence imposed after Lewis "Scooter" Libby's perjury conviction also fit into the architecture of impunity. When outcry first emerged after the leaking of the covert CIA status of Valerie Plame, the administration sought to trivialize the problem. After criticism grew, Deputy Attorney General Comey appointed a special prosecutor, Patrick Fitzgerald, who convened a grand jury. Libby lied to the grand jury to conceal Cheney's role in the events leading to the leak. As a result, a jury convicted Libby of perjury. The administration had the last word, however, when the president commuted Libby's prison sentence. See Amy Goldstein & Robert Barnes, Bush Says He's Not Ruling Out Pardon for Libby: President Defends Commutation of Prison Sentence, Wash. Post., July 4, 2007, A4.

CHAPTER 4

1. See Office of the Inspector General and Office of Professional Responsibility, United States Department of Justice, An Investigation of Allegations of Politicized Hiring

in the Department of Justice Honors Program and Summer Law Intern Program, June 24, 2008 (hereinafter OIG Honors Program Report), at 18, available at http://www.usdoj.gov/oig/special/s0806/final.pdf.

2. See Bruce A. Green & Fred C. Zacharias, "The U.S. Attorneys Scandal" and the Allocation of Prosecutorial Power, 69 Ohio St. L.J. 187 (2008).

3. See Dick Polman, A Crusade to Keep Bench From Liberals: Wary of "Renegade Judges," Conservatives Have Been Tying Up Clinton's Nominations, Phil. Inquirer, March 23, 1997, E1.

4. See Dan Eggen & David A. Vise, Ashcroft Firm in Defending His Record Amid Queries: Democrats Call Answers Evasive and Inaccurate, Wash. Post, Jan. 27, 2001.

5. See JOHN ASHCROFT, NEVER AGAIN: SECURING AMERICA AND RESTORING JUSTICE 90 (2006).

6. Id.

7. Id. at 91.

8. See Toobin.

9. ASHCROFT, 245.

10. See Memorandum from John Ashcroft, Attorney General, U.S. Dep't of Justice, to All Federal Prosecutors, Sept. 22, 2003.

11. See Stephanos Bibas, The Feeney Amendment and the Continuing Rise of Prosecutorial Power to Plea Bargain, 94 J. Crim. L. & Criminology 295, 301 (2004); Daniel Richman, Federal Sentencing in 2007: The Supreme Court Holds—the Center Doesn't, 117 Yale L.J. 1374 (2008); cf. David M. Zlotnick, The War Within the War on Crime: The Congressional Assault on Judicial Sentencing Discretion, 57 SMU L. Rev. 211 (2004) (discussing *in terrorem* effect of congressional hearings).

12. See Linda Greenhouse, Chief Justice Attacks a Law as Infringing on Judges, N.Y. Times, Jan. 1, 2004, at A6.

13. See United States v. Lovett, 328 U.S. 303, 308–9 (1946).

14. Id., 309–10.

15. See Richman, 1388.

16. See Billy House, No Party Has Moral Upper Hand, Tampa Trib., Oct. 18, 2008, 5.

17. See Zlotnick, 227.

18. Id., 228.

19. 543 U.S. 220 (2005).

20. Id., 256–57.

21. Id, 262–63.

22. See Kimbrough v. United States, 128 S. Ct. 558 (2007). The judge's discretion could not eliminate all sentencing disparities; for example, Congress has established mandatory minimums that judges must observe for certain crimes, including a minimum ten-year sentence for possession with intent to distribute of more than fifty grams of crack cocaine. See 21 U.S.C. sec. 841(b)(A)(iii) (2000 ed. & Supp. V). This contrasts with no minimum for distributing powder cocaine. See 21 U.S.C. sec. 841(b)(1)(C) (Supp. V). The Court's recent holding, however, permits a judge to reject prosecutors' arguments for a sentence *exceeding* the minimum.

23. In another case, federal district judge Jack Weinstein decided that the absence of a drug court in the federal forum justified adjourning a federal prosecution and allowing the state to take the lead, where more flexible drug court remedies could come into play. See United States v. Brennan, 468 F. Supp. 2d 400 (E.D.N.Y. 2007); cf. Richman, 1415.

Decisions like *Kimbrough* also suggest that courts can play a meaningful role in stemming the tide of policy centralization, except where centralization is truly needed.

24. See Richman, 1391.

25. See Eric Lipton & Jennifer Steinhauer, Battle Over F.B.I. Policy Against Taping of Suspects Comes to Light in Firing Inquiry, N.Y. Times, April 2, 2007, at A18; cf. Office of the Inspector General, United States Dep't of Justice, An Investigation into the Removal of Nine U.S. Attorneys in 2006, September 2008 (hereinafter OIG U.S. Attorneys Report), at 232, available at http://www.usdoj.gov/oig/special/s0809a/final.pdf (discussing Charlton's position).

26. See John Gleeson, Supervising Federal Capital Punishment: Why the Attorney General Should Defer When U.S. Attorneys Recommend Against the Death Penalty, 89 Va. L. Rev. 1697, 1701 (2003).

27. Id. at 1703.

28. See United States v. Pepin, 514 F.3d 193 (2d Cir. 2008).

29. See John Marzulli, AG Rejects 50-Yr. Sentence, N.Y. Daily News, July 10, 2008, 49.

30. See Alan Feuer, An Aversion to the Death Penalty, but No Shortage of Cases, N.Y. Times, March 10, 2008, B1.

31. Id.

32. See Philip Dine, KC Case Has Relevance in Firings of Attorneys, St. Louis Post-Dispatch, June 15, 2007, A1.

33. See Hearing, Senate Judiciary Committee, Preserving Prosecutorial Independence: Is the Department of Justice Politicizing the Hiring and Firing of U.S. Attorneys?, Chaired by Senator Sheldon Whitehouse (D-R.I.), June 5, 2007 (hereinafter Sen. Judiciary Committee, Preserving Prosecutorial Independence).

34. See Dine.

35. Id.

36. Id.

37. See Rep. Linda T. Sanchez Holds a Hearing on the Dismissal of U.S. Attorneys, CQ Transcriptions, House Subcommittee on Commercial and Administrative Law, March 6, 2007 (testimony of Principal Associate Deputy Attorney General William Moschella).

38. See OIG U.S. Attorneys Report, 281.

39. See 8 U.S.C. sec. 1326(a) (2008).

40. See Solomon Moore, Focus on Immigration Crimes Is Said to Shortchange Other Cases, N.Y. Times, Jan. 12, 2009, A1.

41. See Jennifer M. Chacon, Unsecured Borders: Immigration Restrictions, Crime Control, and National Security, 39 Conn. L. Rev. 1827, 1886–88 (2007).

42. Immigration-related crimes accounted for more than half of the sentences handed down in Lam's cases in 2006. See Dana Wilkie, Top Official Who Defended Lam's Record Now Defends Her Firing, Copley News Service, March 13, 2007; cf. OIG U.S. Attorneys Report, 282–83 (discussing Moschella's favorable letter to Senator Feinstein regarding Lam, and noting that Lam did not hear from superiors at Justice about immigration statistics between the time of the Moschella letter and her firing).

43. Moreover, e-mails later disclosed reveal that Moschella's testimony was reviewed not only in Justice, but also by Deputy White House Counsel William Kelley. See Dan Eggen & Amy Goldstein, E-mails Reveal Tumult in Firings and Aftermath, Wash. Post, March 21, 2007, A1.

44. See OIG U.S. Attorneys Report, 223.

45. Id. at 224.

46. Id. at 225; see also Lipton & Steinhauer (discussing FBI's position).

47. See Westinghouse Elec. Corp. v. Republic of the Phil., 951 F. 2d 1414 (3d Cir. 1991).

48. See, for example, Michael L. Siegel, Corporate America Fights Back: The Battle over Waiver of the Attorney-Client Privilege, 49 B.C. L. Rev. 1 (2008).

49. See United States v. Stein, 541 F.3d 130 (2d Cir. 2008) (affirming dismissal of indictment because of inappropriate prosecutorial conduct involving pressure on accounting firm to limit advancement of defense costs to individual defendants that government viewed as uncooperative). See also Sarah H. Duggin, The McNulty Memorandum, the KPMG Decision, and Corporate Cooperation: Individual Rights and Legal Ethics, 21 Geo. J. Legal Ethics 341 (2008). For less critical views of Justice Department policy, arguing that privilege waiver can serve legitimate law enforcement purposes, see Samuel W. Buell, Criminal Procedure Within the Firm, 59 Stan. L. Rev. 1613 (2007); Daniel Richman, Decisions About Coercion: The Corporate Attorney-Client Privilege Waiver Problem, 57 DePaul L. Rev. 295 (2008). In an earlier piece, I had supported some limits on corporate advancement of defense costs to individual defendants. See Peter Margulies, Legal Hazard: Corporate Crime, Advancement of Executives' Defense Costs, and the Federal Courts, 7 U.C. Davis Bus. L.J. 55 (2006). While corporations should have remedies against executives who have harmed the interests of the corporation and its shareholders, I now recognize that government pressure to limit advancement of defense costs in individual cases constitutes overreaching.

50. See Attorney-Client Privilege Protection Act of 2007, S. 186, 110th Cong. (2007).

51. See United States Dep't of Justice, Principles of Federal Prosecution of Business Organizations, Aug. 2008, at 8–9, available at http://usdoj.gov/opa/documents/corp-charging-guidelines.pdf.

52. Norman W. Spaulding, Professional Independence in the Office of the Attorney General, 60 Stan. L. Rev. 1931, 1975–76 (2008).

53. See Walter Dellinger & H. Jefferson Powell, The Constitutionality of the Bank Bill: The Attorney General's First Constitutional Law Opinions, 44 Duke L.J. 110, 118–20 (1994).

54. See 39 U.S. Op. Atty. Gen. 484, 486–88 (1940).

55. See ELLIOT RICHARDSON, THE CREATIVE BALANCE: GOVERNMENT, POLITICS, AND THE INDIVIDUAL IN AMERICA'S THIRD CENTURY 26 (1976).

56. Id.

57. See CALABRESI & YOO, 7.

58. Id., 199.

59. See 28 C.F.R. sec. 42.1(a), Part 42, Subpart A ("It is the policy of the Department to seek to eliminate discrimination"). See also Curinga v. City of Clairton, 357 F.3d 305, 311 (3d Cir. 2004) (defining political affiliation).

60. See 5 U.S.C. sec. 2301(b)(2).

61. 416 U.S. 134 (1974).

62. See CALABRESI & YOO, 7.

63. Id., 207–8; see also Christopher S. Yoo, Steven G. Calabresi & Laurence D. Nee, The Unitary Executive During the Third Half-Century, 1889–1945, 89 Notre Dame L. Rev. 1, 22–23 (2004).

64. See SAVAGE, 296–300; see also Joseph D. Rich, The Attack on Professionalism in the Civil Rights Division, in Citizens' Commission on Civil Rights, in THE EROSION OF RIGHTS: DECLINING CIVIL RIGHTS ENFORCEMENT UNDER THE BUSH ADMINISTRATION 16 (William L. Taylor et al. eds. 2007).

65. See OIG Honors Program Report.

66. See Office of the Inspector General, United States Dep't of Justice, An Investigation of Allegations of Politicized Hiring and Other Improper Personnel Actions in the Civil Rights Division, Jan. 13, 2009 (hereinafter OIG Civil Rights Report), available at http://www.usdoj.gov/oig/special/s0901/final.pdf.

67. Id., 15.

68. Id., 17.

69. Id., 23.

70. Id., 24.

71. Id.

72. Id., 35–39.

73. See Rich, 14.

74. Id.

75. Id., 15; OIG Civil Rights Report, 37–38.

76. Rich, 13. The Bush-Cheney era was not a total loss for advocates of civil rights. Congress passed landmark legislation, the ADA Amendments Act of 2008, overriding Supreme Court decisions that had defined narrowly who was protected by the Americans with Disabilities Act. The new legislation, championed by both liberals and conservatives like Wisconsin's Jim Sensenbrenner, ensured that people who used devices such as eyeglasses that mitigated the impact of their disability would receive protection under federal law. See 42 U.S.C. sec. 12102(4)(E) (2008); see also Robert Pear, Congress Passes a Civil Rights Bill, Adding Protections for Disabled, N.Y. Times, Sept. 18, 2008, A21.

77. Goodling's job titles were research analyst, senior analyst, and deputy director for research and strategic planning. On her resume, she described her work as involving "a broad range of political research." See An Investigation of Allegations of Politicized Hiring by Monica Goodling and Other Staff in the Office of the Attorney General, Office of the Inspector General, United States Dep't of Justice, July 28, 2008 (hereinafter OIG Monica Goodling Report), at 5, available at http://www.usdoj.gov/oig/special/s0807/final.pdf.

78. Id.

79. Id. It is not clear if Goodling actually tried any cases—presumably her training period extended for a couple of months into her new assignment, and starting in February she would have had to wrap up any pending cases to move to her new job. That would have left a couple of months at best for active casework.

80. Id. at 5–6. This included political positions, career positions, waiver requests, and hiring of IJs. See Benedetto.

81. See OIG Monica Goodling Report, 18.

82. Id., 38.

83. Id., 18.

84. Id., 19. Although other DOJ officials complained about Goodling to Kyle Sampson, Attorney General Gonzales's chief of staff, she was never disciplined. Id.

85. Id., 21.

86. Id., 45–47.

87. Id., 25. The candidate was eventually hired. Id. at 30.

88. Id., 26–27.

89. Id., 32–34.

90. See Charlie Savage, White House Pushed List of "Loyalists" for Hire, N.Y. Times, July 31, 2008, A17.

91. See Charlie Savage, Vetted Judges More Likely to Reject Asylum Bids, N.Y. Times, Aug. 24, 2008, A17.

92. Juliet Eilperin & Carol D. Leonnig, Administration Moves to Protect Key Appointees: Political Positions Shifted to Career Civil Service Jobs, Wash. Post, Nov. 13, 2008, A1.

CHAPTER 5

1. See Peter Margulies, Lawyers' Independence and Collective Illegality in Government and Corporate Misconduct, Terrorism, and Organized Crime, 58 Rutgers L. Rev. 939 (2006).

2. See Robert M. Chesney, Beyond Conspiracy? Anticipatory Prosecution and the Challenge of Unaffiliated Terrorism, 80 S. Cal. L. Rev. 425 (2007).

3. 336 F. Supp. 2d 676 (E.D. Mich. 2004).

4. Cf. Lonnie T. Brown Jr., "May It Please the Camera, . . . I Mean the Court"—An Intrajudicial Solution to an Extrajudicial Problem, 39 Ga. L. Rev. 83 (2004) (arguing for more vigorous judicial oversight regarding extrajudicial remarks by prosecutors and defense attorneys).

5. See Danny Hakim & Eric Lichtblau, After Conviction, the Undoing of a US Terror Prosecution, N.Y. Times, Oct. 7, 2004, A1.

6. United States v. Koubriti, 305 F. Supp. 2d 723 (E.D. Mich. 2003).

7. See United States v. Koubriti, 336 F. Supp. 2d 676 (E.D. Mich. 2004).

8. Cf. LICHTBLAU, ix–xv (discussing collapse of Koubriti case); Bennett L Gershman, How Juries Get It Wrong—Anatomy of the Detroit Terror Case, 44 Washburn L.J. 327, 339–42 (2005) (analyzing prosecutor's conduct). The prosecutor was acquitted of all charges in 2008. See Paul Egan, Free Press Reporter Doesn't Have to Reveal Source, Federal Judge Rules, Detroit News, April 22, 2009.

9. On keeping prosecutors in check, see Bruce A. Green & Fred C. Zacharias, Regulating Federal Prosecutors' Ethics, 55 Vand. L. Rev. 381, 439–41 (2002).

10. See Abraham S. Goldstein, Conspiracy to Defraud the United States, 68 Yale L.J. 405, 409 (1959).

11. See Neal Kumar Katyal, Conspiracy Theory, 112 Yale L.J. 1307 (2003).

12. See Eric S. Janus, The Preventive State, Terrorists, and Sexual Predators: Countering the Threat of a New Outsider Jurisprudence, 40 Crim. L. Bull. 576, 582–97 (2004).

13. See City of Chicago v. Morales, 527 U.S. 41 (1999) (striking down antigang loitering law); Papachristou v. City of Jacksonville, 405 U.S. 156 (1972); cf. David Cole, Hanging with the Wrong Crowd: Of Gangs, Terrorism, and the Right of Association, 1999 Sup. Ct. Rev. 203, 219–21 (arguing that Morales case offers insufficient protection for freedom of association).

14. See Goldstein, at 410.

15. See Phillip E. Johnson, The Unnecessary Crime of Conspiracy, 61 Calif. L. Rev. 1137, 1155 (1973).

16. Krulewitch v. United States, 336 U.S. 440, 447 (1949) (Jackson, J., concurring).

17. Id. at 447–48.

18. See Johnson, at 1155.

19. Krulewitch v. United States, 336 U.S. 440, 454 (1949) (Jackson, J., concurring) ("Jurors . . . are ready to believe that birds of a feather are flocked together").

20. 177 P.2d 315, 316–17 (Cal. Ct. App. 1st Dist. 1947).

21. The court also indicated that the defendant could be held liable for abortions committed *before* she joined the conspiracy, but a later decision disavowed this even more blatant example of unfairness. See People v. Weiss, 327 P.2d 527, 566 (Cal. 1958); see also Johnson, at 1147 (discussing cases).

22. 341 U.S. 494, 497 (1950).

23. See Fisher, 631 (discussing perception of J. Edgar Hoover, long-time Director of the FBI, of links between the Communist Party USA and the civil rights movement).

24. See Krulewitch v. United States, 336 U.S. 440, 445 (1949), citing BENJAMIN CARDOZO, THE NATURE OF THE JUDICIAL PROCESS 51 (1921); cf. Lawrence M. Solan, Statutory Inflation and Institutional Choice, 44 Wm. & Mary L. Rev. 2209, 2236–60 (2003) (describing factors that broaden the scope of criminal liability under federal statutes); William J. Stuntz, The Pathological Politics of Criminal Law, 100 Mich. L. Rev. 505 (2001) (discussing the convergence of interests between legislators and prosecutors that broadens the scope of criminal law).

25. See Goldstein, 406.

26. See Gretchen B. Chapman & Eric J. Johnson, Incorporating the Irrelevant: Anchors in Judgments of Belief and Value, in HEURISTICS AND BIASES: THE PSYCHOLOGY OF INTUITIVE JUDGMENT 120, 120–25 (Thomas Gilovich, Dale Griffin & Daniel Kahneman eds. 2002).

27. Cf. id., 134 (discussing hindsight bias).

28. See In re Winship, 397 U.S. 358, 362–64 (1970) (analyzing basis for reasonable doubt standard).

29. See Fed. R. Evid. 801(d)(2)(E); Bourjaily v. United States, 483 U.S. 171 (1987).

30. United States v. Bruno, 105 F.2d 921, 922 (2d Cir. 1939) (holding that smugglers, wholesalers, and retailers participated in single conspiracy to distribute illegal narcotics in New York, Texas, and Louisiana), reversed on other grounds, 308 U.S. 287 (1939).

31. See Krulewitch v. United States, 336 U.S. 440, 453 (1949).

32. See Goldstein, 411.

33. Krulewitch v. United States, 336 U.S. 440, 446 (1949), citing Conference of Senior Circuit Judges, Annual Report of the Attorney General for 1925, at 5–6.

34. See ADRIAN VERMEULE, JUDGING UNDER UNCERTAINTY: AN INSTITUTIONAL THEORY OF LEGAL INTERPRETATION 38 (2006) (discussing the impact of "salient" facts that are graphic or fit readily into narrative); Timur Kuran & Cass R. Sunstein, Controlling Availability Cascades, in BEHAVIORAL LAW AND ECONOMICS 374 (Cass R. Sunstein ed., 2000) (explaining availability phenomenon); Paul Slovic et al., The Affect Heuristic, in HEURISTICS AND BIASES: THE PSYCHOLOGY OF INTUITIVE JUDGMENT 397, 397–400 (Thomas Gilovich, Dale Griffin & Daniel Kahneman eds. 2002) (discussing interaction between cognition, memory, and emotionally vivid information).

35. See Cass R. Sunstein, Probability Neglect: Emotions, Worst Cases, and Law, 112 Yale L.J. 61, 62 (2002).

36. Because prosecutors must care about both false positives *and* false negatives, their job is extraordinarily difficult. In contrast, terrorists do not care about false positives. They construct elaborate justifications to explain that all victims are complicit.

37. See Lilly v. United States, 527 U.S. 116, 141 (1999) (Breyer, J., concurring); cf. Paul F. Kirgis, Meaning, Intention, and the Hearsay Rule, 43 Wm. & Mary L. Rev. 275, 321, n. 200 (2001).

38. See Edward de Grazia, The Haymarket Bomb, 18 Cardozo Stud. L. & Lit. 283, 315 (2006).

39. See United States v. Spock, 416 F.2d 165 (1st Cir. 1969).

40. See Ellen Yaroshefsky, Cooperation with Federal Prosecutors: Experiences of Truth Telling and Embellishment, 68 Fordham L. Rev. 917 (1999) (describing incentives for dishonesty among cooperators); Daniel C. Richman, Cooperating Clients, 56 Ohio St. L.J. 69 (1995) (discussing cooperation and legal ethics); cf. Ian Weinstein, Regulating the Market for Snitches, 47 Buffalo L. Rev. 563, 614 (1999) (discussing treatment of cooperators under federal sentencing guidelines); but see Peter Margulies, Legal Hazard: Corporate Crime, Advancement of Executives' Defense Costs, and the Federal Courts, 7 U.C. Davis Business L.J. 55, 107–9 (2006) (discussing how cooperation at corporate level can facilitate institutional reform); Michael A. Simons, Vicarious Snitching: Crime, Cooperation, and "Good Corporate Citizenship," 76 St. John's L. Rev. 979, 992–95 (2002) (same); Michael A. Simons, Retribution for Rats: Cooperation, Punishment, and Atonement, 56 Vand. L. Rev. 1, 33–42 (2003) (arguing that cooperation can be reflection of remorse and atonement, instead of merely utilitarian calculus).

41. The Bush administration found this out when it relied on informants with their own agendas to provide intelligence about WMD in Iraq.

42. See William Glaberson, Man Burned at White House Is Called Central to Terror Case, N.Y. Times, Nov. 17, 2004, B1. This evidence led to a conviction, which was overturned on appeal. See United States v. Al-Moayad, 545 F.3d 139, 159–64 (2d Cir. 2008).

43. See generally Daniel C. Richman, Prosecutors and Their Agents, Agents and Their Prosecutors, 103 Colum. L. Rev. 749, 799–801 (2003).

44. Cf. id., 803–4 (discussing barriers to prosecutors reconsidering strength of evidence, particularly in big cases).

45. See Alan Feuer, Tapes Capture Bold Claims of Bronx Man in Terror Plot, N.Y. Times, May 8, 2007, at B1.

46. Cf. DAVID COLE, ENEMY ALIENS: DOUBLE STANDARDS AND CONSTITUTIONAL FREEDOMS IN THE WAR ON TERRORISM (rev. ed. 2005); cf. RICHARD DELGADO, JUSTICE AT WAR: CIVIL LIBERTIES AND CIVIL RIGHTS IN A TIME OF CRISIS 160–61 (2003) (discussing relationships between minorities during crises); Adrien Katherine Wing, Civil Rights in the Post-9/11 World: Critical Race Praxis, Coalition Building, and the War on Terrorism, 63 La. L. Rev. 717, 747–48 (2003).

47. See Jeffrey Rosen, John Ashcroft's Permanent Campaign, Atlantic Monthly, April 2004; Toobin, 50.

48. For a more critical analysis of Kennedy's use of an informant in the investigation of corrupt labor boss Jimmy Hoffa, see Ralph S. Spritzer, *Hoffa v. U.S.: A Retrospective View*, 39 Ariz. St. L.J. 377, 381 (2007).

49. See EVAN THOMAS, ROBERT KENNEDY: HIS LIFE 252 (2000) (noting that Kennedy realized that FBI Director Hoover "grossly exaggerated the communist threat; indeed, the attorney general was always nudging the director to move his agents away from infiltrating the moribund American Communist Party to investigating the real threat, organized crime").

50. See Dan Eggen, Ashcroft's High Profile, Motives Raise White House Concerns, Wash. Post, June 17, 2002, A4.

51. See United States v. Koubriti, 305 F. Supp.2d 723 (E.D. Mich. 2003) (admonishing Ashcroft for inappropriate public comments).

52. See Mayer, 50.

53. See Eric Lichtblau & Josh Meyers, U.S. Will Seek Death for Sept. 11 Suspect, L.A. Times, March 29, 2002, A1.

54. On the third try, the government obtained convictions of most of the defendants in the Miami case in May 2009. See Damien Cave & Carmen Gentile, Five Convicted in Plot to Blow Up Sears Tower as Part of Islamic Jihad, N.Y. Times, May 13, 2009, A19.

55. See Eric Lichtblau, U.S. Spells Out Danger Posed by Plot Suspect, N.Y. Times, June 2, 2004, A1.

56. See Ray Rivera & Matthew Sweeney, Acquaintance of 2 Hijackers Is Acquitted, N.Y. Times, Nov. 18, 2006, B1.

57. See Joseph Kahn, Raids, Detentions, and Lists Lead Muslims to Cry Persecution, N.Y. Times, March 27, 2002, A11.

58. For a description of the case, see United States v. Khan, 309 F. Supp. 2d 789 (E.D. Va. 2004), affirmed in part and remanded in part, 461 F.3d 477 (4th Cir. 2006). Ali Al-Timimi, the scientist convicted of encouraging the young men, has argued that the government failed to disclose exculpatory evidence at his trial. See United States v. Al-Timimi, 2006 U.S. App. Lexis 32554 (4th Cir. 2006) (granting motion to remand to district court for further proceedings on appellant's claim). Al-Timimi's lawyer, Jonathan Turley of George Washington University, has argued that the government wiretapped Al-Timimi's communications without a warrant, as part of the Terrorist Surveillance Program. See Eric Lichtblau & James Risen, Panel to Call for N.S.A. Investigation Into Wiretapping of Muslim Scholar, N.Y. Times, Dec. 8, 2008, A22.

59. See Matthew Purdy, Our Towns; Puzzling Over Motives of the Men in the Lackawanna Qaeda Case, N.Y. Times, March 30, 2003, A21.

60. See April Hunt & Bob Mahlburg, Senate Rivals Exchange Charges on Jobs, Terror: Castor Tries to Link Martinez to Outsourcing as Both Cross the States, Orlando Sentinel, Oct. 30, 2004, B1.

61. See Washington Journal: Suspected Terrorist, White House guest?, St. Petersburg Times, March 2, 2003, 14A.

62. See 18 U.S.C. 2339B (barring material support to group designated as foreign terrorist organization by the secretary of state).

63. See Boim v. Holy Land Found for Relief and Development, 549 F.3d 685, 691 (2008); Humanitarian Law Project v. Reno, 205 F.3d 1130 (9th Cir. 2000); cert. den. sub nom Humanitarian Law Project v. Ashcroft, 532 U.S. 904 (2001).

64. 18 U.S.C. sec. 2339A.

65. See Padilla v. Hanft, 423 F.3d 386 (4th Cir. 2005).

66. See Padilla v. Hanft, 432 F.3d 582, 587 (4th Cir. 2005).

67. See Abby Goodnough & Scott Shane, Padilla Is Guilty on All Charges in Terror Trial, N.Y. Times, Aug. 17, 2007, A1 (citing Professor Michael Greenberger of the University of Maryland, who asserted that the verdict "demonstrates . . . that the United States is fully capable of prosecuting terrorism while affording defendants the full procedural protections of the Constitution"); cf. Kelly Anne Moore, Take Al Qaeda to Court, N.Y. Times, Aug. 21, 2007, A19 (arguing that verdict in Padilla case demonstrates that legal system can both safeguard rights and lead to confinement of terrorists). For a more balanced perspective, see Adam Liptak, A New Model of Terror Trial: Tools for Prosecution Seen in Padilla Case, N.Y. Times, Aug. 18, 2007, A1.

68. See Kirk Semple, Padilla Gets 17-Year Term for Role in Conspiracy, N.Y. Times, Jan. 23, 2008, at p. 14.

69. See Carol J. Williams, Terror Suspect Pleads Guilty: Australian David Hicks's Admission Caps a Day of Legal Wrangling at the Guantánamo Tribunal, L.A. Times, March 27, 2007, A1. For an excellent description of the strategy used by Hicks and his lawyers, including Marine Maj. Michael "Dan" Mori and veteran New York criminal defense lawyer Joshua Dratel, see Ellen Yaroshefsky, Zealous Lawyering Succeeds Against All Odds: Major Mori and the Legal Team for David Hicks at Guantánamo Bay, 13 Roger Williams U. L. Rev. 469 (2008).

70. See Michael Higgins, 21-month Sentence for Salah; Businessman Guilty of Lying in Hamas Case, Chi. Trib., July 12, 2007, C1 (noting the judge's statement that Salah had lied in a civil lawsuit and had been convicted of obstruction of justice as a result, and the judge's view that Salah had also lied about allegations of torture; providing disparate accounts of jurors' beliefs on the defendant's veracity; also reporting that the jury had acquitted Salah of the terrorism charge, for which testimony by Israeli agents was the government's chief evidence).

71. See Ellen C. Yaroshefsky, The Slow Erosion of the Adversary System: Article III Courts, FISA, CIPA, and Ethical Dilemmas, 5 Cardozo Pub. L. Pol'y & Ethics J. 203 (2006).

72. In addition, the legitimation of the shadow government continues at trial. The government has used the Classified Information Procedures Act (CIPA) to have information about sources and methods excluded from conspiracy trials. In some cases, the government has even acted where CIPA is not actually applicable and extended its reasoning to cases involving interviews with detainees who could provide exculpatory evidence in advance of trial. In these cases, at least one court has held that a defendant must rely on cold summaries and transcripts of detainees' interrogations, instead of having the opportunity to secure testimony with appropriate security safeguards, or at least to conduct a deposition. This use of CIPA and related measures, including the state secrets privilege, poses a substantial problem under the Sixth Amendment's fair trial guarantee.

73. United States v. Faris, 388 F.3d 452, 457 (4th Cir. 2004).

74. Since Justice Kennedy did not share his position, Stevens did not command a majority on this view.

75. Cf. Mark A. Drumbl, Enemy Combatants After *Hamdan v. Rumsfeld*: The Expressive Value of Prosecuting and Punishing Terrorists: Hamdan, the Geneva Conventions, and International Criminal Law, 75 Geo. Wash. L. 1165 (2007) (arguing that conspiracy prosecutions may serve valuable expressive purpose under the law of war, even though their pedigree is uncertain).

76. One can argue, however, that the detainees had notice, since Congress amended the federal criminal code shortly after September 11 to prohibit material support to a terrorist group or activity anywhere in the world. See 18 U.S.C. sec. 2339A, B (2009). Moreover, one can argue that Congress has some leeway under the define and punish clause, see U.S. Const., art I, sec. 8, cl. 10, to designate crimes as triable by military commissions. Cf. Curtis A. Bradley, Universal Jurisdiction and U.S. Law, 2001 U. Chi. Legal Forum 323, 335 ("Courts are likely to afford Congress substantial flexibility in making this determination, given that Congress is expressly given the power to 'define'" such offenses). In addition, international criminal law, which a military commission arguably applies, prohibits joint criminal conspiracies (JCEs). JCEs are largely indistinguishable from conspiracies. See Allison Marston Danner & Jenny S. Martinez, Guilty Associations: Joint Criminal Enterprise, Command Responsibility, and the Development of International Criminal Law, 93 Cal. L. Rev. 75, 82–85 (2005) (noting due process problems with JCE doctrine, which in some tribunals has been read to require little in the way of knowledge or intent by defendant).

77. See Scott Shane & Andrea Zarate, F.B.I. Killed Plot in Talking Stage, a Top Aide Says, N.Y. Times, June 24, 2006, A1; see Cave & Gentile (reporting on conviction of some of the defendants in May 2009). In the case that raised the most legitimate concern about violence, an informant whom the government had paid over one hundred thousand dollars entered into an agreement with a young man to plan to explode a bomb at New York's busy Herald Square subway stop, near Penn Station and the original Macy's. In this case, which resulted in a conviction, the views consistently expressed by the young man were profoundly disturbing, and the stakes were huge, given the volume of traffic through the station and the potential for massive casualties. Even in this case, however, the informant seemed to be the prime mover behind the scheme. The actual steps taken to further the plot were tentative, limited to inspecting some bags to determine if they could hold explosives.

78. Whatever the ultimate ambivalence expressed by some of the defendants, the participation of the Fort Dix defendants in a video involving illegal weapons possession justified law enforcement officials' opening of an investigation. In December 2008, a jury convicted the defendants of conspiracy. See Troy Graham, Fort Dix Five Guilty of Conspiracy, Phil. Inquirer, Dec. 23, 2008, A1.

79. See Three Hamas Terrorists Indicted for Racketeering, GlobalSecurity.org, Aug. 20, 2004, at http://www.globalsecurity.org/security/library/news/2004/08/sec-040820-usia01. htm.

80. For discussion of a related prosecution based largely on events that occurred in the early to mid 1990s that culminated in convictions after a mistrial, see Jason Trahan, 5 Ex-Leaders Guilty in Holy Land Trial: Jury's Finding That Charity Aided Hamas Is Victory for Government, Dallas Morning News, Nov. 25, 2008, 1A (discussing government's successful prosecution of leaders of Holy Land Foundation); cf. Boim v. Holy Land Foundation for Relief and Development, 549 F.3d 685 (7th Cir. 2008) (setting out test for causation and intent that will facilitate civil lawsuits against individuals and entities that allegedly aided terrorist groups). I served as counsel to *amicus curiae* 9/11 Families, who filed a brief supporting plaintiffs-appellants in *Boim*.

81. See Katyal, 1351 (discussing incentives in criminal organizations caused by need to monitor associates).

82. See Krulewitch v. United States, 336 U.S. 440, 453 (1949) (Jackson, J., concurring) ("The naïve assumption that prejudicial effects can be overcome by instructions to the jury, . . . all practicing lawyers know to be unmitigated fiction"). See Sheri Lynn Johnson, Black Innocence and the White Jury, in CRITICAL RACE THEORY: THE CUTTING EDGE 180, 181–85 (Richard Delgado ed., 1995); R. Richard Banks, Race-Based Suspect Selection and Colorblind Equal Protection Doctrine and Discourse, 48 UCLA L. Rev. 1075, 1081–89 (2001); cf. Anthony V. Alfieri, Community Prosecutors, 90 Calif. L. Rev. 1465, 1487–89 (2002) (discussing trends in scholarship on bias in criminal justice system).

83. See Johnson, 181–85.

84. See Wing (discussing images of Muslims in American culture and media); Muneer I. Ahmad, A Rage Shared by Law: Post–September 11 Racial Violence as Crimes of Passion, 92 Cal. L. Rev. 1259, 1278–80 (2004) (discussing dynamics of profiling American Muslims and South Asians); Raquel Aldana & Sylvia R. Lazos-Vargas, "Aliens" in Our Midst Post-9/11: Legislating Outsiderness Within the Borders (review essay), 38 U.C. Davis L. Rev. 1683, 1685 (2005) (discussing backlash against undocumented immigrants, occurring despite the fact that all the September 11 hijackers were legally admitted to the United States as students or visitors).

85. See Charles Lawrence, The Id, the Ego, and Equal Protection: Reckoning with Unconscious Racism, 39 Stan. L. Rev. 317 (1987).

86. See Sherman v. United States, 356 U.S. 369 (1958).

87. See United States v. Abdel Rahman, 189 F.3d 88, 114–17 (2d Cir. 1999).

88. See Daniel Benjamin, The 1,776-Foot-Tall Target, N.Y. Times, March 23, 2004, A23.

89. United States v. Abdel Rahman, 189 F.3d 88, 117 (2d Cir. 1999).

90. See 18 U.S.C. sec. 922(d)(5)(A).

91. See Carol Eisenberg, JFK Terror Plot: Credibility of Case in Question, Newsday, June 6, 2007, A5. Experience of other kinds may also be useful. For example, technological expertise may be significant, enhancing the ability to complete a plan.

92. Cf. Angela J. Davis, Prosecution and Race: The Power and Privilege of Discretion, 67 Fordham L. Rev. 13 (1998) (discussing impact of race on prosecutorial decision making).

93. See AM. BAR ASS'N, MODEL RULES OF PROF. CONDUCT, rule 3.8 (2004) (noting duties to refrain from prosecuting a charge except when supported by probable cause, disclose exculpatory evidence, and avoid prejudicial pretrial statements); see generally Bruce A. Green, Prosecutorial Ethics as Usual, 2003 U. Ill. L. Rev. 1573 (2003) (criticizing failure of revisions to ethics code to further specify duties of prosecutors).

94. See AM. BAR ASS'N, MODEL RULES OF PROF. CONDUCT, rule 3.8, cmt. 1 (2004).

95. Kotteakos v. United States, 328 U.S. 750, 770–74 (1946).

96. See Cole, Hanging with the Wrong Crowd; Fisher.

97. See Chesney, Beyond Conspiracy. This issue is also raised in another recent case involving attendance at a terrorist training camp. See United States v. Abdi, 498 F. Supp.2d 1048 (S.D. Oh. 2007) (holding that the government properly pleaded section 956 count).

98. As noted above, this uncertainty should not bar more limited material support liability based directly on the conduct involved in attending a training camp abroad. The problem here is one of imputation under section 956 of an agreement to engage in violence. Lack of fungibility should not bar a section 956 prosecution of an alleged

recruiter of terrorist trainees, since over time the sheer numbers of recruits will overcome contingencies in particular cases. Moreover, an effective recruiter's job consists of winnowing out individuals who may become ambivalent, exhausted, or disillusioned. Anyone who conspires to recruit two or more camp attendees would be culpable on this view of section 956.

99. The government should be able to use section 956 to reach certain kinds of helping conduct even when the location or timing of an attack is uncertain. For example, in United States v. Sattar, 314 F. Supp. 2d 279, 303–4 (S.D.N.Y. 2004), the court held that the government could charge the defendants, who included the noted criminal defense attorney Lynne Stewart, with violations of 956. The defendants allegedly conspired to secure an authorization from an imprisoned cleric, the "blind sheik" Abdel Rahman, for renewed violence. Here, the defendants sought to trigger violence by an established group of the cleric's supporters with a track record of terrorism. See Douglas Jehl, 70 Die in Attack at Egypt Temple, N.Y. Times, Nov. 18, 1997, at A1. This track record supplied a context to the agreement of the defendants sufficiently broad to support section 956 liability, even though the defendants did not agree on specific attacks. Indeed, the blind sheik's authorization was fungible in the way that attendance at a training camp is not, by potentially authorizing myriad violent acts. To the extent that the objection to use of section 956 entails concerns about proportion and context, judges can alleviate those concerns through sentencing. See Semple (noting that the judge sentenced Padilla to term of imprisonment far shorter than the life sentence sought by government).

100. See Humanitarian Law Project v. Reno, 205 F.3d 1130 (9th Cir. 2000), cert. den. sub nom Humanitarian Law Project v. Ashcroft, 532 U.S. 904 (2001).

101. In some cases, such decisions have sparked useful attempts in Congress to clarify the statutory language. See 18 U.S.C. 2339A, B (2004) (amending statute to provide that defendant accused of providing training must provide training in specific skill, while defendant accused of providing personnel to designated group must act under direction and control of that group, and not independently).

102. In an earlier version of this piece (Peter Margulies, Guantanamo By Other Means: Conspiracy Prosecutions and Law Enforcement Dilemmas After September 11, 43 Gonzaga L. Rev. 513, 556 [2007]), I also suggested changes in the entrapment defense that would be more focused on the government's role as the prime mover in the conspiracy. Although I am still concerned about the role of informants, I have concluded that changes in the entrapment defense are not constitutionally required since a conviction also requires proof that the defendant was predisposed to commit the crime. Further, charges in entrapment doctrine might create undue uncertainty for law enforcement, and permit guilty defendants to game the system.

103. 545 F.3d 139, 159–64 (2d Cir. 2008).

104. The defendants in the case had never denied their knowledge of Hamas's violent activities, and offered to stipulate to that effect before the jury. Id., 161.

105. Id., 163.

106. See Robert H. Jackson, The Federal Prosecutor, 24 Am. Judicature Soc'y 18, 19 (1940), available at http://www.roberthjackson.org/Man/theman2-7-6-1/ ("Only by extreme care can we protect the spirit as well as the letter of our civil liberties, and to do so is the responsibility of the federal prosecutor").

107. See 18 U.S.C. sec. 2339B. In some cases, this charge will not be available, if the prosecution lacks evidence to show that a designated terrorist group ran the camp where the defendant received training. Testimony from an expert or a cooperating witness who also attended the camp will be helpful in such prosecutions. In other cases, the defendant could be prosecuted for making false statements to immigration and customs officials about the purpose of his trip abroad. See Chesney, Beyond Conspiracy, 491. Some of the training camp cases will not be easy for prosecutors to make. Given the power of the state, however, prosecutors in a democracy should weigh charging decisions carefully, and decide based on the evidence.

CHAPTER 6

1. See DAVID IGLESIAS, IN JUSTICE 74 (2008).
2. Id., 95–96.
3. Id., 98; cf. OIG U.S. Attorneys Report, 179.
4. IGLESIAS, 92–95.
5. Id., 98; OIG U.S. Attorneys Report, 179.
6. IGLESIAS, 2–5.
7. See Gomillion v. Lightfoot, 364 U.S. 339, 341 (1960).
8. Some states continue to disenfranchise convicted felons, although the trend has been to repeal such laws.
9. IGLESIAS, 83–87.
10. See Bob Drogin, Rights Panel Finds Fla. Vote "Injustice," L.A. Times, June 5, 2001, A1.
11. 531 U.S. 98, 127 (2000).
12. See Bush v. Gore, 531 U.S. 98, 127 (2000) (Stevens, J., dissenting).
13. See Reynolds v. Sims, 377 U.S. 533 (1964).
14. Id., 588.
15. See Joyce Purnick, Stricter Voting Laws Cause Latest Partisan Divide, N.Y. Times, Sept. 26, 2006, A1.
16. Id.
17. 128 S. Ct. 1610 (2008).
18. Absentee ballot fraud is a real concern. Even Bush administration officials who have been overzealous in other areas raise legitimate points on this issue. See Hans A. von Spakovsky, Voting Greene, National Review Online, Sept. 15, 2008, available at http://article.nationalreview.com/?q=NjQzYjE4YTBkNjk5MWI1ZDMwZGRjZTkxNTE3ZDZiM jg= (detailing reports of absentee voter fraud in Greene and Perry Counties in Alabama).
19. IGLESIAS, 83.
20. The most common registration fraud involves filing applications for fictitious voters like Mickey Mouse. Some employees of the community organizing group ACORN filed such applications in 2008. However, few people show up at the polls seeking to vote under fraudulent applications. See Michael Falcone & Michael Moss, Group's Tally of New Registered Voters Was Vastly Overstated, N.Y. Times, Oct. 24, 2008, A1. ACORN supervisors often flagged these applications, which federal law requires them to submit to election authorities, and fired hundreds of workers. But conservative critics rightly noted that ACORN needed to exercise far greater diligence in selecting and supervising employees.

Subsequent revelations about ACORN employees who sought to aid amateur journalists posing as a prostitute and pimp indicated that ACORN had failed to make these reforms. See Scott Shane, Conservatives Draw Blood From ACORN, Favored Foe, N.Y. Times, Sept. 16, 2009, A13.

21. IGLESIAS, 85–88.

22. State Republican operatives had been frustrated that Iglesias had gotten what they viewed as inadequate results in the prosecution of a Democratic state official—the first trial resulted in a hung jury. Id., 81. In the second trial, the Democratic official, Robert Vigil, the state treasurer, was convicted on one of the twenty-four counts—but he received a sentence of thirty-seven months, the longest sentence given to an elected official in New Mexico history. Id. Republican officials, however, were concerned that Iglesias had "dropped the ball." Id.

23. See WHITNEY NORTH SEYMOUR JR., UNITED STATES ATTORNEY: AN INSIDE VIEW OF "JUSTICE" IN AMERICA DURING THE NIXON ADMINISTRATION 79 (1975).

24. See Whitehouse Criticizes Bush Administration's "Systematic Effort" to Conduct Government in Secret, States News Service, July 24, 2007.

25. SEYMOUR, 90.

26. See Sen. Judiciary Committee, Preserving Prosecutorial Independence.

27. OIG U.S. Attorney Report, 17.

28. The account in this and the following paragraph is based on OIG U.S. Attorneys Report, 150–57.

29. The alleged source of the charge—a subordinate of Iglesias—denied making such a charge at any time. Occasionally, as a naval reserve officer, Iglesias was away from his office, but such absences would not justify the "absentee landlord" label.

30. Id., 175–76.

31. See IGLESIAS, 71–72. The Justice Department inspector general found that Graves's firing resulted from pressure brought on Main Justice and the White House by the senior staff of Missouri Republican senator Christopher Bond. See OIG U.S. Attorneys Report, 112–13. This pressure stemmed from Graves's reluctance to mediate a political dispute between Bond's office and Graves's brother, a U.S. congressman from Missouri. Id.

32. IGLESIAS, 74.

33. Id. Schlozman had a record of indifference regarding the effects of restrictive voting legislation. For example, he had as chief of the Voting Rights Division overruled staff lawyers on both Georgia's restrictive voter ID law (which required a photo ID and declined other proof of identity, including birth certificates and Social Security cards—id. at 73), and on Texas's reapportionment plan, masterminded by Tom DeLay, then House majority leader—a portion of which was later invalidated by the U.S. Supreme Court. Id. Schlozman later gave inaccurate information to the Senate Judiciary Committee about the ACORN prosecution, asserting that he had been directed to bring it when apparently it was his idea. See Eric Lichtblau, Grand Jury Said to Look at Dismissals of Attorneys, N.Y. Times, June 17, 2008, A12.

34. IGLESIAS, 133.

35. OIG U.S. Attorneys Report, 256. The Inspector General was unable to confirm that this episode prompted Sampson to place McKay on the list of federal prosecutors to be fired. Id. at 257. But the Inspector General did observe that when McKay met with White

House Counsel Harriet Miers about a possible federal judgeship, Miers first asked McKay why Washington State Republicans were so angry at him. Id. at 260–61. The Inspector General reported that the most likely reason for McKay's firing was his clash with Deputy Attorney General Paul McNulty about the Justice Department's adoption of an information-sharing program. Id. at 266.

36. See David Johnston & Eric Lipton, Ex-aide Disputes Gonzales Stand Over Dismissals, N.Y. Times, March 30, 2007, A1.

37. See Charlie Savage, Gonzales Gets Grilling, Vows to Stay: Senators Voice Anger, Express Doubts with AG, Boston Globe, April 20, 2007, A1.

38. See Jonathan D. Silver, Many Questions Surround Wecht Retrial, Set for May, Pittsburgh Post-Gazette, April 9, 2008. Federal prosecutors subsequently dropped all charges. See Paula Reed Ward, Wecht Charges Dropped; U.S. Attorney Blames Court Order That Suppressed Evidence; Forensic Pathologist Calls Buchanan "A Sore Loser," Pitt. Post-Gazette, June 3, 2009, A1.

39. See Sean Hamill, Pathologist Accused of Profiting from Office, N.Y. Times, Jan. 28, 2008, A12.

40. See United States v. Wecht, 541 F.3d 493 (3d Cir. 2008).

41. Id., 511.

42. Id., 512.

43. See Dawson Bell, Don't Bet on Fieger Fallout: Case Won't Faze Campaign Finance Law, Experts Say, Detroit Free Press, June 8, 2008, 1.

44. Id.

45. See Adam Nossiter, A New Twist in the Prosecution of a Former Governor of Alabama, N.Y. Times, Nov. 22, 2008, A11.

46. There are troubling aspects about Siegelman's conduct. Scrushy, who has also been acquitted of fraud charges in connection with his company, HealthSouth, potentially stood to benefit from his membership on the Alabama Certificate of Need Board, which determined whether and where new hospitals would be built in the state. It is also notable that while the government must show intent to influence a government official and intent to be so influenced, see 18 U.S.C. sec. 666, 18 U.S.C. sec. 1341, 1346, it need not show an express quid pro quo between the parties. In the case, Siegelman received one check from Scrushy for $250,000 *before* naming Scrushy to the board, and one check shortly thereafter. The circumstances, along with testimony from a Siegelman aide that Siegelman told him the checks were in exchange for a seat on the board, could allow a jury to find the intent required under the federal statutes. See United States v. Siegelman, 2008 U.S. Dist. Lexis 133 (M.D. Ala. Jan. 2, 2008), at 11–13.

47. See Ex-Ala. Governor Seeks Special Prosecutor, Wash. Post, Feb. 26, 2008, A2. The federal prosecutor in the case heatedly denied Bailey's claim that the prosecution knew of Bailey's notes, saying that the witness "did not share that with us." Id.

48. See United States v. Siegelman, 561 F.3d 1215 (11th Cir. 2009).

49. See John Schwartz, Ex-Governor of Alabama Loses Again in Court, N.Y. Times, May 16, 2009, A9.

50. See United States v. Thompson, 484 F.3d 877, 879 (7th Cir. 2007).

51. Id.

52. This event is rare—typically a federal court will merely order a new trial, not free a defendant who has been convicted.

53. Id., 880.

54. Id., 882.

55. Scott Horton, Vote Machine: How Republicans Hacked the Justice Department, Harper's Mag., March 2008, at 37, 43.

56. During the tenure of Attorney General Mukasey, the Justice Department prosecuted one high-profile Republican politician, Senator Ted Stevens of Alaska, for allegedly accepting and failing to disclose gifts from a contractor involving home renovations. Unfortunately, this prosecution turned out to be a disaster, since prosecutors did not share evidence with the defense, as the Sixth Amendment's fair trial guarantee requires. After obtaining a conviction, prosecutors had to move to have the conviction set aside because of these deficiencies in the case, even though some of Stevens's conduct was arguably illegal and unethical. See Neil A. Lewis, Dismissal for Stevens, But Question on "Innocent," N.Y. Times, April 12, 2009; Charlie Savage, Elite Unit's Problems Pose Test for Attorney General, N.Y. Times, May 8, 2009, A20.

CHAPTER 7

1. See Iraq and Afghan Defense Contract Fraud, Senate Appropriations Committee, Fed. News Service, July 23, 2008 (statement of Senator Dorgan); cf. Electrical Systems in Iraq, House Oversight, and Government Reform Committee, CQ Cong. Testimony, July 30, 2008 (testimony of Jeffrey P. Parsons, executive director, U.S. Army Materiel Command) (explaining difficulty of maintaining showers, and noting that KBR inspection of quarters where fatality occurred had failed to discover grounding problem).

2. See Lichter v. United States, 334 U.S. 742 (1948).

3. See JEREMY SCAHILL, BLACKWATER: THE RISE OF THE WORLD'S MOST POWERFUL MERCENARY ARMY (2007); James Risen, Blackwater Chief at Nexus of Military and Business, N.Y. Times, Oct. 8, 2007, A6.

4. In December 2008, the Justice Department unsealed indictments against the Blackwater guards involved in the shooting of seventeen Iraqis. See Ginger Thompson & James Risen, Plea by Blackwater Guard Helps U.S. Indict 5 Others, N.Y. Times, Dec. 9, 2008, A12.

5. See Special Inspector General for Iraq, Agencies Need Improved Financial Data Reporting for Private Security Contractors, Oct. 30, 2008.

6. Id. at iii.

7. Democrats restored funding for the special inspector general after the 2006 elections. See James Glanz, David Johnston & Thom Shanker, Dems to Resurrect Agency That Exposes Corruption in Iraq: New Bills Aim To Void Termination Date Of An Office That Embarrassed the White House, Hous. Chron., Nov. 12, 2006, A6. Contractors elsewhere who have provided weapons and ammunition have also performed poorly, but they experienced little accountability. For example, a little known company with a headquarters at an unmarked office on Miami Beach and a vice president whose primary training was as a masseur provided hundreds of millions of dollars of ammunition to Afghanistan's security forces. See C. J. Shivers, Supplier Under Scrutiny for Aging Arms to Afghans, N.Y. Times, March 27, 2008, A1; cf. Casualties of a Scandal, St. Petersburg Times, Feb. 23, 2008, 12A. American and NATO forces had already determined that the ammunition, which came from aging Communist bloc stockpiles, was unreliable. Ammunition actually

delivered to Afghanistan was found wanting by army officers. Moreover, the company worked with others accused of international arms trafficking. Nevertheless, the military has delayed investigating the company and has permitted shipments of faulty ammunition to continue.

8. See Casualties of a Scandal.

9. See Office of the Special Inspector General for Iraq Reconstruction, Falluja Waste Water Treatment System, Falluja, Iraq, Oct. 27, 2008 (summarizing findings).

10. See RAJIV CHANDRASEKARAN, IMPERIAL LIFE IN THE EMERALD CITY: INSIDE IRAQ'S GREEN ZONE 103 (2006).

11. Id.

12. Id. at 106.

13. 31 U.S.C. 3729 et seq.

14. See United States ex rel. DRC, Inc. v. Custer Battles, LLC, 444 F. Supp. 2d 678 (E.D. Va. 2006).

15. See United States ex rel. McBride v. Halliburton Co., U.S. Dist. Lexis 48112 (D.D.C. 2007).

16. See Senate Democratic Policy Committee Holds a Forum on Iraq, April 28, 2008, CQ Transcriptions.

17. Cf. United States ex rel. David L. Wilson v. Kellog Brown & Root, Inc., 525 F.3d 370 (4th Cir. 2008) (holding that lawsuit by former employees of contractor alleging deficiencies in contractor performance did not state claim under federal False Claims Act).

18. See James Risen, Limbo for U.S. Women Reporting Iraq Assaults, N.Y. Times, Feb. 13, 2008, A1.

19. For a critical analysis of the Republican campaign to discredit trial lawyers, see CARL T. BOGUS, WHY LAWSUITS ARE GOOD FOR AMERICA (2001).

20. See Eric Lichtblau & Myron Levin, In Reversal, U.S. to Seek Tobacco Suit Settlement, L.A. Times, June 20, 2001, A1.

21. See David E. Rosenbaum, Divided Senate Begins Debate on Tobacco Legislation, N.Y. Times, May 19, 1998, A17 (quoting Ashcroft as asserting that bill proposing tax on cigarettes "is nothing more than an excuse to raise taxes and expand Government").

22. Id.

23. See Neil A. Lewis, S.E.C. Chief Rejects Calls for His Resignation, N.Y. Times, July 15, 2002, A10 (noting complaints of congressional critics, including Senators Joseph Lieberman, Democrat of Connecticut, and John McCain, Republican of Arizona).

24. See Stephen Labaton, S.E.C.'s Leader Evolves Slowly in a Climate Enron Altered, N.Y. Times, May 3, 2002, C1.

25. See Interim Report of the Committee on Capital Markets Regulation, Nov. 30, 2006 (hereinafter Interim Report), available at http://www.capmktsreg.org/pdfs/11.30Committee_Interim_ReportREV2.pdf. Paulson commissioned a Treasury Department report that endorsed many of the task force's regulations, including its recommendation that the SEC abandon the clear guidance established by what the Treasury Report called "outdated" prescriptive rules, in favor of a more amorphous discretionary regime. See Dep't of the Treasury, Blueprint for a Modernized Regulatory Structure, March 2008, at 111, available at http://ustreas.gov/press/releases/reports/Blueprint.pdf.

26. See John C. Coffee Jr., Law and the Market: The Impact of Enforcement, 156 U. Pa. L. Rev. 229 (2007).

27. See Interim Report, 60.

28. Id., 63.

29. Id., 65.

30. See Eric Dash & Julie Creswell, Citigroup Pays for a Rush to Risk, N.Y. Times, Nov. 23, 2008, A1.

31. See Stephen Labaton, Accounting Plan Would Allow Use of Foreign Rules, N.Y. Times, July 5, 2008, A1.

32. Id.

33. See H. David Kotz, Inspector General, SEC, Re-investigation of Claims by Gary Aguirre of Preferential Treatment and Improper Termination, Sept. 30, 2008 (hereinafter Improper Termination Report), available at http://finance.senate.gov/press/Gpress/2008/prg100708.pdf.

34. Id., 46–54.

35. Id., 69.

36. Id., 79–87; see also 17 CFR sec. 200.735-3(b)(7)(i) (setting out policy).

37. See Improper Termination Report, 96.

38. Id., 139.

39. Id., 151. In an unusual maneuver, the SEC asked an administrative judge to respond to the Inspector General's recommendation that a number of Aguirre's superiors be referred for possible discipline. The administrative judge, acting outside her usual jurisdiction, produced a report clearing virtually all the officials. The Inspector General and a number of senators criticized both the substance and process of the administrative judge's report. See Walt Bogdanich, S.E.C. Judge Finds Agency Didn't Mishandle Hedge Fund Inquiry, N.Y. Times, Nov. 11, 2008, B3.

40. See Raymond H. Brescia, Capital in Chaos: The Subprime Mortgage Crisis and the Social Capital Response, 56 Cleve. St. L. Rev. 271, 292–93 (2008).

41. See Rep. Henry A. Waxman Holds a Hearing on the Role of Federal Regulators, CQ Transcriptions, Oct. 23, 2008; Possible Responses to Rising Mortgage Foreclosures, House Financial Servs. Committee, Fed. News Service, April 17, 2007 (testimony of Sheila Bair, chair, FDIC) (hereinafter Waxman Hearing).

42. See E. Scott Reckard, 6 Firms Act to Help Avert Foreclosures, L.A. Times, Feb. 12, 2008, C4 (noting that some borrowers were moving to refinance subprime mortgages for customers who qualified for a fixed-rate loan).

43. Brescia, 286; cf. Richard D. Marsico, Subprime Lending, Predatory Lending, and the Community Reinvestment Act Obligations of Banks, 46 N.Y.L. Sch. L. Rev. 735, 742 (2002–3) (defining predatory lending).

44. Brescia, 295.

45. See Stephen Labaton, Agency's '04 Rule Let Banks Pile Up New Debt, and Risk: Plans to Increase S.E.C. Scrutiny of Firms Faltered, N.Y. Times, Oct. 3, 2008, A1.

46. Id., A23.

47. Id.

48. Id.

49. See Office of Inspector General, SEC, SEC's Oversight of Bear Stearns and Related Entities: The Consolidated Supervised Entity Program, Sept. 25, 2008, at 17–18 (noting that SEC staff was aware of Bear Stearns's dangerous reliance on mortgage-backed securities, but did nothing to address problem).

50. Brescia, 298; cf. Waxman Hearing (Bair testimony).

51. Id.

52. See Patricia Sullivan, Fed Governor Edward M. Gramlich, Wash. Post, Sept. 6, 2007 (noting Gramlich's warnings about lending practices); Waxman Hearing (testimony of Alan Greenspan) (acknowledging Gramlich's warnings as early as 2000).

53. See Marsico.

54. See Waxman Hearing (Greenspan testimony).

55. See Labaton, Agency's '04 Rule, A23.

56. Id.

57. See Subprime and Predatory Mortgage Lending: New Regulatory Guidance, Hearing of the Financial Institutions and Consumer Credit Subcommittee of the House Financial Servs. Committee, Fed. News Service, March 27, 2007 (testimony of Sheila Bair, chair, FDIC) (hereinafter Bair Testimony) (noting that regulation by Federal Reserve would be more effective than new legislation).

58. See John Cassidy, Anatomy of a Meltdown: Ben Bernanke and the Financial Crisis, New Yorker, Dec. 1, 2008, at 48, 55.

59. See Bair Testimony.

60. See Maura Reynolds & Jonathan Peterson, No Silver Bullet for Borrowers: The Bush Loan Plan Helps Only a Subset of Struggling Homeowners, L.A. Times, Dec. 7, 2007, A1.

61. See Hearing of the Senate Finance Committee, TARP Oversight: A Six-Month Update, Fed. News Service, March 31, 2009.

62. See Bell Atlantic Co. v. Twombly, 550 U.S. 544 (2007).

63. 551 U.S. 308 (2007).

64. See Stoneridge Investment Partners, LLC v. Scientific-Atlanta, Inc., 128 S. Ct. 761 (2008).

65. See Robert A. Prentice, Stoneridge, Securities Fraud Litigation, and the Supreme Court, 45 Am. Bus. L.J. 611, 623–25 (2008).

66. Cf. JOHN C. COFFEE, GATEKEEPERS: THE PROFESSIONS AND CORPORATE GOVERNANCE (2006) (discussing importance of lawyers and accountants in preventing securities fraud, and diminishing legal incentives for professionals' performance of this role).

67. 549 U.S. 497 (2007).

68. Id., 504.

69. Id., 506–07.

70. Id., 516–20.

71. Id., 523–25.

72. Id., 534.

73. Id.

74. See Riegel v. Medtronic, 128 S. Ct. 999 (2008). In a later decision, the Court voted 5–4 to cut back on preemption doctrine, upholding a jury verdict against a drug manufacturer for faulty labeling leading to medical treatment that caused the amputation of the right forearm of the plaintiff, a professional musician. See Wyeth v. Levine, 129 S. Ct. 1187 (2009). In his opinion for the Court, Justice Stevens wrote that the drug manufacturer could have complied with both state law and federal labeling requirements.

75. See Gardiner Harris, F.D.A. Scientists Accuse Agency Officials of Misconduct, N.Y. Times, Nov. 18, 2008, A15.

76. See Juliet Eilperin, Mines to Get Freer Hand to Dump Water: New Rule Eases Water Protections, Wash. Post, Oct. 18, 2008, A6.

77. See Inspector General, Dep't of the Interior, OIG Investigations of MMS Employees, Sep. 9, 2008, available at http://www.doioig.gov/upload/RIK%20REDACTED%20 FINAL4_082008%20with%20transmittal%209_10%20date.pdf.

78. Id. at 2.

79. See Inspector General, Dep't of the Interior, Investigative Report: MMS Oil Marketing Group—Lakewood, Aug. 19, 2008, 5.

80. Id., 7–8, 20.

AFTERWORD

1. 128 S. Ct. 2229 (2008).

2. See Alex Berenson & Diana B. Henriques, S.E.C. Issues Mea Culpa on Madoff, N.Y. Times, Dec. 17, 2008, B1.

3. See Stephen Labaton, S.E.C. Image Suffers in a String of Setbacks, N.Y. Times, Dec. 16, 2008, B6.

4. See *Boumediene*, 128 S. Ct. at 2259.

5. Id. at 2246.

6. Id. at 2257–58.

7. Id. at 2253.

8. Id. at 2269–70.

9. In one case, a federal district judge found that the government could support its claim of enemy combatant status against one individual in a group of five detainees. See Boumediene v. Bush, 579 F. Supp. 2d 191 (D.D.C. 2008). In another case, the same judge ruled that the government had demonstrated that the detainee was an enemy combatant by virtue of his stay at a Taliban and Al Qaeda safe house, receipt of military training at a terrorist camp, and direct support of Taliban fighters. See Al Alwi v. Bush, 593 F. Supp. 2d 24 (D.D.C. 2008).

10. See Bob Woodward, Detainee Tortured, Says U.S. Official, Wash. Post, Jan. 14, 2009, A1.

11. See Richard A. Serrano, In Court, Two 20th Hijackers Stand Up, L.A. Times, April 3, 2006, A1.

12. See John Schwartz, Path to Justice, But Bumpy, for Terrorists, N.Y. Times, May 2, 2009, A9.

13. See Hearing of the Administrative Oversight and the Courts Subcommittee of the Senate Judiciary Committee Chaired by Sen. Sheldon Whitehouse (D-RI), Fed. News Service, May 13, 2009.

14. Id. (discussing the roles of both Bellinger and Secretary Rice).

15. See Mayer, 316–18.

16. See Senate Armed Services Full Report, 84 (discussing Bowman's role).

17. See Eric Lichtblau, Nominee Wants Some Detainees Tried in the U.S., N.Y. Times, Jan. 16, 2009, A1.

18. Another indication of the new administration's change of course was Obama's choice for Assistant Attorney General heading the Justice Department's Office of Legal Counsel, Professor Dawn Johnsen of Indiana University. A veteran of the Clinton administration,

Johnsen had sternly criticized the OLC's opinions authorizing the detours that formed the Bush administration's stock-in-trade. See Dawn E. Johnsen, Faithfully Executing the Laws: Internal Constraints on Executive Power, 54 UCLA L. Rev. 1559 (2007). With Johnsen at OLC, it seemed likely that adherence to established processes and practices would again become the rule, and that the officials would recognize the virtues of constraint. Unfortunately, an unfair campaign depicting Johnsen as a "radical" delayed her confirmation, which was pending as of August 2009. See Editorial, The Confirmation Game: It Remains, as Tony Lake Once Said, 'Nasty and Brutish Without Being Short,' Wash. Post., Aug. 30, 2009, A22.

19. The later also allow hearsay to prove the command responsibility of high-ranking officials for acts of genocide committed by subordinates. See Drumbl, 1191.

20. See Sheryl Gay Stolberg, Obama Would Move Some Terror Detainees to U.S., N.Y. Times, May 22, 2009, A1.

21. See WITTES, 74–79.

22. See Hamlily v. Obama, 2009 U.S. Dist. Lexis 43249 (D.D.C. May 12, 2009), at 25–32, 35–36 (holding that substantial assistance to Al Qaeda or Taliban is evidence that detainee is "part" of one or both of these organizations, and finding that the Geneva Conventions support this result); cf. Bradley & Goldsmith, 2109–15 (discussing interaction of law of war and Congress's post–September 11 Authorization for the Use of Military Force); Ryan Goodman, The Detention of Civilians in Armed Conflict, 103 Am. J. Int'l L. 48, 53–55 (2009) (discussing authority under law of war for detention of civilians indirectly assisting combatant groups).

23. As of August 2009, the Justice Department had not yet released a report from its Office of Professional Responsibility (OPR) on the drafting of the torture memos. Reports indicated that the OPR report would not recommend prosecution of any of the lawyers, but would refer issues surrounding the lawyers' conduct to state bar authorities. See David Johnston & Scott Shane, Torture Memos: Inquiry Suggests No Prosecutions, N.Y. Times, May 6, 2009, A1.

24. See 28 U.S.C. sec. 2241(e)(2) ("No court . . . shall have jurisdiction to hear or consider any . . . action against the United States or its agents relating to . . . treatment . . . of an alien who is or was detained by the United States"). See generally Daniel L. Pines, Are Even Torturers Immune from Suit? How Attorney General Opinions Shield Government Employees from Civil Litigation and Criminal Prosecution, 43 Wake Forest L. Rev. 93 (2008); Benjamin G. Davis, Refluat Stercus: A Citizen's View of Criminal Prosecution in U.S. Domestic Courts of High-Level U.S. Civilian Authority and Military Generals for Torture and Cruel, Inhuman, or Degrading Treatment, 23 St. John's J.L. Comm. 503 (2008).

25. For example, a prosecutor could argue that the OLC opinions were so outrageous that official reliance on them was not reasonable. In addition, the MCA provision may be vulnerable as violating the separation of powers, since decisions about whether to prosecute or pardon individuals are typically the province of the executive, not the Congress.

26. See Vicki Divoll, Congress's Torture Bubble, N.Y. Times, May 13, 2009, A31 (arguing for expanded notification to Congress).

27. 542 U.S. 466 (2004) (holding that statutory writ of habeas corpus extended to Guantánamo).

28. See Daryl J. Levinson & Richard H. Pildes, Separation of Parties, Not Powers, 119 Harv. L. Rev. 2311, 2354 (2006).

29. See Jenny S. Martinez, Process and Substance in the "War on Terror," 108 Colum. L. Rev. 1013 (2008).

30. See United States v. Al-Moayad, 545 F.3d 139 (2d Cir. 2008).

31. See United States v. Odeh, 552 F.3d 177 (2d Cir. 2008) (upholding modified Miranda warning in case of defendant convicted of role in 1998 bombing of U.S. embassies in Kenya and Tanzania).

32. See United States v. Odeh, 548 F.3d 276 (2d Cir. 2008).

33. Id. at 284–86.

34. See generally Robert M. Chesney & Jack L. Goldsmith, Terrorism and the Convergence of Criminal and Military Detention Models, 60 Stan. L. Rev. 1079 (2008) (arguing that criminal adjudication of terrorism cases is becoming more flexible, while other forums such as military commissions are providing more procedural safeguards to defendants, leading to common ground); Zabel & Benjamin (arguing that federal courts fashioning flexible rules should be first resort for prosecution of terrorism cases). Some have argued that to ensure flexibility Congress should establish a National Security Court. See Kevin E. Lunday & Harvey Rishikof, Due Process is a Strategic Choice: Legitimacy and the Establishment of an Article III National Security Court, 39 Cal. W. Int'l L.J. 87 (2008); Glenn M. Sulmasy, The Legal Landscape After Hamdan: The Creation of Homeland Security Courts, 13 New Eng. J. Int'l and Comp. L. 1 (2006). Unfortunately, a National Security Court could institutionalize shortcuts, while military commissions and detention under the laws of war have the virtue of being temporary measures that would more readily fade into disuse if the need diminishes. For a useful debate, see Amos N. Guiora & John T. Parry, Debate, Light at the End of the Pipeline? Choosing a Forum for Suspected Terrorists, 156 U. Pa. L. Rev. Pennumbra 356 (2008), available at http://www.pennumbra.com/debates/pdfs/terrorcourts.pdf.

35. See Timothy Egan, The Pre-blame Game, N.Y. Times, Dec. 28, 2008, WK8.

36. See SAVAGE, 21.

Index

Gonzales, Alberto, 5; conspiracy prosecutions, 108–11; immigration policy, 27; interrogation and legal advice, 64; politicized hiring in Justice Department, 93; showdown with administration officials who opposed TSP, 185n. 69; U.S. Attorney firings, 132–35; War Council on interrogation, 59

Goodling, Monica: and challenge to merit-based hiring for career Justice Department positions, 76, 94–95; role in U.S. Attorney firings, 133

Graham, Lindsey: criticism of legal memos on interrogation, 61; questioning of interrogation techniques, 187n. 102

Gramm-Leach-Bliley Act of 1999, 148

Grassley, Charles, on NSLs abuses, 21

Graves, Todd, 134; dispute as U.S. Attorney seeking tougher sentence for hate crime, 87–88; fired by Bush officials, 76; questioned evidence in vote fraud case against ACORN, 134

Greenpeace, politically motivated prosecution, 25

Greenspan, Alan, failure to predict subprime collapse, 152

Guantanamo, 4; conspiracy prosecutions for detainees, 114–16; detention of suspected terrorists, 34–36; difficulties facing lawyers for detainees, 46–47; difficulties with closing, 160–61; military commissions, 15, 57; restrictions on habeas struck down, 157–58; Kurnaz case, 34–35

habeas corpus, 16; Military Commissions Act limits, 58; limits struck down in *Boumediene*, 157–58

Halliburton, 5; Iraq role, 141. *See also* Kellog Brown & Root

Hamdan, Salim, Guantanamo detainee, 46

Hamdan case, 57, 115

Hamdi case, 49, 56–57

Hayat prosecution, 117

Haynes, William "Jim": interrogation techniques memo on, 41; testimony before Senate Armed Services Committee, 68–69, 187–88nn. 100, 102; War Council member, 59, 68–69; Pentagon Working Group, 61, 184n. 50

Hicks, David, 113, 115

Holder, Eric, described waterboarding as torture, 160

Humphrey's Executor decision (Roosevelt administration), 13

Iglesias, David, 2, 5; firing, 127, 133–35, 139; refusal to target foes of New Mexico Republicans, 76, 131

immigration, 4; anti-immigration politics, 11–12; asylum policy, 30–33; court decisions, 12; Haitian refugees and detention, 31; *Iqbal* case, 75; judges, politicized hiring of, 96; raids, 33–34; round-up after September 11, 28–30, 75; tail-wagging-the-dog criminal prosecutions, 89; unsafe detention conditions, 34

imperial presidency, courts' response, 13

Inspector General for Justice Department: immigration round-up, 75; record as watchdog, 162; Terrorist Watchlist, 45

Insular Cases, 55

international law, torture, 37. *See also* interrogation and coercion; torture, ineffectiveness of

interrogation and coercion, 36–42, 187n. 94; Justice Department legal opinions, 59–66

Iqbal case, regarding officials' liability for immigration round-up after 9/11, 75

Iran-Contra, 8–9

Jackson, Robert, Attorney General (Roosevelt administration): on conspiracy prosecutions, 102, 125; on dangers of overzealous prosecutors, 138; on destroyer deal with Britain, 91; *Youngstown* decision, 14, 107

Japanese-American internment, 17, 27; government lawyers unethical conduct, 65

Jayyousi, Kifah, conspiracy prosecution, 116

Johnsen, Dawn: criticism of OLC opinions, 210 n. 18; delay of hearings on nomination to head OLC, 210 n. 18
Johnson, Lyndon, and law and order, 10
Johnson v. Eisentrager, 54

Katrina, Hurricane, 7, 21–23
Katyal, Neal, lawyer for Guantanamo detainee Salim Hamdan, 47
Kellog Brown & Root (KB&R), Iraq role, 141, 145
Kennedy, Anthony, *Boumediene* decision, 157–58; *Iqbal* decision, 75
Kennedy, Edward, support for State Secrets Protection Act, 72
Kennedy, Robert, Attorney General, 85, 107, 198n. 49
Kleinman, Steven, disclosures on interrogation techniques, 41
Koubriti case, 100–101, 108, 118. *See also* conspiracy prosecutions
Kurnaz, Murat, Guantanamo detainee, 34–35

Lackawanna Six, 109
Lam, Carol, federal prosecutor, fired, 88–89, 110
Lanier case, applied to extraordinary rendition, 74
law and order: as political strategy, 10; and presidential power, 8
lawfare, 4, 9, 45
lawyers, disproportionate penalties sought for misconduct, 45–49
Leahy, Patrick, heads hearings on U.S. Attorney firings, 134
Lee, Sheila Jackson, 171
Levin, Carl, heads hearings on interrogation techniques, 67–68
Levin, Daniel: interrogation advice, 63–64, 160; pro bono work, 186n. 72; testimony before Senate Armed Services Committee, 69–70; waterboarding experienced, 64, 69
Libby, Lewis, Valerie Plame episode, 50, 190n 151

Lieberman, Joseph, pushed for creation of DHS, 171n. 94
Lincoln, Abraham, 6; habeas corpus, 16, 164; risks to preserve Union, 161
Lindh, John Walker, 47–48, 108; analysis of *Miranda* warnings provided, 180n. 143
Luttig, Michael, *Padilla* case, 113

Madoff, Bernard, financial scandal, 157
Maseth, Ryan, victim of contractor abuses in Iraq, 141
material support of terrorism, 111, 126, 201–2n. 98, 202n. 99
material witnesses, 17, 42–44
Mayfield, Brandon, material witness abuses, 43–44
McKay, John, U.S. Attorney fired by Bush officials, 76, 134
McNulty, Paul, 109; role in U.S. Attorney firings, 134
Mercer, William: politicized hiring in Justice Department, 79; testimony on U.S. Attorney firings, 133
Miers, Harriet: executive privilege asserted, 76, 77; and U.S. Attorney firings, 132
military commissions: Ashcroft defense of, 15; *Hamdan* decision, 57. *See also* Military Commissions Act of 2006
Military Commissions Act of 2006, 58; conspiracy charges, 115; immunity provisions, 161; provision struck down in *Boumediene*, 157–58. *See also Boumediene* decision; *Hamdan* case
Minerals Management Service, 155–57
Miranda decision, 11, 37; need to tailor Miranda warnings for use abroad, 163–64
Mohammed, Khalid Shaikh, coercive interrogation, 36
Mora, Alberto, opposed interrogation, 61
Moussaoui, Zacarias, 108
Mueller, Robert: in group forcing changes to TSP, 185n. 69; questioned interrogation practices, 160; warned about detours in trying terrorists, 15

Mukasey, Michael, in Attorney General confirmation hearing, testimony on waterboarding, 53, 160

Nadler, Jerrold, hearings on interrogation techniques, 67, 188n. 104
National Security Agency (NSA), surveillance, 18
National Security Court, proposals for, 212n. 34
National Security Letters (NSLs), abuses in obtaining, 19–21
New York Times, reveals existence of TSP, 18
Nixon, Richard, 4, 6; executive privilege claims, 76–77

Obama, Barack, 6; commitment to dialog, 161; release of Office of Legal Counsel memos, 162; reform of military commissions, 160; wariness on prosecuting Bush officials, 161
O'Connor, Sandra Day, *Hamdi* opinion, 56–57
Office of Legal Counsel (OLC), Justice Department: Guantanamo, 4; interrogation, 37–42, 69–66; religious discrimination in anticrime programs, 1–2
Office of Professional Responsibility (OPR), Justice Department, 162–63

Padilla, Jose, 16–17; conspiracy prosecution, 99, 112–13, 123, 125–26
Pakistan, cross-border raids, 161
Patriot Act, 15, 19–21
Paulson, Henry, 147; bank bail-out, 153
perjury, false claims of memory loss by witness, 67–68
Philbin, Patrick: key figure in changes to TSP operations, 185n. 68; role in OLC memo on Guantanamo, 183n. 27
Pitt, Harvey, 147. *See also* Securities and Exchange Commission
Plame, Valerie, 26, 50
pleading requirements, imposed by Supreme Court in lawsuits against corporations, 153

politically motivated prosecutions, 5, 132–39
politicized hiring, 92; in Coalition Provisional Authority (Iraq), 144; contrasted with law and tradition on merit-based hiring for career positions, 92; in Justice Department, 92–96
preemption doctrine and limits on state regulation of business, 155
presidential power, 8, 13–14. *See also* imperial presidency, court's response
prosecuting Bush administration officials, 161–62
prosecutors, difficult choices faced by, 197n. 36
protesters targeted, 44–45
prison-industrial complex, 13

qualified immunity of officials from lawsuits, extraordinary rendition case, 74–75
Quirin case, 16–17

Radack, Jesselyn, Justice Department lawyer fired over John Walker Lindh case, 47–48
raids on Northern Virginia Muslim schools, 109
Randolph, Edmund, Attorney General strove to give independent advice, 91
Rasul case, 49, 163
Reagan, Ronald, 6
Reed, Jack, criticized regulatory failures, 148
Rehnquist, William, criticizing effort to list judges for lenient sentences, 82
Reynolds case on state secrets, 71
Reynolds v. Sims decision on voting rights, 129–30
Rice, Condoleezza, efforts to reform interrogation practices, 159–60
Richardson, Elliott, Attorney General, independence of, 91
Rockefeller, Jay, surveillance questions, 18
Roosevelt, Franklin, 3; *Curtiss-Wright* decision, 13–14; Japanese-American internment, 17; *Quirin* case and German saboteurs, 16–17; risks to decrease danger to U.S., 161

Rosenbaum, James, federal judge targeted by House Judiciary committee for allegedly lenient sentencing, 84

Rove, Karl, 4; strategy on terrorism, 15, 110; and U.S. Attorney firings, 76, 132–33, 190n. 138

Rumsfeld, Donald, interrogation policy, 41, 68

Salah, Muhammad, 113, 117–18

Sampson, Kyle, role in U.S. Attorneys firings, 12, 132–35

Schlozman, Bradley: as Justice Department senior official, sought lenient sentencing for hate crime, in opposition to U.S. Attorney Todd Graves; 87; politicized hiring within Civil Rights Division, 93–94; replaced Graves, 88; role in U.S. Attorney firings, 134. See also Graves, Todd

Scott, Hal, task force on curtailing securities regulation, 147

Securities and Exchange Commission (SEC), 3, 5; Christopher Cox as chair, 147, 151–52; William Donaldson as chair, 147; Harvey Pitt as chair, 147; role in subprime collapse, 151–52

Sensenbrenner, James: and ADA Amendments Act of 2008, 194n. 76; and DHS, creation of, 21; and House Judiciary Report against sentencing practices, 84; and Patriot Act, 19

separation of powers, 2, 53

SERE training, 38–39. See also interrogation and coercion; torture, ineffectiveness of

Sessions, Jeff, questioning by, on interrogation methods, 187n. 102

Seymour, Whitney North, on prosecutorial independence, 131–32

Siegelman, Don, governor of Alabama, corruption prosecution, 136–38; questionable conduct, 205n. 46

signing statements, 169n. 50

sleep deprivation, 40. See also interrogation and coercion; torture, ineffectiveness of

soft power, 53–54; Guantanamo impact, 58

Specter, Arlen: against challenge to attorney-client privilege, 91; in support of State Secrets Protection Act, 72

state secrets, 70–72

Stevens, John Paul, and Hamdan opinion, 57, 115

Stevens, Ted, problems with prosecution of, 206n. 56

Stewart, Lynne: prosecuted for role in defense of Omar Abdel Rahman, 48–49, 202n. 99

subprime mortgage crisis, 2, 150–53

Supreme Court: Boumediene decision on habeas corpus, 157–58; cases limiting government regulation, 153–55; Hamdan case on military commissions, 57, 115; Hamdi case on detention, 49, 56–57; Iqbal decision ruling out senior officials' liability for immigration round-up after 9/11, 75

surveillance, warrantless, 4, 17–19; opposition of Ashcroft and Comey, 109. See also Terrorist Surveillance Program (TSP)

Swift, Charles, lawyer for Guantanamo detainee Salim Hamdan, 46–47

Taliban, as not party to Geneva Convention, 55–56

Taylor, Sara, and executive privilege defense in U.S. Attorney firings, 76

Tenet, George, 50

Terrorist Surveillance Program (TSP), 17–19; key administration legal figures bring change to, 185n. 69; state secrets and, 71

Terrorist Watchlist, FBI, 44–45

Thompson, Georgia, corruption prosecution viewed as politically motivated, 138–39

Thompson, Larry, 108; surveillance program qualms, 19

Thomsen, Linda, SEC lawyer shared information with Morgan Stanley, 149

Thornberry, William, urged creation of DHS, 21–22

Thornburgh, Richard, criticized politicized prosecutions, 136

torture, ineffectiveness of, 37

torture statute, 15, 60

Troubled Asset Relief Program (TARP), government bailout, 153

Truman, Harry, 6; opposed to profiteering during World War II, 142; steel seizure case, 6, 14

truth commission proposals, 162

Turley, Jonathan, lawyer for Ali Al-Timimi, argued that Terrorist Surveillance Program figured in conviction, 198n. 58

Uighurs, as detainees at Guantanamo, 160, 175n. 71

unitary executive theory, 8, 10, 13; politicized personnel decisions, 93

United States Attorney firings, 12, 88; executive privilege claims by Bush officials, 75–77; political motivations, 127–28, 131–35; and Karl Rove, 190n. 138

Verdugo-Urquidez decision, 55

vote fraud, 128; absentee ballots, 203n. 18; concern about undocumented immigrants, 130; photo ID requirement as burden for elderly, 130–31; and U.S. Attorney firings, 133

vote suppression, 128–31; racial history and consequences, 128–29

voting rights, 128

walling technique used on detainees, 39. *See also* interrogation and coercion; torture, ineffectiveness of

Warren, Elizabeth, skepticism about government bailout, 153

waterboarding, 16, 39; guidelines, 176n. 95; *Lee* case, 60; medical safeguards inadequate, 65–66. *See also* interrogation and coercion; torture, ineffectiveness of

"water cure," 176n. 94

Waxman, Henry, and congressional oversight, 146; resists formation of DHS, 22

Waxman, Matthew, role in interrogation reform, 159–60

Wecht, Cyril, target of politicized prosecution, 135–36

White, Mary Jo, 149

Whitehouse, Sheldon: questioned Attorney General nominee on waterboarding, 53; supported independence of federal prosecutors, 87–88, 132

Wilson, Heather, phone call to David Iglesias on targeting New Mexico Democrats for prosecution, 127. *See also* Iglesias, David

Wilson, Joseph, 26, 50

Wittes, Benjamin, 35, 160–61

Working Group, Pentagon: and Bybee Memo, 184n. 50; on interrogation issues, 61

Yoo, John: interrogation advice, 59–60, 69–70; legal opinions of, 53–53, 161, 163; presidential power advocate, 8; statutes twisted to justify coercive interrogation, 61; testimony before Senate Armed Services Committee, 69. *See also* Office of Legal Counsel

Youngstown decision (Truman administration), 14; *Hamdan* role, 57; ignored in Justice Department legal memos on interrogation, 60

Zelikow, Philip: efforts to reform interrogation, 159–60; questioned results obtained with coercive techniques, 177–78n. 112

Zubaydah, Abu: official interference with inquiry into interrogation of, 70; waterboarding, 16, 40. *See also* waterboarding

About the Author

PETER MARGULIES is a professor of law at Roger Williams University School of Law. He has represented groups in the Supreme Court and other tribunals seeking fairness and access to the courts, including immigrants, people with disabilities, and victims of terrorism.